W9-BEZ-587

Marriage and Christian Life

A Theology of Christian Marriage

Daniel Hauser

University Press of America,® Inc.
Lanham · Boulder · New York · Toronto · Oxford

Copyright © 2005 by
University Press of America,® Inc.
4501 Forbes Boulevard
Suite 200
Lanham, Maryland 20706
UPA Acquisitions Department (301) 459-3366

PO Box 317
Oxford
OX2 9RU, UK

Library of Congress Control Number: 2004113392
ISBN 0-7618-3057-X (paperback : alk. ppr.)

Table of Contents

Preface

Today, some would argue that Christianity is needed more than ever. It is certainly true that during every period of history there have been needs and since the coming of Christ, his Church has struggled to administer to the needs of the time. No doubt the needs of the modern secular culture that now dominates the west are different from the needs of other generations, yet in many ways they are the same. At the core of all human needs is the desire for those things or persons which fulfill human life. To fulfill a human life requires many things. Our culture and most of the West, has been quite successful in securing the material goods necessary for life. Quite frankly, the West is very well off. In addition to all of the things necessary for life, to live a "good" human life one needs human community. But in the West we have greatly failed at this. In particular, individualism, with its false sense of freedom, has led to the isolation of people from one another, be it from the family, friends, community, and country. Modern man sees himself first and foremost as an individual and has a difficult time understanding the needs of others and his responsibility for others. As a result the human community has become fragmented in so many ways. It is not uncommon for people to live feeling isolated living within walking distance of thousands of people.

In the Roman Catholic Church, marriage and family have always been considered to be the center of human life. As a sacrament, marriage was understood as a participation in the New Covenant, the One Flesh union of Christ and his Church. Through the total gift of themselves, a man and women enter into the nuptial mystery of that covenant. In their mutual love they partake of the grace by which they are redeemed. Their love completes their lives, touching upon the deepest dimensions of human life, bringing them closer to God.

It is precisely the kind of self-sacrificial love, the love of Christ for his Church, that is essential to marriage and so difficult in any age, but especially today. Such a love cannot be born of persons focused on themselves. Such a love cannot be found in a person wounded by abuse or by divorce. Such love becomes almost impossible in a society where one is solely judged by one's success in a career or other function. Again, such a love is difficult in any age, and especially one like ours with a culture that does not support it. But such a love does remain possible in Christ.

One of the lost insights of our age is that love is procreative. That is, if a man and a woman gives themselves totally to another in marriage, they should be open to having children. Roman Catholicism is often mocked for its support of procreation in marriage. Living in our anti-natal culture, the opponents of the Church often refer to other important things that people can do besides have children. But the Church's response has been, like what? No doubt people do many things with their lives that are good and many are called to serve God in ways other than marriage. But what is more important than bringing children into the world and raising them? But today we are confused on this issue. Ask any person who has children and they will talk about them as if they were the most important things in their lives, yet they will often ignore them, be absent from them, and neglect them in all sorts of ways. In effect people are divided about the meaning of children.

The Catholic response to modern culture is that something very important for human life takes place in marriage and the family. Chesterton called the family "the great adventure." He argues that unlike the rest of life it is not narrow. For example, outside of the home you get to choose whom you want to associate with. Each chooses friends that think and act like they do. On the other hand, in the family you are forced to deal with all sorts of people. Also, and most importantly, the family is where one learns the most important lessons about life. It is the seminary for life. It is in the family that one learns how to love and care for others. The relationships in families touch upon the foundation of human life. They cannot be replaced by schools, day care, or the state. In fact, real love is self-sacrificial and is nuptial. It is marital and reflects the relationship between husband and wife. It is out of this nuptial love that children should be born and nurtured. Unfortunately today that is less and less the case, but that does not mean that we should abandon this good.

The family is also the place where the education of the children takes place. In the family, from the example of the parents, the children learn their faith, morality and the way in which they should treat others. The most profound lessons in life take place there. At the heart of the family stand marital love, the communion of persons, a product of the love born of the New Covenant, Christ's sacrifice for the Church.

This book is a contribution to understand the nature and purpose of marriage from a Roman Catholic theological position. In it, marriage as a sacrament is defined and its purpose in human life is described. As a sacrament, marriage touches upon the most profound dimensions of human life, making the husband and wife holy, through the total gift of self, which mediates the redemptive grace of Christ. It is this profound nature of marriage that has been lost to modern culture and needs to be restored. Only by reclaiming the sanctity of marriage and family will human sexuality once again be properly understood.

Daniel C. Hauser
University Of St. Francis
Joliet, Illinois
July 14, 2004

Acknowledgments

During the course of any human effort there are many people who are involved. Some people have not been directly involved with this work but supportive of the effort such as my wife Lori and our children Meagan, Alyssa, Sarah, Tom and Emily. I would also like to include in this category many of my colleagues and my parents Bernard and Elaine Hauser. There have also been a couple people without whom this book would still be a stack of notes in a pile in my office. I would like to thank Karla Gonzalez who helped with much of the early editing of the text. I would especially like to thank Cheryl Koren for her help with the final editing and preparation of the book. Her effort has been essential to the completion of this task. Finally, I need to recognize Fr. Joseph Murphy, S.J. who helped from some of these theological ideas on marriage years ago and Fr. Donald Keefe, S.J. whose theology has provided much of the foundation for what is in the book.

Introduction

If one examines the curriculum of most colleges and universities in the United States, one finds that many institutions have general education programs that claim to address those "larger questions" that human beings must answer about human life. Such curricula are often described as "educating the whole person." In most cases, the means by which this is accomplished is that the student is required to take a series of the courses that touch upon what are considered to be the fundamental issues of human life. Philosophy courses, for instance, not only advance skills such as critical thinking, but also engage the student to consider such questions as the nature of reality, the nature of the human person, and the problem of what constitutes the "good life." In religious institutions, many of the same questions are addressed in theology courses, where the nature of God, the meaning of faith in God, and living out of the life of faith are considered. But there is one area of life that is almost totally ignored by undergraduate education and that is the topic of marriage and family.

This is not to say that one does not find some reference to love, marriage and family in university curriculums. Sociology and economics courses, no doubt, consider marriage and family from the perspective of their disciplines. In the past, courses in literature used to find love as a common theme. Yet, there are few general education courses found in any discipline that address this issue in a direct and comprehensive manner. Such an omission is astounding when one considers that almost ninety percent of the people in United States get married, and that this primary human relationship will consume much of their time and energy. Many will attest to the love of their spouse as the most important relationship in their lives. Their children will be the recipients of an overwhelming proportion of their love and resources. In short, marriage and family will engage the graduates of our institutions in the most fundamental way. Yet, we ignore those topics in our curriculum.

There may be a number of reasons why college and university curriculums do not address these issues. First, one might argue that what people know about marriage is learned from experience and not suitable to university instruction. It is certainly true that much of one's understanding of the meaning and purpose of marriage and family comes from one's own experience of family life. Therefore, one might argue that what educational institutions would add to a student's understanding of marriage would be insignificant compared to real life experience. Second, others might argue that marriage is a private choice, one choice among many lifestyle choices that people must make in their lives. They might add that marriage and family are social conventions, which, as all such realities, are in constant transition. At any time, there are competing social realities that are possible options for living a human life. As a private choice, universities ought to stay out of the business of influencing any such decisions.

Interestingly, many colleges and universities offer courses in the sociology of the family that describes changes in the family and the effects of changes in the social order upon the family. But within such areas of study, the significance of marriage and the family are redefined and their importance for society is often minimized. More often than not, in such sociological accounts of the family, no place has been given to a religious understanding of marriage and family.

Third, another reason that the family is not discussed in colleges and universities is because of political considerations. At least in the academy and in some other institutions, there are certain ideologies at work depicting marriage and the family as the true enemy of human freedom. They are often seen as the remains of an antiquated social order which needs to be overcome if there is to be equality among people. They would hold that only when marriage and family are abolished could real freedom be achieved. It is therefore politically incorrect to give attention to the family, except in a negative sense.

The Roman Catholic intellectual tradition, on the other hand, continues to defend the importance of the marriage and family for human life. Within this religious tradition, it is believed that the order of marriage was established by God in creation and that the love between a man and woman was a way in which they affirmed the goodness of the order created by God. Marriage, in this tradition, is a sacrament in which the married couple participates in the love of God. Thus, marriage is not simply a social reality to be measured in terms of the social sciences or politics, nor is it only a "natural" and foundational human relationship, but it is a religious event. Marriage, as a sacrament, is a religious commitment founded upon the covenantal relationship between God and creation, a unity that finds its completion in the New Covenant.

In addition to being a sacrament, and therefore a redemptive action, within the Roman Catholic intellectual tradition marriage is thought to be the primary human society, the source of both the love and life that sustain the larger human community. Within the Catholic intellectual tradition, human beings are understood to be social beings. And since humans are social beings, one can never isolate the good of the individual person from the common good. Therefore, the individual always has a responsibility to sustain the common good, and in return, the individual will reap the benefits of living in a society in which the common good is supported by its members. Within this understanding of political life, marriage and the family were the most basic human community upon which the larger social order was built and by which it was sustained. Marriage and a family that was built upon marriage were thought to be a normative good for human living.

Today, many challenge this belief, holding an interpretation of human sexuality that is ideological. They argue that the family is, at best, incomplete or, in fact, unsuited for modern social life. In many instances, these modern cultural trends support the radical autonomy of the human person, insisting that any form of sexual expression is legitimate. Such trends are by no means new in history; yet, the radical individualism at the heart of this philosophy is certainly aimed at freeing human sexuality from any normative expression.

The Roman Catholic Church has responded to such challenges by noting that in marriage and the family real human freedom is expressed in a radically unique fashion. First, by the true giving to another in marital and familial love, humans become human. Nowhere else is there a context in which humans are free to live as completely as in the family. Second, through the procreation of children, the very continuation of human life is made possible. Both find their unique expression in marriage and the Christian family.

The significance of marriage for human life, according to Catholic teaching, is not limited to marriage itself, but the marital relationship is the norm by which the rest of human sexuality must be understood. Within the Catholic tradition, marriage is understood as the context in which the human sexuality finds its completion. From the beginning, the Judeo-Christian tradition has held that there is an order to the created universe. There is a complementarity between male and female, so that in the love for one another they become complete. One way in which the Christian tradition has described the normative nature of the male/female relationship is to say that human sexuality finds its completion in marriage as the fullest form of sexual expression. All other forms of sexual expression fall short and are, in the end, a turning away from the good that was established by God "in the beginning." What is at stake in marriage, as the most complete form of sexual expression, is nothing less than the most profound dimensions of our being. In this love, one discovers the true meaning of life, one's own being and the true love of God. Marriage then becomes a fundamental vocation for the Christian. In and through the love of one's spouse and one's children, the believer is called to serve God.

The foundation for the Church's examination and judgment of human sexuality has its origin stems in the sacramental nature of marriage. The Church contends that what is given in the sacrament of marriage is holy, and therefore, it is more than simply the satisfaction of natural sexual attraction. From a Christian perspective, the love between a man and woman in marriage is thought to be redemptive. That is, in and through the love of man and woman, the believer is called to participate in the triune love of God. This nuptial order was established in creation, where man and woman are created in the image and likeness of God, male and female, and this nuptial order remains the order of redemption. It is within this framework that men and women are called to the one flesh unity of marriage, a unity given in Christ.

To understand the meaning and purpose of marriage, one must see it from a larger perspective than one's own. That is, one needs to see it in the light of faith. Today many understand the significance of human life to be given by the individual alone. In the past, the purpose of human life was answered by a truth or meaning that transcended the individual. Usually, it was thought that meaning was given by the culture, religion, or state. But today, there is a general distrust of any external claim to authority. Instead, meaning no longer is thought to come from without, but from within. Something has meaning only if it has meaning for me. I give meaning to my life. A Christian, on the other hand, would not deny the significance of the human freedom in shaping human life, but the Christian would see the meaning of life as not originating in human efforts, but in the work of God. Human beings do not create their own world, but live into the truth of the world, a truth given in Christ. So, unlike many today who claim that religion is a mere private affair, the Christian faith claims that the whole truth about life is given in the faith. It is not a mere private belief, but a living into the truth of the faith given in Christ. God has created the world with an order and a purpose that is placed there by God.

If there is such an order or purpose to life that is placed there by God, then living a "good" human life is to live according to that order. This would include marriage. I do not create marriage, it is a truth that is beyond my creation, but I do decide to live a married life. At the heart of marriage is the call to respond to the love of God. In the process of responding to God's love, I give myself to God and others in order to come to myself. Notice that the order of creation that comes from God is not an oppressive determinist, limiting structure, but it is covenantal. It is an order circumscribed by freedom and love, not power. Human beings are created out of the generosity of God's love so that they might live in the love of God. As all love, this requires the free response of the one to whom the offer of love is made.

As the foundation of human life, this love defines human life. In one's love of God, one gives oneself totally over to that which alone completes one's life, and in return for giving one's life, one gains one's life. "If any man wishes to come after me, let him deny himself and take up his cross and follow me. For whoever would save his life will lose it; and whoever loses his life for my sake and the gospel's will save it. For what does it profit a man, to gain the whole world and forfeit his life?" (Mark 8:34-36) This sacrificial love is the central act of human life. Such faith demands the complete response of the believer. It is the proper response to the truth and life and love that is God alone.

This approach to understanding marriage in terms of the larger economy of salvation also reveals the sacramental nature of marriage. Marriage not only opens up one's life to one's spouse, but as noted, it opens one up to the salvation given in Christ. It becomes a means in which one comes to participate in the New Covenant. As one of the sacraments, marriage is an event and action through which one enters into the events by which one is saved: the life, death and resurrection of Christ. It is precisely by these events that the believer shapes his/her life. One of the many great contributions of Pope John Paul II has been his phenomenology of the human person. He teaches that through their actions, human beings shape their lives. This is derived from a view of the human person that in each human act the entire person is involved. There is an integrity to the human person that does not permit it to be divided and so in each human act the whole human person is involved and shaped by that act. For instance, if one commits a sin, eats too much, it is not just the body that is affected, but the whole person is shaped by that act. Likewise, when one does a good deed, the whole person is shaped by that deed. What this means, then, is that in the life of faith, the whole life of the believer is shaped by the actions and events of Christ, whose actions are redemptive for every human being. In marriage, as a sacrament, one enters into the life of the New Covenant through the love of one's spouse and children. It is to this vocation of love that the Christians give themselves over to in marriage.

If education in American Catholic colleges and universities is really about the most fundamental issues that affect the lives of our students, it is hard to imagine that it cannot but include a theological reflection upon the nature and purpose of marriage. Perhaps more than ever, our universities and colleges need to affirm and clarify the significance and meaning of marriage, since presently, our culture no longer possesses a clear understanding of marriage. Within such a situation, perhaps one of the most profound acts of Catholic colleges and universities will be to continue to affirm the normative nature of marriage and family, and the good that they are.

This book is written for students who are looking for an understanding of the faith and place of marriage in that faith. It presupposes that most of those who read it are or will marry, and that ultimately the best way of serving those students is to reaffirm the religious significance of marriage, explaining what is at stake and why it is a sacrament. For to live one's life correctly one needs to understand things correctly. That means one needs to see things in the light of the truth of Christ, who reveals the whole truth about man.

Chapter I:
Marriage and Family in Today's World

If one were to take a moment to reflect upon the state of marriage and family at the beginning of the twenty-first century, one would see two very different interpretations of the meanings of these realities. First, one would notice that certain people argue that marriage and family, as traditionally understood, is in a process of decline as the result of sociological changes.[1] Some of the evidence is found in the divorce rate, the decline in birth rates, the number of abortions, the growing hostility between men and women, and the amount of violence within American households. One of the many reasons for the pervasive decline of marriage and the family is the adherence to the prevailing ideology that holds that the traditional understanding of the family is too narrow, appropriate for a time now past, and in need of redefinition within a broader and more contemporary social context. Of course this "new" approach to marriage and family includes a new definition of the family that no longer places marriage at the center of the family and promotes an understanding of human sexuality quite different from traditional Christian understanding of human sexuality and marriage.

At the same time that these efforts toward the dissolution of the family are occurring, one cannot help but notice some very vocal groups who continue to argue for a privileged place for marriage and the family in American culture. In almost all instances, the defenders of the family hold that marriage and family are not simply social constructs that can be redefined according to the time, but that they are part of the "natural order" of things. Many of these groups, especially the Christian groups, believe that the family has a divine origin, established by God at creation. Other defenders of the traditional family, including some secular theorists, see marriage and the family as the foundation of human society. Simply, they argue that marriage and family are "natural" social units that provide a basis for societal stability. What takes place in marriage and in the family, such as the begetting and the raising of children, cannot be done as well in any other context. That is, the traditional family provides a context of real security and love fundamental to the proper development of human life. One might say that the family is the "seminary" for life. It is the place where new life comes into existence, where it is fostered and where it grows. Therefore, the societal functions that marriage and family perform are fundamental to human society and need to be preserved if freedom and "real" human develop-

---

[1]The traditional view of family has at its foundation heterosexual marriage, where the children are the offspring of those parents. The other forms of human associations now called families would have been unrecognizable in the past.

ment are to continue to take place in one's culture. To deny the importance of marriage and family, or to try to redefine them, will lead to disastrous social and religious consequences.

In trying to understand some of the reasons for the present decline in marriage and family, some defenders of the marriage and families claim that the decline is the result of the anti-marriage/anti-family ideologies now promoted by "liberal" ideologues; e.g., feminist and gay activists represent a couple of the primary sources of these challenges. The conflict between the "liberal" view of marriage and the family and those who hold more traditional views of marriage and family has led to what has been labeled a "culture war." At the core, this struggle is over different ways of viewing what is the "good" human life, each giving answers that are fundamentally irreconcilable. And because of their importance, marriage and family have found themselves at the center of this struggle.

The problems associated with what has become known as the culture war may seem to be unique to our time, but G.K. Chesterton was writing about many of these issues earlier in this century.[2] In those writings he took up a defense of marriage and the family against feminism and other ideologies that wanted to discard the family in the name of social progress and economic change. In short, Chesterton saw himself fighting against those "utopians" that sought the power to manipulate the social structure for what they viewed to be "progress." And no different from today, those ideologues understood marriage and family to be the greatest impediment to such social change.

In response, Chesterton noted that real freedom and real human living took place in its most intense form in the family. (It was also for this reason that the family was hated by the utopians, since they could not control the freedom and allegiances that are rooted in the family.) For it was here that the most profound relationships within human life took place. In the family, one learned to be a human: one learned to love, to trust, to care, to moderate one's behavior. The family was a place of growth and freedom protected from the influences of public life. Other social relationships, such as political or economic allegiances, are never as profound as familial relationships, nor are they subject to the same freedoms, always being controlled by a set of rules. (Which of you is not freer in your own homes than at work?) As a matter of fact, at one point Chesterton calls marriage and family "the great adventure," since it is in this context that most important dimensions of human life are realized. Attempts to replace it

---

[2]I found it fascinating that G.K Chesterton in the earlier part of the last century found the same issues already being discussed. See *Brave New Family: G.K. Chesterton on Men & Women, Children, Sex, Divorce, Marriage & the Family*, ed., Alvaro de Silva (San Francisco: Ignatius Press, 1990). This series of essays are both insightful and entertaining.

with some new social program or economic career were doomed to be superficial, artificial, and in all likelihood, totalitarian.

Since Chesterton was fighting against an ideology whose ideas had not yet taken firm root, his defense of marriage and the family was in some sense easier than it might be today. The overwhelming majority of people of the time were still rooted in the Judeo-Christian tradition, respectful of the order that God created. In contemporary society, those who try to defend marriage and family are doing so in a climate where those anti-family philosophies have been at work for over three-quarters of a century. The defense of the family has become much more difficult. Nevertheless, the culture war has come to define contemporary Western culture, and it is a war that will continue well into the next century.

a. The Decline of Marriage and the Family

As one looks around today, it often appears that the evidence of the decline of marriage and the family, and its corresponding consequences, is overwhelming. On almost a daily basis, we are confronted with signs of this degeneration and all indications are that the decline and its effects will continue to undermine Western life for some time to come. The reasons given for the decline of the family are multiple, yet one could contend that the decline is not simply the result of problems in our culture, but that there is a concerted effort to disestablish the cultural significance of the family as it was traditionally understood. One can characterize the opposition to the family in the following ways. First, some argue that the decline of marriage and family is simply part of our social and cultural evolution. According to this theory, often promoted by those in the social sciences, morality and culture and social structures are human conventions established in reaction to the environment in which people find themselves. As the situations in which societies find themselves change, so too must the social structures change. Not only do the structures that underlie the social order within a particular culture change, but there are also different structures in different cultures. Since the beliefs and practices of any culture are the product of that culture, one should expect differences and changes from culture to culture. No one set of cultural beliefs can be said to be better than another, they are simply different.

If one accepts this account of the development of cultural structures, one should no longer cast a judgment upon other nations or cultures. One needs to "accept" others and cultural changes and the corresponding social and cultural effects.[3] Cultural changes are understood to be simply facts beyond dispute. This position presupposes that there is no enduring order within history. Over time all that was once thought to be relevant and normative is rendered irrelevant since there are no natural or transcendent foundations that the social or moral structure of a culture tries to embody. Again, nor is there any structure or order that can be said to be better than another. One needs simply to accept the present order as the product of the times.

If one begins with the premise of this "evolutionary theory," that cultures are human conventions that evolve, then such institutions as marriage and family, as the products of social development, can be changed, rearranged, and replaced at any time by some other social construct. According to these theories, many of them driven by certain ideologies,[4] humans are thought to have absolute power over their lives. They are believed to be able to define and give meaning to their lives in and by themselves. So it is not surprising when periods of the social evolution occur in which the dissolution of one structure, as a matter of course, leads to its replacement by another. As a matter of fact, according to this theory all social structures will eventually be destroyed and replaced by others. In the case of the marriage and family, the needs that marriage and the family once met will disappear or be provided for by other social structures. As an example, they might argue that one can look to history to see how the family has evolved from the tribe to the extended family, to the nuclear family and now beyond. What comes next can only be imagined.

According to this historicist interpretation of the social order, today the family is in a process of transition through which a new family structure or an alternative social structure is emerging. Already this process is underway, and to a great degree this redefinition has already taken root. Many of my students tell me that in their social science and education courses the family is usually defined as a "microcosm," a group of people whose unity is based on some sort of common interest or affection. This, of course, then makes the family unit

---

[3]See Dinesh D'Souza's, *Illiberal education : the politics of race and sex on campus*, (New York : Free Press , 1991). He criticizes cultural diversity on the grounds that not all aspects of a culture are good and therefore should not be accepted. He raises some critical questions about the kinds of social "judgements." He asks whether or not all forms of behavior should be incorporated into cultural life. He assumes that there is a rational basis beyond culture and power by which one can make judgements about what is good and bad in culture.

[4]An ideology entails an understanding of the world that is comprehensive, interpreting all of reality in the light of an overriding idea. Those who hold such beliefs tend to want to impose them on all those around them, believing that they have discovered the truth to life. In most cases, they are overly simplistic and have a distorted view of reality. In the end, they are imposed on others through power of one group over all others, often claiming that it is for their own good.

malleable in almost any of the infinite number of ways that human interests and affections may vary. The critics of such definitions of the family claim that if the family can mean any association of people, the term family becomes almost meaningless. Others argue that this is simply the present understanding of the family, a stage in its evolution.

Often, as part of this attempt to explain the difficulties that are now prevalent in the area of marriage, sexuality and family, you will hear people say that the "times have changed," indicating that the mere passage of time erodes or changes the social realities, and, of necessity, causes the formation of new and different forms of behavior and new social structures better suited to the times. This way of thinking, consistent with the "evolutionary" principle cited above, rests upon the premise that nothing in the world has a basis outside of the realm of change, transcending the realm of change. There are no enduring norms for human social interaction.[5] The social dimension of our world is understood to be self-contained: there are no higher norms to which one can appeal. Intrinsic to this world is a set of fundamental laws that order the social life of men. One of the fundamental laws is that everything changes. In the end, all one can expect is that the present order will pass away and another will take its place. The struggle of human life is for man to adapt to these changing structures that shape the present world. Human life is open to an almost infinite manipulation.

This evolution not only includes social structures but also the moral structure that undergirds the social order. What is evident to all in American culture today is that the moral structure of American life has undergone a radical change. For example, it is only recently that many Americans have come to believe that pre-marital sex, homosexuality, artificial contraception, or in some cases even adultery are no longer morally wrong or sinful. Many argue that as long as these acts are done by mutually consenting adults, they are moral. This was not the case a generation ago, nor for the Americans of the generations before that. Yet despite the historical weight against their new moral insights, many people today believe themselves to be living in a new and unique time with a new and better understanding of human sexuality which fosters a more "open" approach to sexuality, including the acceptance of "alternative lifestyles." One needs only to note the changes in language to get a sense of the changes in attitudes. One no longer has a spouse; one has a "domestic partner." One no longer has a lover, but a "significant other." Such language is laden

---

[5]This reflects a historicist interpretation of temporal existence. See Pope John Paul II, *Fides et Ratio*, para. 87. According to the historicist premise, one's view of the world is defined by the intellectual horizon represented by the particular historical period. There are no enduring human truths. Therefore, from the historicist perspective, humans becomes infinitely malleable, his life can be changed in any number of ways. There are no transcendent truths. Concerning the significance of historicism see, Leo Strauss, *Natural Right and History* (Chicago: University of Chicago Press, 1953), pp. 9ff.

with values, relativizing traditional sexual mores, accepting any number of possible "arrangements." Clearly, within such a view, marriage and family no longer hold a privileged position.

What is perhaps most interesting about these contemporary moral changes is that often the defense of these changes in activity and attitude has been based on the assumption that we now possess a new knowledge of human sexuality. Yet when asked about what this new knowledge about sexuality is, a knowledge that must have been denied or unknown in other eras, there is never a clear answer as to what is its content. As a matter of fact, the answers given are usually so unclear that one soon becomes convinced that the acceptance of these other forms of sexual behavior does not rest on some special insight or knowledge, but instead is the result of a real confusion about the nature of sexuality. (One need only look at the modern experts on human sexuality that populate American television talk shows to see examples of this confusion). And today, despite the increase in formal education among some Americans, they seem to know less about sexuality than prior generations, and therefore, are less able to judge what is good and what is evil when it comes to matters of sexuality.[6]

In the same vein, those arguing that today we have a new attitude and openness about sexuality by which our own attitudes about sexuality should be guided, never conclusively show how this openness is better than the moral norms that controlled sexuality in the past. Is this openness better? Should we accept wider parameters for human behavior? Or has this openness lead to all sorts of problems? Is it not simply an argument for the acceptance of previously prohibited forms of sexual behavior? Is this not simply a way of attempting to legitimize a variety of sexual passions?

The second line of reasoning associated with the contemporary attacks upon the family finds its locus in a specific philosophical position. It is a position that believes that marriage and the view of sexuality underlying the traditional understanding of marriage are simply wrong and in some cases oppressive. In defense of their position, those who espouse this new understanding of sexuality often state that Catholics and others who hold more traditional views of sexuality are simply too preoccupied with sex and sexuality, arguing that Catholics take it "too seriously." They contend that the old morality was too rigid, and especially oppressive of human sexuality, particularly female sexuality. The proponents of the "new sexual morality" hold that people must learn to be more open and casual about sexuality. After all, many argue, are we not sexual beings? Should we not exercise this "natural" function when we want? Is it not

---

[6]In a speech given at the University of Bologna, May 3, 1988, Cardinal Ratzinger speaks about a different approach to sexual knowledge. Citing Claus Westermann, Ratzinger indicated that knowledge of human sexuality is not objective knowledge or physiological knowledge, but "personal," "rather the understanding which grows from encounter. *Avvenire*, May 14, 1988.

destructive not to exercise our sexuality? Should we not strive to have a healthy sex life whether married or not, heterosexual and homosexual?

Proponents of the contemporary arguments for the casual nature of sex attack the idea that sexuality may have some transcendent purpose. They begin with what can be described from a religious perspective as a denial of the belief that human sexuality is sacramental. That is, they deny the traditional Christian idea that human sexuality has a significance or meaning beyond brute nature, or beyond any meaning that the individual might ascribe to it. This is a key point. For to accept a purpose or to find meaning in sexuality itself, would be to say that sexuality has an intrinsic intelligibility and purpose beyond any human manipulation. It would be to say that sexuality is part of some larger order, and that the true meaning and goodness of sexuality can be found only within that order. For example, the traditional understanding of sexuality was that man was created male and female, based on the idea that God, in creating the world, established a particular order. In that order, man images God and was created in his likeness as male and female (Gen. 1:24-27). The complementarity between the sexes was understood to be part of the original good creation, therefore, a norm by which the proper living out of one's sexuality could be understood. But the modern philosophy that reduces the significance of human sexuality to necessary drives, rejects any such understanding of human sexuality, undermining any attempt to root the intelligibility of human sexuality in any higher order.

In most past cultures and even in many cultures today, sexual morality commanded great respect. The reason for this was that most cultures understood sexuality to be a powerful human force, a power that could be used for good, but could also be destructive. This understanding of the power of sexuality required that every society structure its social life in such a way that the destructive possibilities of abuses of human sexuality could be avoided or controlled. For instance, adultery and homosexuality were condemned in many cultures as destructive forms of sexual behavior. It was thought that such acts violated the natural order and at the same time undermined the human community. Today, however, such norms are believed by many to be historically conditioned, belonging to the past and no longer binding on the individual. One now finds that many of the norms once governing sexual behavior have been undermined, freeing sexual passion to be lived out in any variety of shapes and forms. The contemporary ideal appears to be for individuals to choose a lifestyle that best fits them, but unable in the end, to say why one is better than another. Such ideologies leave man alone in the world, to create his own world. There is no revelation, no introduction of transcendent norms. Human creativity and power become the primary virtues in a world where each is left to find one's own happiness, establish a lifestyle, and seek self-fulfillment.

One of the resulting characteristics of this emphasis on individuals and their need to create the world is the radical individualism so evident today.[7] Here is the most blatant manifestation of the belief that there can ultimately be no transcendent meaning, order, or goodness. From such a perspective, there is no appeal to truth in order to determine which is the best way to live; rather, order and the meaning of goodness are believed to be determined by power. If power determines what is right and wrong, then one ends up with a fundamental relativism, limited only by the "will to power" of human creativity. Each person or culture makes his or her own world. This is simply the way it is.

Even further down at this end of the ideological spectrum is the more aggressive utopian belief that not only is marriage and the family confining when it comes to individual human choices, but that they need to be "overcome" in order to bring about a better world.[8] Such efforts are based on the belief that social changes are the product of human manipulation where the objective is to "engineer" the best possible society. From their ideological perspectives, many of these utopians understand marriage and family to be an impediment to the best social changes and human development, an impediment that cannot be tolerated.[9] They see the claims to the normative nature of marriage and family as contrary to human freedom and human equality. For example, consistent with contemporary efforts to establish an egalitarian society, many utopians attack the family as unfair, since families provide unequal starting points for humans, ultimately leading to inequalities. Since some families are better than others, those people coming from better families have an advantage over those coming from less adequate families. Accordingly, many of these utopians claim that the family is not only a dated institution, no longer capable of preparing people for living in the complex world in which we now live, but an unjust institution. A recent and popular example of the this philosophy, is the saying that Hillary Clinton made so popular, "It takes a village to raise a child." She could have

---

[7]Joyce Little, *The Church and the Culture Wars* (San Francisco: Ignatius, 1995) pp. 88ff. She speaks of the contemporary emphasis on the individual as the "Imperial I."

[8]For a summary of these arguments, see Bryce Christensen, *Utopia Against the Family* (San Francisco: Ignatius Press, 1990), pp. 1ff.

[9]A contemporary example of this is the philosophy of John Rawls. In his work, he cites the family as being the basis for the present inequalities in society. If such inequalities are to be overcome, the family must go. In discussing distributive justice, he notes that inequalities will remain as long as people have different starting points, " . . . . the inequality cannot be done away with as long as something like the family is maintained." John Rawls, "Distributive Justice," *Philosophy, Politics and Society*, 3rd series, ed. By Peter Laslett and W.G. Runciman (Basil Blackwell, Oxford: Barnes & Noble Books, Div. Harper & Row, Publishers, New York, 1967).

said the village should help the family to raise the child; but stated as it is; it presupposes that the family no longer has priority in the child-rearing process. If that is the case, then governments have the right and obligation to usurp the rights of parents, since those rights and responsibilities are only secondary to those of "the village." Even more concrete examples of the usurping of family and parental authority are the laws that allow minors to have an abortion without parental consent. In this instance, civil authority usurps the authority of the parents.

Many of these utopians and ideologues argue that the family hinders human freedom because it limits the choices of the individual. Today, the resistance to the normative claims of the family is especially evidenced by those who talk about "children's rights." For example, the family is a place in which children are subject to the authority of another, the parents. In this subjection, their freedom is limited and the family is understood to be an "oppressive" social institution. Notice that those rights are usually understood to be in opposition to the authority of the parents, not in terms of the other cultural forces. Are not social forces more tyrannical than one's family? Another area where one finds attempt to undermine the authority of the family is in the discussion of alternative forms of sexual and social interaction. The traditional understanding of the family stands against such expressions of human sexuality and it is consequently attacked as an oppressive structure by those who desire to live in such a manner. Universally, these alternative lifestyles require the undermining of the family if they are to find social acceptance; e.g., homosexual marriage.

Notice that these latter arguments do not presuppose that the times have changed and that we simply need to blindly follow along. Rather, they presuppose that we now understand the true meaning of sexuality, and that marriage and family are no longer adequate to provide for social or individual development. The traditional configurations of marriage and family are contrary to human freedom. So the utopians demand that these archaic social structures be erased in the pursuit of a better world. These changes in attitudes and beliefs may be based on a new knowledge; but more likely, such a new attitude is based on a different evaluation of the meaning of the good life. Today, then, if one is to understand the reasons for societal change, one needs to look beyond simply the blind social forces to the intellectual basis of that change, to the human motivation and power that is prompting that change.

b. In Defense of Marriage and Family

If, as we have seen, there are currently popular beliefs that hold that the traditional understanding of marriage and the family is no longer viable, other commentators will claim that marriage and family are part of the enduring natural order of human life. According to them, the decline of the family is not because it is not useful, nor is it simply the effect of a social evolution, but it is the result of certain destructive intellectual forces that are undermining it. Many describe these intellectual forces as having their origin in the liberal ideologies in the West, that have relativized most traditional values, while at the same time substituting a new set of values unfriendly to the family. Others describe the present as a time of spiritual corruption. These critics of the modern world claim that contemporary Western culture has lost its sense of the higher and nobler ends of human life, resulting in the continued dehumanization of the world. For other critics, the present decline is the result of both the triumph of modern ideologies and moral decay. Two of the best examples of those who find the present an age of both spiritual corruption and intellectual decline are John Paul II and Alexander Solzhenitsyn. They understand the intellectual changes caused by modernity and the spiritual decline of the West to go hand in hand.

According to these men, the present is a time when the sacredness and nobility of human life have been lost. Both have indicated on a number of occasions that the loss of the spiritual dimension of life has led to the present decline in the modern West. Perhaps the best way to summarize their positions is by referring to Augustine's insight that a person becomes what he loves. If you love humans and seek their good, you become more human. Likewise, if you "love" what is less than human, you become less than human. And, since almost everywhere today man has chosen to pursue wealth, power, ideological utopias and other forms of "this worldly" agendas, Western man is becoming less human in the process. In an effort to identify the destructive nature of these forces and to stand against them, both Pope John Paul II and Alexander Solzhenitsyn have spoken out against the individualism, the materialism, and moral relativism of West.

In Alexander Solzhenitsyn's Harvard address "A World Split Apart," he characterizes the West as having lost its moral courage as a result of having lost its spiritual direction. According to him, this has had a devastating effect on Western culture. When speaking of the historical development of the West after the Middle Ages, he says,

> Then, however, we turned our backs upon the Spirit and embraced all that is material with excessive and unwarranted zeal. This new way of thinking, which had imposed on us its guidance, did not admit the existence of intrinsic evil in man, nor did it see any higher task than the attainment of happiness on earth. It based modern Western civilization on the dangerous trend toward worshiping man and his material needs. Everything beyond physical well being and accumulation of material goods, all human requirements and characteristics of a subtler and

higher nature, were left outside the attention of
the state and of the social system, as if human life
did not have any higher meaning.[10]

The consequent loss of a higher meaning has led to a loss of order and subsequent corruption and weakness in the West where people no longer have any
control over their passions, can no longer identify evil, and are paralyzed with
weakness when the time comes for confronting and stopping evil from being
perpetuated.

The heart of this spiritual crisis as understood by Solzhenitsyn and Pope
John Paul II, is man's turning away from God. This new form of idolatry, ele-
vates the human, more importantly today, the individual, to the highest authority
in life, leading to the kind of moral relativism that is now prevalent in the West.
Within this framework, human beings no longer have norms beyond the individual's wants and desires that provide a basis for making moral judgments. For
instance, in many cultures it was assumed that innocent life was an intrinsic
good that needed to be protected. Thus, all members of that culture were bound
by the recognition of this good, and required to foster and protect innocent life.
Today, however, the majority of people in the West no longer accept any universally transcendent norms binding upon the conscience of every individual.
There is seemingly no particular framework within which one can identify that
innocent life is good and should be protected. An individual may agree to protect an innocent life, but that does not mean that another person has to. Morality
is understood simply to be a matter of personal preference.[11]

Much of Pope John Paul II's criticism of Western culture has been aimed at
this idolatry.[12] What has happened is very simple: people in the West have
fallen into a kind of idolatry, an age-old problem that has always plagued people
throughout history, of which the traditions of Judaism and Christianity remind
us. For instance, in Christianity, either Christ is the center of one's life or something else is. To place something else other than Christ at the center of one's
life is idolatry. The real problem today, as in every age, is that as people lose
faith in Christ and the fact that the whole truth about man is given in Christ.
They opt to place something else at the center of their lives. These idolaters no
longer live in the truth, since, as Christians claim, Christ is the way, the truth,

---

[10]Alexander Solzhenitsyn, "A World Split Apart: commencement address delivered
at Harvard University, June 1978," translated from the Russian by Irina Ilovayskaya Alberti (New York: Harper & Row, c1978).

[11]In *Veritatis Splendor*, 38-40. Pope John Paul II speaks out about the inadequacy
of contemporary moral relativism.

[12]Pope John Paul II, *Veritatis Splendor*, 1.

and the light. As a result, they cannot understand the world in which they live, nor can they understand the truth to which all men are called.

Recently, the theologian Joyce Little has noted in her book *The Church and the Culture War* that more people in the United States profess to believe in God than ever before. But, she asks, what kind of God do they believe in? Is it the Christian God, or some other God? If one compares the actions of those who profess to believe to the actions of others, one might be left wondering what sort of God most people have created. This is not simply to say that there is a gap between what one believes and how one lives, but it is to question what sort of "God" do people believe in today?

The question of what kind of God people believe in must also be asked of Christians. By their faith, Christians profess to believe in a God who is Trinitarian in nature; yet today, Christians no longer image the Trinity in their actions. This is especially evident in much of Christian life where the self-sacrificial love, which is constitutive of the Christian life, is no longer clearly evidenced. Little indicates an effect of this loss in her description of some changes in attitudes towards marriage.

> Americans are less inclined than they were a generation ago to value sexuality fidelity, lifelong marriage, and parenthood as worthwhile personal goals. Motherhood no longer defines adult womanhood, as everybody knows; equally important is the fact that fatherhood has declined as a norm for men . . .. Fewer than half of all adult Americans today regard the idea of sacrifice for others as a positive moral virtue.[13]

If self-sacrifice is no longer a virtue essential to living a full human life, one must wonder, as Little does, how can those Americans who profess to be Christians can believe in God, a Trinitarian God, where the Father sends the Son, who dies on the Cross, and who even in his death does not abandon sinful humanity, but sends the Spirit? Can American Christians, who seemingly reject sacrificial love, believe in a God whose essence is self-sacrificial love? According to Little, it is no wonder that Christianity continues to decline since we no longer are willing to "follow Christ."[14]

---

[13]Here, Little quotes Barbara DefoeWhitehead, "Dan Quayle Was Right," *Atlantic Monthly*, vol. 271, no.4 (April 1993), 57-58. It should be noted that a recent poll noted that most men thought that the most important way in which they supported their country was by staying in shape. Also see, Walter Kasper, *Transcending all Understanding*, (San Francisco, Ignatius Press, 1989), pp. 13-16. Here, he discusses the problem of identifying the contemporary understanding of "belief."

[14]Little, *The Church and the Culture War*, 105-106.

Of course, such a loss of faith seems to disturb very little the many who claim to have faith. As a matter of fact, in many instances, whether one has faith or not does not seem to influence how people act and live. The majority of people in the West have been taught that whether one has faith or not is simply a matter of choosing a particular lifestyle or a particular belief system. One may not agree with the beliefs of another, but if they are what others believe in, then we should tolerate them. Often today people are taught not to judge the beliefs and actions of others, but to simply accept them no matter what. One is expected to respect the person who holds even the most false ideas. But the demands of the Christian faith exceed such respect, calling the believer to love their neighbor, and in the process bring them to the truth of Christ.

Christians, on the other hand, have always claimed that certain ways of living are good and consistent with the faith, and others are not.[15] For instance, anyone who is an idolater cannot live well. The reason is simple. If the truth of existence is given in Christ, then to reject that truth means to live a falsehood, a lie. Notably in scripture, especially in the Old Testament, whenever the Jews forsake their God and chase after idols, they always become so corrupt that they no longer know what is good and have to relearn it (Isaiah 1:17). Also, during these periods of corruption, the Jews persecuted the most helpless people in their society, widows and orphans (Isaiah 10:2). The reason for this is simple: without the truth - the worship of the one true God - one cannot make good choices, one cannot identify good and evil, one loses one's way.

From the biblical perspective, this means that if the Christian understanding of God as Trinity is lost, substituting another understanding of God, or simply substituting something for God, then those people who accept this "different" understanding of God no longer live in truth, and consequently, cannot live well. Therefore, as the spiritual decline in Western culture continues, resulting from the loss of the belief in the triune God, the corruption and decline of culture is

---

[15]In human history, periods of decline are periods when people can no longer recognize good and evil. In such periods, of course, there is no defense against evil, since the first step in fighting against an evil is recognizing the evil. In the introduction to her book *The Church and the Culture War*, Little notes that today most people, in the name of "inclusivity," embrace what she calls the "both/and" approach to morality. They cannot say one thing is better than another. But the Christian must make an "either/or" decision. We believe or do not believe. We are charitable or we are not charitable. Thus, Christians must and do distinguish between actions that are better and worse. Also, see *Veritatis Splendor* where John Paul II reaffirms that the morality of an act is not contingent upon the intention of the individual alone; there are intrinsically evil acts: i.e., abortion, the practice of artificial contraception. (Para. 67) In this document, the pope repeatedly affirms the significance of moral choices.

inevitable. The hope of reversing this trend can only come from regaining the truth given in Christ.[16]

What is perhaps most dangerous today is not simply the deviation from Christian norms, but that there is a general rejection of all norms. Nevertheless, this rejection of norms and consequent spiritual decline has an intellectual basis. As noted, contemporary thought is founded upon a philosophy that explicitly rejects any transcendent truths, relegating all norms for human behavior to the realm of human convention.[17] There have always been philosophies of life like this, but none came to dominate Western thought until the triumph of Machiavelli, who rejects the traditional belief that man had an exalted place and noble end in the cosmic order. Implicit within Machiavelli's philosophy is the rejection of the Judeo-Christian tradition and the classical philosophical tradition. His philosophy begins with an understanding of human life where transcendent norms do not exist or are insignificant when it comes to how men actually live. Accordingly, he lowered the horizon for man, beginning with how men actually live rather than how they *ought* to live. Machiavelli argues that humans can, and most often do, act like beasts so that one must learn "not to be good" lest the good man perish among the many who are not so good.[18] According to Machiavelli, what motivates humans most is not faith or virtue, but fear. Life in this world is a struggle among men, and in the end, people with power determine the order of human life. There is no room for God or some other transcendent order. There is no transcendent law, natural or religious, which might regulate human behavior. Those with power are left to make the world the way they wish.

Later, building upon the framework of modernity introduced by Machiavelli, other philosophers such as Thomas Hobbes and John Locke write philosophies that begin with human beings who are by nature beasts. Human nature is now understood to be defined by the instinctual dimension of human life, what is less than human. By nature, man is neither moral nor social nor rational. He is a beast and nature is brutal, a state of warfare. According to Hobbes the fundamental struggle of man is for survival and in the process of this struggle for

---

[16]The particular nature of this Christian view of reality will be worked out in the first part of this book. The belief that Christ is the truth is affirmed by the gospel and lies at the center of Christian teaching. The precise meaning of this has been lost to modern man and is evidenced in the life of the Church in the sacramental life and teachings of Pope John Paul II. It is precisely the challenge of modern Christianity to recapture the meaning of this truth.

[17]Leo Strauss, "The Three Waves of Modernity," in *Essays in Political Philosophy*, ed. Hilail Gilden (Indianapolis, 1975).

[18] Nicolo Machiavelli, *The Prince*. See chapter 15.

self-preservation man comes to transcend his nature, to become rational and moral, and in the process, create history. But within modernity (modern philosophy), there is no intrinsic meaning or teleology for human life that is used to guide man in his quest for order, outside the primary instinct for self-preservation. Man is left to himself to determine the purpose and meaning of life, which is not given apart from his own effort. Human life and conduct, therefore, are infinitely changeable, since man can create them in any number of ways. Those changes are reflected in the cultural changes that determine and shape human action.

In the end, philosophers like Hobbes, Locke and Friedrich Nietzsche have influenced modern life by stripping away the final vestiges of any transcendent order. According to Nietzsche, the "will to power" is the source of human greatness and creativity, not natural or divine truth. Through power, humans create morality and values, since such things are conventional, having no basis in nature. Each society or individual is left to give meaning to their lives. Marriage and family are simply one among the many options that one might choose.

If this description of the "spiritual decline of the West" and the philosophical underpinning for that decline is at all accurate, then it is difficult to see what role marriage and family will have in the future. In contemporary society, where this philosophical shift is now deeply in place, not only is support for marriage lacking, but just as important, people no longer have the vision and virtue to sustain married family life. The kind of social, psychological, and spiritual developments that would enable someone to live a "good" married life are no longer handed down from one generation to the next, nor supported by society in general. For according to contemporary gurus of happiness, what makes one happy - one's self-fulfillment - is the primary end of human life, not self-sacrificial love. To try to live a married and family life with the primary purpose of seeking one's own fulfillment and goals certainly will not work.

It is not surprising, then, that those who defend marriage and family see the world in a different way from the ideologies that now dominate American life. These defenders of marriage and family understand themselves to be part of a larger order that transcends individual preference or social convention. In many instances, because of their understanding of marriage and family, it is not unusual to find defenders of the family and marriage among people with traditional Christian religious values, often supported by the evangelical churches.[19] Within the churches that defend these traditional values, the members almost universally accept the importance of marriage and family, since their doctrines are founded upon the word of God, which established marriage and family as normative for human life. In fact it has been the case that the evangelical

---

[19]This discussion has become obscured in the American political landscapes, all sides claiming to be "for the family." Yet, there are major differences as to how marriage is understood by the different participants.

churches in the United States have been vocal in promoting the family and traditional family values. They stand against modern relativism, believing that marriage is from the very beginning part of the divinely inspired order. God created man as male and female, commanding them to be fruitful and multiply. Marriage and family are understood to be part of the "good creation" and therefore provide a basic norm for human living. Those who reject this order, and live in such a way that the importance of marriage is relativized, are refusing the good of the created order. Those who defend a traditional biblical view of marriage believe that marriage and family are not negotiable, changeable or able to be replaced. The biblical truth about men and women, marriage, family and sexual sins, endures.

Another contemporary defender of the family is the Roman Catholic Church. Like the evangelical Christians, the Catholic Church teaches that the truth about human sexuality is not created by psychology or philosophy or sociology, but comes from God in his revelation. Consequently, they accept the fact that there is a biblical basis for marriage and the family. Catholics accept the creation story, believing marriage to be part of the order of reality created by God. And like the evangelicals, they have resisted the historicist temptations of seeing marriage as the product of a certain cultural period.[20] Instead, they accept the normative nature of the biblical revelation for "revealing" the true order and meaning and purpose of human life. Yet, unlike these evangelical churches today, it is not its theologians or the laity in general who are the defenders of the traditional understanding of the family, it is the *magisterium*.

c. Catholics in America

Within contemporary Roman Catholicism in the United States, most lay Catholics have been "successfully" acculturated into American life. Since the great immigration of European Catholics, beginning with the Irish in the 1850's and culminating with the coming of southern Europeans in the early part of this century, Catholics have struggled for acceptance into American life. The prejudice against Catholics by the Protestant establishment allowed for only a slow acceptance of Catholics into the various aspects of American life. Nevertheless, despite how the established institutions treated Catholics, the goal of most Catholics was to "fit" into American life. It is only recently, that much of the external hatred directed at Catholics has diminished, although occasional instances still occur. Most of the early Catholic European immigrant groups are now established, many living in the most affluent areas of the country, sending

---

[20]One does find this historicity premise rampant among Catholic theologians. For an example, see Joseph Martos, "A New Conceptual Context For The Sacramentality of Marriage," *Horizons*, 22/2 (1995), 214-36.

their children to the best colleges in the land. Catholics have now "made it" in America and participate in all aspects of American life.

But as part of this process of integration into American life, in order to "fit in," many Roman Catholics began to relinquish those ideas and beliefs that were identifiably Catholic. One need only look at some recent Catholic politicians who claim to be Catholic, at the same time rejecting the Church's teachings on any number of issues, e.g., abortion. And if one were to interview Catholics in the United States, one would find that many have opted for a different set of values than those promulgated by their Church. For example, if you interviewed Catholic graduates of Georgetown University, Boston College, Marquette University, or the University of Notre Dame, you would be hard pressed to finding anything distinctively "Catholic" in their attitudes towards marriage, divorce, family, children, artificial contraception, and even abortion. There is a definite gap between their church's teaching and the beliefs of many American Catholics.[21]

One key factor in understanding Catholics today is that unlike the evangelicals who voluntarily joined their churches, accepting from the start the teaching of those churches concerning a variety of doctrinal and moral issues, many Catholics are "cradle Catholics," whose membership may not include a profound knowledge of or an intellectual assent to the teachings of the Church. In some instances, they are Catholics because they have always been Catholic and at the same time their acculturation into society has led them to a set of beliefs different from those of the Chuch. In many instances, they knowingly reject their Church's positions, or in some instances, their knowledge of the faith is not adequate to understand the demands of the faith. Nevertheless, today some theologians presuppose and argue that American Catholics are a new breed of Catholics, more independent and better educated than other generations, and therefore, they should be granted an autonomy when dealing with moral and doctrinal issues that other generations of Catholics might not be prepared for. In addition, our culture asserts the myth, often under the influence of contemporary ideologies now so pervasive in Catholic intellectual circles, that each of us finally determines what is true for ourselves. This has no foundation in any Christian teaching; rather, such views reflect the influence of contemporary individualism.

And, although we have a well-educated laity in the United States, (at least in terms of numbers of years that they have attended school), the nature and range of their religious and theological education continues to remain limited. As a matter of fact, what one discovers upon examining the "products of Catholic education" is that many lack a genuine knowledge of the foundations of their faith. More often than not their "religious" perspectives are not informed by their faith or a Christian view of the world, but by current sociological, or eco-

---

[21]See Patrick Reilly, "Are Catholic Colleges Leading Students Astray?", *The Catholic World Report,* March 2003, 38-46.

nomic, or some other secular viewpoint. For instance, most Catholics are said to oppose the Church's position on artificial contraception. I am always curious as to what this means. Thus, I often ask people I meet why they think people are against this particular teaching. What I find are a number of interesting things. First, almost no one I ask can give an account of why the Church says what it says. Seldom have I met a non-theologian who has read and studied *Humanae Vitae*, or can in any way relate in detail the Church's teaching on this issue. This has always seemed incredulous to me.[22] If one really does not know the position of the Church, how can one reject it? Are they simply following cultural trends or personal selfishness? Second, people seldom, if ever, give "religious" reasons in defense of artificial contraception. They use "practical" explanations about not being able to care for more children, either psychologically or economically. Or they want to space children for some reason, even putting them off indefinitely to pursue a career or some other objective. There are, no doubt, a variety of valid reasons for putting off children within a marriage, *Humanae Vitae* admits that, but ultimately such decisions should not be economic, political, or sociological, but religious.[23] One needs to ask whether one is fulfilling one's commitment to God by refusing to have children. And how might the use of artificial contraception affect one's sexuality, one's marriage and one's salvation? But such questions are usually seldom, if ever, raised in a discussion of this issue.

This last example of the contemporary situation of the Catholic faith is anecdotal; yet, it could be argued that it reflects the contemporary secular understanding of marriage and sexuality that now dominates Western culture. Since the religious dimension is seldom of concern in the matters of marriage and family, it is hardly surprising that most people not only fail to accept the Church's teachings on sexuality, but find them kind of "strange." This inability to accept the Church's teachings on sexuality parallels the "profanation of the holiness of sexuality" that has occurred today, where our understanding of sexuality and

---

[22]To dissent in good conscience from the teaching of the Church one would have to know what the Church says and why she says what she says. To fail to do this would seem to be a matter of bad faith. Also, since dissent is a matter of conscience, another cannot do this work for you, i.e., you cannot dissent based on what your theology professor in college might have told you. Since theology is an attempt to understand and articulate the faith, it is hypothetical and subject to error. See the role of conscience and conscience formation *Catechism of the Catholic Church*, 1783-1794, especially 1791.

[23]In addition, as *Humanae Vitae* points out clearly, one needs to separate the question of number of children from the means of spacing them. It holds that the use of artificial contraception is immoral, recommending natural forms of birth control. This doctrine affirms that some acts are intrinsically sinful.

family is reduced to the understanding of the reigning contemporary ideology.[24] As noted, these ideologies articulate the meaning of human life, in this case human sexuality, in the light of some particular insight into human life. Those who espouse such ideologies, since their insights are on the cutting edge, always try to impose them on others. Yet in all cases, despite in some instances the limited usefulness of such theories, from a Christian perspective, they all fall short.

The effects of the reductionisms that result from inadequate theological anthropologies influenced by contemporary ideologies are numerous today. In many instances, their effects are most obvious in the theories concerning sexuality, where they deny the sacramental nature of human sexuality. Against this, the Catholic tradition has held that human sexuality is sacramental, that it is connected with the depths of human life, revealing the very truth about our human existence as male and female. According to the faith, a full account of sexuality and human life cannot be given apart from the revelation. Any other approach to human sexuality is bound to fall short.

One result of looking at the human life from a non-Christian perspective is the dehistoricization of human sexuality and the subsequent morality. This means that in such theories, people become "abstract persons,"[25] (which is the only alternative to a sacramental view of human sexuality). For instance, one might hear people argue that even though they sleep around quite a bit, they are not promiscuous. Or that as long as people are consenting adults it is acceptable to do whatever they want to do. In such instances, the persons separate themselves from their actions. In those descriptions of human actions it sounds as if the people involved are abstract souls; i.e., souls that are not united with the body to form the complete human person, but souls that are separate from the body and now imprisoned in the body awaiting release. So they would argue that their acts do not affect who they are. Yet, despite such arguments, the human experience is quite different. The body and soul are different aspects of the whole human person which cannot be separated. For example, when I am sick, it affects my whole being. When I am in good physical condition that also affects my whole being. The human person is a whole, an integrity that cannot be abstracted from its actions and its physical existence.

In fact, one of the emphases within the thought of Pope John Paul II has been his insistence that the human act is central to human life, constituting who we are. One needs only to look at daily life to see this. If I am to be a charitable person, I must do charitable deeds. If I am to be faithful, I must do faithful acts. To say that we can somehow separate ourselves from what we do is contrary to

[24]Donald Keefe, *Covenantal Theology: The Eucharistic Order of History* (New York: University Press of America, 1991), p. 40.

[25]Keefe, *Covenantal Theology*, p. 52.

our most basic experience. And in the end, of course, the failure to see the person in terms of their wholeness as created by God always leads to an inadequate, oppressive and limiting of human life. The best cure against the temptation to such limits is to see the human person for what he is in the light of the activity of Christ. Only then, can one begin to understand the full mystery and significance of human life.

Despite efforts on the part of the Church to defend the full dignity of human life, the influence of these rationalist ideological interpretations of human life and sexuality now seemingly dominate the western culture. Such rationalisms always hold a reductionistic view of human life. They fail to see the mystery and depth of human life, often reducing the person to one or more of their animal components. Such views are not Catholic. In the end, the Catholic view of life affirms that man's proper response to the human person is religious; it is seeing life through the eyes of faith.

d. The Catholic World View and Modern Trends

The guide to Roman Catholic teaching on doctrinal and moral issues is found in the magisterium. The magisterium of the Church is its official teaching authority.[26] Its purpose is to guide the faithful in their faith and guard them from being led astray. This teaching office is ancient. It is an authority that can be traced back to the apostles and has been handed on to their successors, the bishops. The New Testament often speaks of the leaders of the Church guiding the faithful in the "correct" living out of the faith. In the Roman Catholic tradition, the official teaching office is identified with the priestly authority of bishops and the pope.[27] In both cases, they are called, as successors of the apostles, to proclaim the truth of the gospels.

---

[26]The Magisterium of the Church has a teaching authority which it receives as part of its mission in the world, that is, proclaiming the gospel to the world. One function of this office is to protect the true understanding of the faith and promulgate that faith. It has an authority which is more than that of the individual or the majority of the believers. It does not make the faith, but protects the faith. It can do this because the Church is made holy by the sacrifice of Christ. Because she is holy and thereby free the Church is able to interpret the true nature of the faith; i.e., a definitive understanding of the faith, something no individual or group can achieve. This role of teacher was entrusted to the apostles and to their successors, the bishops. In particular, the power to teach universally is given to Peter and his successors.

[27]The Church's teachings distinguish between the *ordinary* and the *extra-ordinary* magisterium. The former refers to the teaching authority of the local bishop, whose duty it is to teach and protect the faith of the members of his diocese. The extra-ordinary magisterium refers to the authority of the pope to teach universally in the name of the Church.

Today, as in the past, the magisterium was called upon to answer the questions raised by the new situations in which Christians find themselves. Their primary concern is to preserve the faith and apply that faith to the contemporary concerns of Christians. At the heart of its teaching is her belief that although Christians are *in* the world, they are not *of* the world. That is, the Christian view of the world is different from others, and although it is different, it is not simply one among many ways of seeing the world, but the **only** way of seeing the world. In *Veritatis Splendor*, John Paul II says:

> The light of God's face shines in all its beauty on the countenance of Jesus Christ, "the image of the invisible God" (Col. 1:15), the "reflection of God's glory" (Heb. 1:3), "full of grace and truth" (Jn 1:14). Christ is "the way, and the truth, and the life" (Jn. 14:6). Consequently, the decisive answer to every one of man's questions, his religious and moral questions in particular, is given by Jesus Christ, or rather is Jesus Christ himself...[28]

This comprehensive and definitive claim to truth strikes the modern reader as exaggerated. On the one hand, in the West we have divided the world in compartments separating the religious from most of the public aspects of our lives, relegating it to a private affair.[29] On the other hand, there is a call today to recognize different cultures and their views of life. Consequently, the idea that any religion can be true and universal is not supported today. Nevertheless, Christianity claims that the Christian faith is comprehensive; it is the truth for all men, concerning all dimensions of reality. It demands the full response of the

---

[28]Pope John Paul II, *Veritatis Splendor*, 2.

[29]The expelling of religion from public life was the invention of modern philosophy. Hobbes and Locke, in particular, wanted to separate religious beliefs from public discourse. They thought that since religion could not be proved to be true according to the parameter assigned to truth and logic by modern philosophy, it ought to be relegated to the realm of private opinion. At the core of the philosophy of Hobbes and Locke, and also Spinoza, is the belief that the world is a closed rational system governed by certain laws. Within such a system, there can be no revelation, for that denotes an understanding of the world as not locked into the structure of necessitarian laws, but a free creation, open to the presence of the infinite. The latter is the covenantal order of the good creation, which views the world as sacramental and marriage as a sacrament. The former, which now dominates modern intellectual life, reduces human life to the product of impersonal cosmological forces. It is against this modern worldview that Christians now struggle and have always struggled.

believer, a response that fundamentally orders the whole of one's life. Since the act of faith makes such a comprehensive claim on believers, the faith itself must be as comprehensive, touching upon all aspects of life. That is, if the Christian is called to place the whole of his life at the service of Christ, the Christian message must be broad enough to fulfill the whole of one's life.

The comprehensive nature of this faith is something lost or ignored today. As a matter of fact, many Christians feel uncomfortable about "those fundamentalists" or others like them, who see the hand of God in all things and judge the world from a biblical perspective. In contrast with those who see religion as fundamental to human life, the majority of Christians have been taught that religion only affects certain aspects of life. Recently, a man told me that he was disciplined at work by his boss (who thought himself to be a devout Catholic), for pointing out that a problem of a co-worker was really a spiritual problem. Evidently, the boss did not think it appropriate to analyze business from a religious perspective. What the boss failed to realize is that from a Christian perspective, each person has at the center of their lives their relationship to God. So that one might argue that if on this deeper level one's life is in turmoil, will not this affect the whole of one's life? Do not questions about the meaning of life, purpose and human mortality raise such universal basic issues? And, are not the questions on this level religious questions?

The statement by John Paul II, noted above, proclaims the comprehensive nature of the faith in two ways. First, it means that the faith given in Christ is the whole truth about reality. In Christ is revealed the meaning and purpose of the whole created order. Therefore, there is no set of data or truths that can be properly understood apart from the incarnation of the Son of God. Everything true is given in Christ. The second meaning of the universal nature of truth given in Christ is that whole truth necessary for the fulfillment and redemption of an individual human being is given in Christ. Men need not look elsewhere, for the complete happiness and truth about man is revealed in Christ.

What happens in coming to faith, then, is that one is called to participate in the truth of Christ. This is **the** truth, not a possible truth, or a truth just for me, but the truth for all mankind, the truth of all things. Also, this truth given in Christ is not a series of "facts" or philosophical teachings or abstract insights or moral precepts, rather it is a personal truth given in His person. What it means to say that this truth is personal is to say that within the Christian tradition, truth is inextricably bound to history, where the covenantal faith in the Lord of history is revealed in the New Covenant. In the life of a particular man, Jesus of Nazareth, the fullness of God is revealed in history. All the great advances in knowledge in modern times pale in comparison to this truth in Christ. After all, he is the Son of God, who is sent by the Father to do the will of the Father. There can be no fuller revelation, no more definitive knowledge of whom God is and what it means to have faith than what is given in Christ. The knowledge of faith, then, is not simply knowing some "things" about Christ, but knowing

Christ. Faith is best described as a personal relationship, and like all personal relationships, it engages one on a most basic level. Such relationships are not simply emotion or whim. For instance, when a person falls in love with someone, that love is based on a knowledge about that person. Yet, when the person in love is asked what that love means, that person cannot simply list all the reasons why he or she loves the beloved. Thus, love is not simply an emotion, but presupposes a knowledge that comes from each person revealing oneself and giving oneself to each other.

Since the truth that grounds faith is more than simply knowing some "things" about Christ, it demands a different kind of response. This response is described as a *metanoia*, a conversion, a change of heart that reflects a change at the very core of one's being. The truth given in the person of Christ is a truth that engages us and calls us to conversion. Anyone who is serious about the Christian life is well aware of his or her own personal failures in responding to the love of Christ, i.e., we all are aware of sin. Nevertheless, as one grows in faith, one comes to realize that there is no other truth that one can turn to; there is nowhere else to go. At the heart of the world, each individual is called to be for or against God. There is no neutral place, no zone that one can step into and wait to see what will happen. What is unfolding in each of our lives, at every moment of our lives, is the center and meaning of all history: mankind's relationship to God.

Faith is the response of the believers to the gift of grace offered to them in and through Christ. But there is prior reliance on the grace of Christ, which makes faith possible. It is the gift of God's love, the offer of his very self, the offer of grace that fulfills one's very life. Faith, then, is an act whereby the believer responds to the call of Christ. It is a response to the salvation accomplished in Christ by His death and resurrection. It is a free act, where the believer receives the offer of salvation and grace.

Since this is a free act, the believer can never be compelled to have faith. Just as one cannot compel another to love, one cannot compel another to believe. Unlike most contemporary attempts to explain the world in terms of natural forces, thereby understanding human life as product of those forces: i.e., evolution, Christianity understands faith to be a free act, requiring the free response of the free creature to the free offer of love. In the act of faith, the believers freely accept a relationship with Christ, entering into the Trinitarian life, informing their lives according to that love.

This offer of grace and man's response are free acts. And as free, they are acts of will rooted in the truth of Christ. This means that freedom is more than having the ability to choose, it means choosing God. One is only free when one chooses to live in the truth of Christ. Apart from this truth, which is given in Christ, there can be no real freedom, since freedom requires truth. Freedom does not mean self-determination; rather, it means to be freed to live in the truth of the faith. In the Christian tradition, freedom stands in opposition of living in sin, to be free means to be free from the bondage of sin. So faith must not be understood as some servile obedience, which negates human life, but it is in faith, the giving of oneself to God, that one comes to oneself.[30]

Many today are confused about the relationship of truth and freedom. They believe that to accept some truth is a loss of freedom, but quite the opposite is true.[31] In this act of love, which constitutes the act of faith, one is freed from other false claims upon one's life. To be without this truth means to be enslaved to some other false claim to truth. Only in the light of faith can the believer now sees things in truth. There is no other alternative. As a matter of fact, it is in the decisions concerning faith that we become free; we are free to live the truth of our existence according to the love of Christ who is both the means to – and the end of this life. The freedom given in Christ is the only real freedom. All other "attempts" at freedom end in the tragic submission to an ideology, a system of thought, which can never satisfy the fundamental needs of a creature created in Christ and for Christ. Submission to such systems can only mean slavery.

Nevertheless, today as before, many have turned away from the truth of the gospel, substituting for it with other alternative philosophies. As noted earlier, such idolatry cannot but end in tragedy to which the modern world bears witness. For not to live in truth is to live in falsehoods, substituting some other "claims to truth" for the truth of the gospel. The Church, in her mission, guided by the Holy Spirit, continually bears witness to the truth of the gospel. One sees this in her sacramental life and in her magisterial teachings. Today, just as in every age, she calls all people to fidelity in Christ. It is precisely the presence of this truth that makes her an "expert in humanity" struggling to defend the "civilization of life" against the forces of the "culture of death," whose presence is ever evident in abortion, artificial contraception, genetic manipulation, fetal experimentation, and euthanasia.

Summary:

Today, the meaning and purpose of marriage and family are a matter of dispute. The particular meaning that one gives to marriage and family reflects the manner in which one understands the world and the place of human life within that order. The dispute is fundamentally between those who see marriage and family as the product of social convention, thereby able to evolve, change, or even be eliminated according to cultural development or historical progress, and those who view marriage and family as part of the created or natural order. In

---

30. Veritatis Splendour argues that living a moral life requires great courage.
    [31]Keefe, *Covenantal Theology*, 336.

the latter case, marriage and family reflect the order of how things ought to be and therefore need to be sustained. Any movement to change or to eradicate that order is understood to be a sign of cultural decline.

Many of those who support the family do it from a religious basis. They believe that God has placed an order in creation and marriage is part of that order. In marriage, man and woman are united in a unique relationship, a unity that later gives birth to offspring. This understanding of marriage and family is most evident among the evangelical churches and the Roman Catholic Church. They reject the relativism and individualism of contemporary society, claiming instead that the truth of the faith is the only real truth. In the truth of the biblical revelation, the real nature and meaning of marriage and sexuality is given.

At the heart of the Christian position is the claim that there is only one truth and that truth is given in Christ. The act of faith is not simply a part of life, but a choice to accept God or to reject God. Because of the comprehensive and fundamental nature of such a decision, faith leaves no part of life untouched. Consequently, only within this comprehensive act of faith can the true nature and meaning of marriage be understood.

Marriage is an act of faith. It is a religious act whereby the people getting married come to share in the grace of Christ in a special way. I often tell students that the only reason I can see to get married is for the salvation of their souls. Within the Catholic tradition, this means that marriage is a sacrament. Consequently, the full significance of marriage can only be understood from a religious perspective, and all attempts to view it from another perspective end in idolatry and lead to the decline of marriage.

Suggested Readings:

Alexander Solzhenitsyn, "A World Split Apart"
Bryce Christensen, *Utopia Against the Family*
Pope John Paul II, *Letter on the Family*
Pope John Paul II, *Veritatis Splendor*

Study Questions:

1. Do you think that there is a spiritual crisis in the West as described by Solzhenitsyn and Pope John Paul II? In what ways might you differ in your assessment from what they say? With what points might you agree?

2. What does it mean to have faith? What is the relationship of faith and marriage?

3.   Do you think this characterization of the modern attitude toward marriage and the family is accurate?   How might you contribute to or change this description?

4.   What does it mean to be a Christian in the modern world?   Is it still possible? In what ways is faith necessary in every age?

5.   Why is marriage, fundamentally, a religious event?

Chapter II:
The Christian View of the World

If one observes the different Christian denominations and other Christian churches today, one is immediately struck by the variety of ways in which they live and express their faith. Some churches, for instances, demand that their members be "born again," and that they continually bear public witness to their redemption accomplished by Christ. Within this interpretation of Christianity, the focus is on the point of conversion, before which one was in sin, now one has faith. Catholics, on the other hand, understand this same dynamic to be the focal point of faith but see it expressed in a different way. They tend to see faith development as part of a life-long process where one grows, sometimes slowly and sometimes more quickly and deeply, in the love of God. Through the particular events, acts, and decisions within one's life, faith is understood to develop over time. In Catholicism, this "growth" in faith is centered in the reception of the sacraments, especially the Eucharistic worship of the Church, through which the believers continually grow in the life of Christ. Nevertheless, despite the differences between the Christian approaches to faith, they share the belief that faith means a change of heart, a conversion, and a consequent change in the way in which one views the world and in the way in which one lives. The failure to make such a conversion is to continue to live in sin, to reject God's grace given in Christ. One result of this rejection is the inability to recognize the truth.[32]

a. Faith and the Christian View of the World

Christians believe that in the act of faith the individual undergoes a change of heart that leads to a greater participation in the truth that is given in Christ. At the center of the act of faith is twofold realization. First, the believers come to realize the gratuitous nature of their lives and their total dependence upon God as the source of all life. At the same time, this is the realization that one's very existence, as well as the existence of others, is the product of God's love. Human beings do not cause their own existence, but are totally dependent upon

---

[32]Such an interpretation of the faith may seem narrow in an age such as ours when diversity seems to demand that one accept the beliefs of others, even if the beliefs of others are contrary to our own set of beliefs. Diversity presupposes that truth is culturally determined and that one culture should not impose itself upon another. It ends in cultural relativism. Christianity, on the other hand, holds that there is a truth for all people given in Christ. He is the truth. Real freedom and salvation can only be found in him. Apart from this freedom and truth, one can only live in error.

others and ultimately upon God for their life. As the creation story indicates, the whole of the created order comes from God and it is good. The very order of creation has its origin in the trinitarian love of God. It is from this love that the grace of Christ, the Word, proceeds from the Father bringing forth the created order. There is no other source of reality, including human life.

Because of the fundamental nature of faith in human life, the act of faith cannot simply be considered an act to be accomplished at some point in time and then it is over. Rather, since it touches upon the very core of our being, the act of faith has a lasting significance. In this act one comes to rest in the triune God and, consequently each human being will find this relationship to be at the heart of everything that one does. Faith is an act that takes one to the very heart of existence.

An analogy for this relationship to God might be one's relationship with one's family. Prior to marriage, most people see themselves in terms of their relationship to their family. After marriage they see themselves in terms of their spouses and children. These are defining relationships that are more important than the other aspects of one's life. So that even though one might spend many hours working, one would give up one's job, sacrifice one's wealth and even one's own life for those people that we love. In a like manner, faith should define one's life, because the most important things in life are at stake in the act of faith.

The second component of the act of faith is the realization that human beings are in need of redemption. Because of sin, humans have lost the freedom of the original integrity of the good creation. Sin has so completely affected the good creation that Christians understand the world to be fallen. That is, the world, though good as created by God, is experienced as fallen and, therefore, estranged from the unity with God to which it is called. On account of this fallenness the whole created order suffers from this estrangement; e.g., suffering, sin, hatred, etc. The human experience of the fallenness of creation is so profound and so pervasive that they sometimes assume that this fallen state is "just the way things are." In fact, there is no other experience for human beings. Under the conditions of fallen creation, man moves away from God and cannot stop this movement through his own efforts. Sin leaves humans helpless and in radical need of salvation. In the end, man finds himself in a particular dilemma. He finds himself without the ability to save himself in a world that is fallen, but should not be that way. Because of sin, the whole created order is in need of redemption. Man needs to be saved.

The Christian tradition affirms that creation is good; it came from God who is good. As free creatures human beings are called to the love of God, and every human being is free to accept that offer of love or reject it. Sin is the choice to reject Christ and to place at the center of one's existence something other than the love of Christ. The result of this choice is a disorder in creation. Once this fall has begun, under the bondage of sin, humans are bound to continually move away from God. Only the redemptive activity of Christ can reverse this tendency. Except for the grace of Christ, redemption is not possible.

The act of faith is shaped by both the insights of God as creator, and the human experience of their radical dependence upon him, and God as redeemer, who alone can save creation from the radical nature of sin. Both the grace of God and sin touch human life in its most profound dimensions. Sin is a rejection of what is good, the truth of reality, which results in one's own destruction. Each sin alienates one from the order given in creation and from the love of God to which each person is called. Only by the grace of Christ can the alienation due to sin be overcome.

In the redemptive act of Christ, the very nature of man as created by God is restored. By the redemptive act of Christ, the person is not called to be other than what one is, but is now able to be what one is at one's most fundamental level. Thus, faith is not alien to human life, something foreign to human nature or imposed on it.   Rather, grace is man's relationship to God, the offer of love given in the sacrifice of Christ, that makes it possible for each person to love God, thereby bringing their nature to its completion as ordered in creation. For man this means that it is precisely in faith that one is called to love. This is the very love to which each human being is called by God; a love that overcomes sin and provides the basis for a good human life. It is love that demands fidelity to the triune God who alone is the proper object of human love.

As all real love, the love of God demands fidelity and is unable to tolerate any form of idolatry or polygamy. It requires an either/or decision. As one grows in the faith, one must realize that all of the other options offered by the world are inadequate. In fact, there are no other options since the truth of the created order and the whole truth about man is given in Christ. The only other option other than faith is to accept those idolatries that form the basic challenge to faith. These idolatries have plagued human existence from the beginning, either putting man in the place of God (as depicted in the story of the Fall in Genesis) or placing something else from the created order in the place of God. This dynamic struggle between faith and idolatry is, of course, the struggle that is at the heart of human life, both within each individual and within the community.

In the end, the only redemptive option is given in Christ. For it is Christ who is the source of our existence, and it is in Christ that redemption takes place. Only in Christ can the radical destructiveness of sin be forgiven. By his death on the cross, sin is overcome. It is through this redemptive process that the believer is called to participate in the love of Christ so that we might become the "new creation," redeemed and restored in the only truth there is: the redemptive love of Christ. In the act of faith, the Christian is called to believe and grow in the love of Christ.   Christ is the source of all that is true and all that is good, there is nowhere else to turn.

As noted, today, this claim that the truth and redemption of the created order is only given in Christ may seem strange. In our pluralistic age, we are often
taught we can believe all sorts of things, even contradictory things at the same
time. In many instances, people continue to attend churches where the enthusi-
asm for the gospel message and urgency of its preaching has waned. In such
churches, one finds little said about the importance and difficulty of believing
and often finds the gospel "watered down." Often, the preaching is not only
diluted, but it takes on a strange mixture of beliefs, sometimes failing to distinguish between certain traditional beliefs and contemporary cultural opinion.
Seldom is one confronted with the Cross and the scandal of the faith in a world
that fails to believe. Quite simply, many believers and churches belong more to
this world than to Christ. Yet, the gospel demands a complete giving of oneself
to that which alone fulfills human life.

The nature of this relationship between the believer and Christ seems to be
governed by a paradox, which lies at the heart of faith. First, in faith we enter
into the fullness of the *mystery* of God, whose existence and meaning always
transcends our own lives. As humans we seek an infinite love, wholeness, unity,
and peace which is never achieved in this world, not even by the saints. In the
gift of the Son, the Father offers us a participation in the infinite love of God. In
faith, we enter into this mystery, give ourselves over to this mystery, and are
united with this mystery. Yet, we are not the mystery, we do not create the mystery, neither do we ever control it; rather, we give ourselves over to its control.
In one sense, it is like "falling in love." You do not plan it or try to orchestrate it
(such manipulations are usually disastrous). Something happens to you, yet
nothing is imposed on you. A person offers himself or herself to you, an offer
you either accept or reject. Yet, even if you accept the offer of the other, you
do not possess the other nor do you lose yourself, since no human can completely control another. The other always remains other, a mystery, not because
the other is unknowable, but because of its fullness that can never be completely
known or possessed.

One way to say this is that every human being possesses an openness that
corresponds to the truth of existence given in Christ. If this were not true, then
the redemptive grace of Christ would be something foreign to us, imposed on us
from the outside. Since the object of human love is the creative and redemptive
love of the Trinity, humans must possess the ability to participate in that love.
That is our "nature." Though not *the* mystery of God, each person is a mystery,
even to themselves, a mystery that finds its complete fulfillment in Christ.

Second, despite the fact that in the act of faith the believer is called to unity
with the divine, the act of faith is *historical*. This historical dimension at the
heart of the Christian faith finds its completion and fullness in the revelation of
Christ. So, the great mystery of the love of the Triune God, which is the "object" of our faith, is concretely offered to us in history. We need not escape time
and space to "find God." One could even say that the great salvific message of

Christianity is that the God of all creation has entered into history, becoming man and dying on the Cross for us. He is here among us, most concretely in the Incarnation and the Church, his Body, his continued presence in history. History is where one finds God. History is sacramental.

The tension between these two poles, the transcendent, mysterious dimension of the faith and the concrete, historical nature of the faith find their unity in Christ. This truth is no doubt the source of the scandal of the Christian proclamation. Nevertheless, this teaching becomes the measure and center of all life, and anyone following this way of life must perceive the world in a manner different from others.

b. Faith, Christ and the Trinity

If the role of the Christian faith is to bring all people to God, then who God is will certainly affect the nature of the mediation and the kind of faith that the believers will have. Within the Christian tradition, faith is mediated by the *revelation* of Christ, who in this process reveals Himself as divine. The Christian faith is always faith in Christ, since He is not only the means to God, but God Himself. In the traditional language this is expressed in the doctrine that Jesus Christ is one person with two natures: i.e., He is both God and man. Despite the presence of these two natures, which remain distinct, there is perfect unity within him. One of the things that this reveals to us is that the divine and human do not stand in opposition to one another. Instead, it reveals there is a fundamental openness in the created order so that it is able to mediate the grace of God. This is a novel idea in the history of religions. It also makes it possible for the faith to be mediated by a historical reality such as the Church.

Unlike Christianity, many religions hold that at the heart of reality is a cosmic dualism, which separates the eternal from the limited multiplicity of the material order. The divine, the eternal, the immortal, stand outside the limits of physical existence. On the other hand, notice that within Christianity, one does not find God by escaping the world or by being transported into the realm of the divine, but God acts in history, saving His people and the whole of created order by His redemptive power. In the revelation (the words and deeds of God in space and time), man is offered salvation. It is precisely this unity between God and man, the Creator and creature, divine and human, that is the scandal of Christianity, a scandal that does not permit human manipulation of the truth. Instead, it demands a conversion to the truth who is Christ.

In the Christian doctrinal tradition, the final and complete affirmation of the ability of God to enter into creation is the Incarnation – God becoming man. From a Christian perspective, it is the central event of all history. There can be no greater revelation, no greater event, no greater truth, than the unity between God and man made possible by the Father's sending of His Son. The incarnation opens up history in such a way that not only is the divine now present in human history, but humans are now able to enter into that fullness and grace for which they were created. This is the final affirmation of the goodness of creation and God's love for us, the sign and source of our redemption. It is the event by which we enter into the Trinitarian life of God.

What should be noted here is that in the incarnation, Christ is not simply a redeemer God, playing a role and passing from the scene; rather, He continues to redeem human beings throughout history. Just as He entered into history saving man by His death on the cross, Christ remains present in history continually offering salvation to mankind. It is to His person, His being, and His love that the believer is called. Faith, then, is not a set of laws or precepts but a call to respond to the redemptive acts of Christ. This call is given in Christ whose authority extends both to the order of creation and redemption. One might say that both reality and faith are Christocentric. Yet, even Christ finds the Trinitarian love of God to be the source of His life and His relationship to the other persons of the Trinity shapes the interpersonal nature of His redemptive actions.

1. Christian Faith and the Trinity

When one listens to people speak of their faith, one most likely will hear people say that they "believe in God." One probably assumes that what they mean is much the same as what we mean when we say that we believe in God, but that might not be the case. Amid the growing diversity in the West, there is bound to be a greater variety of definitions of God. For example, one possible meaning of the statement "I believe in God" would be the belief that God is some infinite force or powerful being who is reality itself and controls the order and ultimate purpose behind all things. Such a God would be a power removed from history, an impersonal force, revealing himself from time to time as a cosmic force. This definition of God as an impersonal force often takes the form of pantheism, where God is considered to be in all things. Even among Christians there are a variety of ways in which they understand God. Even though they are all monotheists, there is still a variety of ways in which to understand God; i.e., forgiving, compassionate, just, etc. Yet, seldom does one hear of anyone, even Christians, saying that they believe in the Trinity, though many Christians do pray in the name of the Father, the Son, and Holy Spirit.

The traditional teaching on the Trinity states that there are three persons in one God. To set this in the broadest context: this is a rejection of both tritheism (three distinct gods) and a kind of modalism, where a single divine being simply takes on different forms. Against these ideas about God, Christians believe themselves to be monotheists, while at the same time insisting that there are three distinct persons within the Godhead.[33] All of the persons are completely

---

[33]*Catechism of the Catholic Church*, para. 249ff.

divine. There are no gradations between them, none being more or less God than the others.

The origin of this understanding of God is found in the Old Testament. The Jews understood God to be the Lord of history, departing from the nature religions of their neighbors. In the Old Covenant, God revealed Himself to be a God who, although infinitely above man, acts in history to save His people. He was a personal God, who chose the Jews according to His purpose, making a covenant with them, freeing them from idolatry, inviting them to the worship of the one true God. Nevertheless, the infinite distance between God and His people is never completely bridged under the Old Covenant. For despite the fidelity of God, His people continue to sin. They are unfaithful to the Lord, giving themselves to all sorts of idols, awaiting the coming of the messiah, the one who will stand before God.

With the coming of Christ, however, what was only partially revealed in the Old Covenant is made complete in the New. Since Jesus is the Son of God, He perfectly bridges the gap between God and man, something not accomplished under the Old Covenant. It is also in the revelation of Christ that the mystery of the Trinity is revealed. One sees in scripture that Christ is sent by the Father, comes from the Father (Jn. 5:19ff, 10:25ff) and is in union with the Father. Notice, Christ, despite the insistence of His unity with the Father ("I and the Father are one"), is not the Father. It is only in and through the mission of the Son that the Father was revealed. What was revealed by the use of the name Father is that "God is the first origin of everything and transcendent authority; and that he is at the same time goodness and loving care for all his children."[34] The Father is the source or center from which all things come. The Son is begotten of the Father from all eternity. This does not mean that there was a time when there was only the Father, since the persons of the Trinity coexist from all eternity, but it says something about the relationship of the Father and the Son.

The Father, as the source from which all things come, sends the Son, who sends the Spirit. The sonship of the Son can only be understood in terms of his relationship to the Father, as the one who is sent by the Father. The mission of the Son reflects his relationship to the Father. He is begotten of the Father who is the origin of all. And the Son, as the First born of all creation, is the center, the prius of the whole of the created order. Christ "bridges" the gap between the Father and creation, both in the process of creation and in the process of redemption. Through Christ, the order of creation moves out of the Godhead. Through Him all things came to be (Col. 15ff). And in the end, Christ will restore all things to their proper order and return them to the Father. Or, as Paul states, "so that they might be all in all" (Eph. 1:10). Christ is the beginning and

---

[34]*Catechism*, para. 239.

the end, uniting the created order and the order of redemption. The whole of reality is Christocentric.

At the same time, the believer comes to know the Spirit through the activity of the Son. It is through the love of the Father for the Son, and the love of the Son for the Father that the Spirit is sent. The Nicene Creed states that the Holy Spirit "proceeds from the Father and the Son." This is not a temporal procession, the Spirit coming last, but a means of expressing the mission of the Spirit in terms of the mission and activity of Christ whose acts are always in perfect harmony with the will of the Father. For just as the Son is with the Father from all eternity, the Spirit is active from the beginning. The scriptures speak of the Spirit as active in creation and throughout the Old Testament. Later, the Spirit is active in bringing about the mission of the Son and then bearing witness to that mission, revealing its true meaning. One sees the Spirit particularly active in preparing for the coming of Christ into history with the incarnation, and by the continued presence of the Spirit in history during the time of the Church.

What is important here is not only the ontological description of the nature of God within the Trinity, but the relationships themselves. No longer is God understood as simply an impersonal infinite being or power, but as an interpersonal being who is defined by His infinite loving relationship. The relationship between the divine persons is directly reflected in their activity and relationship to the created order. The Son, in his perfect obedience to the Father and love for the Father, not only dies to redeem man, but is the Logos through whom all things come to be. Likewise, the mission to send the Son to give the Spirit "terminates in the creation of the New Covenant, which is the creation, in Christ, of humanity as the context and condition of the freedom of his immanence in creation."[35] In His obedience to the Father, the mission of the Son is both creative and redemptive, restoring fallen creation to its unity within God. Therefore, a creation that is created by such a God must be essentially a free creation whose existence must reflect the free grace of its origin (God). Within such a view of the world, God is not all things, nor does He absorb all things to Himself, but He is a personal God who creates that which is other than God and relates to the other in love.

Faith in Christ, then, has a personal Trinitarian dimension. We are called in and through Christ, and now through the Church, to participate in the triune love of God. This love is radically personal and radically free. The created order does not have a necessary origin within the Godhead, but is a free act of love. Issuing from that love is the whole of the created order, an order conceived from the personal love of God, as the persons of the Trinity give themselves to each other in the full freedom of divine beings. In faith, the believer is called to participate in both the order of creation and redemption, which, as graced, as love,

---

[35]Keefe, *Covenantal Theology*, p. 344.

depend solely on Christ.[36]   In the end, one might say that all things issue forth from the Trinity and are dependent upon the Trinity.   In faith, the believer is called to participate in the love of the Triune God. The whole of salvation history, then, is the history of the Trinity.[37]

2. Christ and Creation

It has been stated that if God is Father, Son and Holy Spirit, such an understanding of the nature of God leads to a certain understanding of the faith. This means that if everything in creation is utterly dependent upon God for its being and salvation, then the order of creation and redemption must reflect the personal nature of the Godhead. Creation must reflect its origin.

This might sound like a strange idea to most people living at the end of the twentieth century, a century dominated by positivism and pragmatism, where many of man's primary accomplishments have been in the realm of science, technology, and productivity. Since the Enlightenment, there have been many attempts to try to find an understanding of creation on other than religious grounds. One result has been to replace the Christian idea of creation with a theory of cosmic evolution or the "big bang theory," where the universe is generated by and governed by a set of natural laws and forces. From this modern empirical perspective, the "natural world" is understood to be an object, admittedly vast and beautiful, which should be studied by science to discover the truths about the universe.

This knowledge procured by the sciences has a dual purpose. First, one seeks such knowledge for its own sake. It is good to understand the order of the universe. Second, humans want to understand the universe so that they can better control human existence in that universe and live better. Now, such knowledge and power are in most instances good. But often hidden in such a view of the world is the belief that God is not an integral factor for understanding the cosmos. According to the modern secular vision of reality, one can give a completely coherent and complete account of reality apart from God. Since within such an understanding of reality, with its own order, rationality, and integrity, God and his grace are not necessary. This "natural" order is thought to stand on its own. In this worldview, the world has an origin and order apart from God.

This view of the world, assumed by many today, stands in opposition to the Christian view, which believes that reality itself is created by God and dependent upon God. In this world view, if there is such a thing as grace, it is some-

---

[36]Walter Kasper, *Theology of Christian Marriage*, trans.by David Smith (New York: Seabury Press, 1980), pp. 37ff.

[37]*Catechism*, para. 257.

thing that is added later, but it is not essential to the workings of the universe. This modern empirical approach to reality has certain benefits and provides insight into the nature of the physical world, but from a Christian perspective, it fails to give an adequate account of the created order.

Many Christians today hold this view of reality although it is incompatible with the Christian belief in creation. Within the Christian tradition, the created order comes from God and is dependent upon God. It is created in Christ, who as the New Covenant, bestows the order of that covenant upon creation. This means that the created order is graced from the very beginning. For it is given in and through Christ. Therefore, the created order is not an object, "out there," to be studied, but is radically dependent upon Christ, issuing forth from the "Word" "through whom all things came to be, apart from which nothing came to be" (John 1:3). The created order, then, is not an order closed in upon itself, subject to some necessitarian order established by the laws of nature, but a free gift given in the New Covenant, an offer made to us to which we are called to respond. The created order, "nature," now must be understood to be graced; therefore, this grace is the prior condition or ground upon which the created order is possible.

The ramifications of such a way of thinking are of course enormous. In the academic world, it would require the placing of Christianity and Christ at the center of all disciplines. This does not mean that the knowledge gained through the practice of the different sciences must be abandoned, but that they need to be reexamined in the light of the truth of the faith. For instance, the hard sciences, such as biology, would have to abandon its present metaphysical basis (or anti-metaphysical bias) and replace it with a Christian metaphysics. If that would happen, then one could only imagine the changes that would take place in biology. Would they not see the meaning and purpose of the created order differently? Would biologists not look upon the value of human life and the meaning of all life from a much different perspective? You can imagine the effects on other areas of study, such as having an economic system that integrates the Christian view of the world, rather than beginning with the assumptions of present day economic theorists.

Also, such an understanding of creation and "nature" will certainly affect the way in which marriage is understood. From a Christian perspective, all creation is graced. Marriage is not, then, some natural estate to which grace is later added. Rather, marriage reflects the order of the good creation. As it pertains to the creation of man in the Genesis account, it is an order that is male and female. Thus, if the created order is graced from the beginning, and man is created male and female from the very beginning, then human sexuality is graced and therefore sacramental. As sacramental, our sexuality becomes the means by which we image God and the means by which we enter into the divine life. The grace of marriage is rooted in who we are as sexual beings before God.

In addition to the Christian view of the world standing against the reductionism of modern science, where all metaphysical truth is reduced to empirical reality, the Christian view of the material world stands against those dualisms that separate form and matter, the divine and human, good and evil, men and women. According to the dualist worldview, what is real is the unlimited, the eternal, the divine. The material realm is evil, limited, finally to be overcome. Salvation is, in the end, an escape from the limits of space and time. Such dualistic ways of thinking have greatly influenced much of world thought. One finds it at the heart of much of eastern philosophy, in the work of the Greek philosophers and operative in any variety of ways still today. In particular, one sees the influence of this way of thinking in contemporary theories of sexuality.

The Christian tradition, on the other hand, says that salvation takes place in space and time. This is possible because of the nature of reality and the nature of God. In the Christian tradition, the material and spiritual worlds are not antithetical. The problem for the Christian is not the material world, but sin. The created order, as created in Christ, is good. And unlike the dualist view of matter, which understands it to be an impediment to the divine, Christians have a sacramental view of the material order. In this view of things, the material order is capable of mediating the divine. Remember, as created in Christ, the order of creation and the order of redemption are free. Their structure is covenantal. God acts in the created order to offer to His creation His redemptive grace. Within the biblical view of the world, the order of creation is not a closed system: i.e., closed to the mediation of the divine, separating man from God. Rather, Christ, the New Covenant, the one through whom all things were made, becomes perfectly united with His creation in the incarnation. His very existence as the New Covenant is the source of all grace and establishes the created order, an order created in and through Him.

Another way to state this is to say that the goodness of creation is affirmed in the fact that it can mediate the divine. The only other option is to say that creation stands in opposition to the divine. In the latter case, the significance of the created order is lost amid the limits of temporal existence that prevent the union of God and man in fallen creation. In such an instance, the physical world would be evil. It would prevent one from "knowing" God.

Some Christians see the world as created good in the beginning and at that time the physical creation could mediate the divine. But they would argue that since the original creation, sin has entered the world and the created order is now closed to the mediation of the divine. Those Christians, who interpret the historicity of the faith in this manner, understand the fall to be overcome only at the end when Christ comes and destroys the sinful world, creating an entirely new heaven and earth. On the other hand, most Christians hold that despite sin, the created order remains good. Sin has certainly affected the whole of creation in a profound manner, but the original grace of the good creation cannot be overcome by sin. If creation ceased to be substantially good, it would cease to exist. Therefore, despite sin, God continues to be present in fallen creation.

Again, it needs to be noted that the goodness of creation is not given *ab extra*, from the outside. It is not "good" because God likes it, or indicates that it is good. Rather, creation is substantially good, since it is the product of the grace of Christ. In the same way, marriage, then, cannot simply be thought to be holy or good because it was decided at some point that it should be. Rather, as created by Christ, marriage is substantially graced and reflects the order of the workings of that grace. In marital love, one enters more completely into the New Covenant, whose order informs the good creation and the process of redemption. Marriage becomes an act of worship whereby we enter into the life of the New Covenant given in the Cross of Christ.

3. Christ and the Order of Redemption

In order to understand the meaning of creation, it has been necessary to look at the meaning of the redemptive activity of Christ. For what one sees is that the center of Christian history is the incarnation, death and resurrection of Christ. This event, the Christ-event, as the full revelation of God - God Himself becoming man - contains, summarizes and reveals the truth about the whole of creation, including man. This means, of course, that despite the fact that creation is chronologically prior to the incarnation, the New Covenant is the center of all things and creation takes its meaning from this event. The historical event of the incarnation of Christ, including the death and resurrection of Christ as the New Covenant, is the metaphysical *a priori* of the act of creation. The person of Jesus and the events of His life are the revelation of this truth. They are not only the basis for understanding individual lives and the process of redemption, but they are essential to discerning the truth of the created order. And although the Christ-event is an event in history, it is at the same time the source and end of history. Christ is the "end" (in the sense of fullness and completion of history) of history because in Christ the full revelation of God is given and the final redemption of man in Him and through Him is offered. Christians await no further revelation of the truth, no second act, no sequel.

Despite the fact that all things are given in Christ, as the truth, fulfillment and completion of history, the redemptive activity of Christ is not an afterthought to fix the world that is broken because of sin, but His salvific presence "fits;" i.e, is in harmony with the order of the good creation. The redemptive acts of Christ are the completion of the salvation history which fulfills what is given in creation. This revelation of Christ was known before the foundation of the world, and as the complete revelation of God in time and space, all of history moves towards it and away from it.

In contrast to this Christian view of history that measures all things in terms of the Christ-event, today it is often thought that what is given in history is man-made and stands in conflict with what is given in nature. Many argue that nature is antagonistic to human life; humans need to conquer nature and control it. An example might be the argument for artificial contraception. According to this view of things, one's fertility, as part of the natural order of the body, is understood by some to be simply a natural, neutral, "pre-moral" power that is in need of control. Accordingly, one needs to control fertility. What is thought to be good and bad does not depend on the intrinsic meaning of the power or act, but on how something is used. This position places humans at odds with their nature, exalting human freedom and mastery over the natural order. This mastery over nature is thought to free human beings from the bondage to our bodies and enable them to live a more human life. From such a perspective, human history is the struggle to overcome nature.

Another way of viewing this tension between man and nature is found among those who see humans as enemies of nature and want to limit human activity so that one might preserve the natural order. Often this position lapses into a kind of pantheistic reverence for the "pristine" order of nature. This is evidenced quite often in the ecological movement, where other human goods are secondary to the preservation of the ecological order. In both cases, the tension between man and nature is understood to be real and irreconcilable.

In contrast, the Christian tradition understands that in the covenantal order of creation there is no conflict between human beings and creation. In the good creation, man is at home in the world. Yet, man often experiences himself to be at odds with the created order. This begins with our experience of the world as fallen, radically under the power of sin. Because of sin, human alienation is so profound that it is often described in terms of man being divided against himself.

This experience of alienation resulting from sin is expressed by the idea of original sin. Original sin describes the state of man as he is separated from the grace of Christ. It points to the radical alienation of man as he tries to give meaning to his own existence, turning away from the redemptive love of Christ. The effects of the "fall" seem to be evident, extending beyond personal sin to the created order itself.[38]

The experience that there is "something wrong with the world," particularly the problem of sin and evil, has been the starting point for many theologies. People suffer physical pain, do evil to each other, die in catastrophes, and endure other innumerable hardships. Since the tradition has held that this evil cannot come from God, since God is good, how does one make sense of such experiences? The answer of course has always been that sin enters the world through the free agency of the creature in his rejection of God and of the order of the

---

[38]For an account of the radical nature of sin, see St. Augustine's *Confessions*.

good creation.[39] The effects of this agency are universal: not only all men, but the whole of the created order falls. Nevertheless, sin does not destroy the created order. Creation, since it is in and through the grace of Christ, can never be completely overcome by sin. The grace of the Christ remains stronger than sin. This is also true of the covenant. Despite the fact that humans are unfaithful, the covenant remains sustained by the grace and fidelity of the Lord, who remains faithful to His people despite their sin. God, in His graciousness, sustains that order in love, in the hope of our repentance.

The Fall, this opposition to the order of the good creation, this disorder in creation, can only be overcome by the redemptive activity of God. The biblical accounts describe this redemptive activity of God as taking place in salvation history. In the historical circumstances in which the people find themselves, God acts. Within the Christian tradition, just as within Judaism, it is from the historical revelation of God that Christians come to their unique way of understanding the meaning of their existence in the world. They see God choosing them, entering into a covenant with them, providing for them, and finally saving them. This whole process, revealed in part over time, constitutes their salvation history.[40]

In each instance, the covenant, whether with Moses, Abraham or with Noah, refers to a relationship between man and God. From the biblical perspective, it is precisely this relationship between God and man that is at the center of all things. The whole of the created order, its meaning, purpose, and significance must be measured in the light of this relationship. Remember that man is the only free creature who "images" God. (This is very different from the cosmologies of the ancient world where the significance of human life is diminished amid vast natural forces.) From the biblical perspective, man is the crown of creation, the one who stands before God and the rest of the created order can only be understood in the light of this relationship.

Within this covenantal relationship, if His people will be faithful to the Lord, the Lord will save them and provide for them. God promises Abraham the land, Moses the Law, and David a Kingdom. This covenant is a free covenant,

---

[39]Here, a more detailed account of the nature of sin and the teaching of original sin might be helpful. What is important, though, is that the fall, the rejection of the good creation, is free act without any prius. It is *ex nihilo*. See Keefe, *Covenantal Theology*, pp. 307.

[40]Today, one often finds that the literal, historical reading of the Bible is neglected. Many scholars claim that one needs to abstract from the events to some deeper truth. Yet, the scandal of Christianity is that the particular historical events do mediate the grace of God. Jesus was not an abstraction, but a unique human being. By neglecting the event character of the faith, the significance of our own actions in history is diminished.

initiated, as all things salvific, by God and ultimately fulfilled by God. The Jews are asked to freely respond to this initiative. They are called to fidelity to God. In each instance, the covenant reestablished the relationship between God and man lost to sin.

In the Christian religions the New Covenant is Christ. As "New" it is not simply better in degree, but as "New," Christ's redemptive activity reestablishes in a fundamental way the order of the good creation. What was lost to sin is now restored. When one thinks of this restoration, what comes to mind first of all is that the unity between God and man is restored in and through the perfect obedience of the Son to the Father, an obedience that culminates in His death on the Cross. By the grace of Christ, the believer is now redeemed in the Cross of Christ, the one true sacrifice by which all are saved. In the act of faith, the believers should experience this redemption in their personal lives, since in the act of faith the believer is united with Christ in the New Covenant. The offer of the grace of the New Covenant is given in Christ, in and through the sacramental life of the Church.

Yet in this process of redemption, not only is the individual brought to faith and experiences grace in his or her own life, but the salvific activity of Christ extends to the whole of the created order. In Christ, the "old man" enslaved to sin and death is replaced by the "new creation" (Eph. 4:17ff). This "new creation" takes its life from the resurrection, which is not simply a resurrection in spirit, or of the soul, but a bodily resurrection. Here, in a most evident way, the extent of the salvation is revealed. This salvation is not simply restricted to some "spiritual dimension," but is a transformation of the whole created order, including the physical order of creation. This restoration of the created order is particularly evident in the redemption of man.

Man, as created in Christ, has various dimensions. The way in which any culture speaks of the human person varies from age to age; yet most commonly, we talk about the physical and the spiritual dimensions of man, the body and soul. Both are part of the good creation created in Christ, and both suffer the effects of the fallenness of creation. In the process of redemption, then all that which is fallen will be redeemed. For example, Christians believe in the bodily resurrection, not only of Christ, but that all those who believe will be raised with Christ on the last day. In the resurrection, Christ overcomes death, the effect of sin, saving the whole person, not simply plucking a soul from a body. The Christ who was born, suffered and died is the Christ who is raised from the dead. The bodily resurrection, then, points to the integrity of the human person. We are bodily creatures and the significance of the body is important for our life and our salvation.[41]

---

[41]Later, in chapter six, Pope John Paul II's understanding of the body will be discussed.

Since the bodily resurrection reasserts the goodness of the whole created order and its inclusion in the process of redemption, it is not surprising that in the Bible the covenant is often described in terms of marital imagery. This nuptial imagery is not merely metaphorical, but tells one something about the nature of the covenant and something about marriage.[42] First, the use of marriage as an image for the covenant reveals that the covenant is personal, based on the free relationship of God and His creatures. Neither is compelled to enter into this covenant. It is a relationship of love, a relationship only possible for personal beings. Second, comparing the covenant to a marriage raises fidelity to a primary category of human living. Noticeably, God's fidelity is of a higher order than that of man; nonetheless, only in fidelity to God does man become human. Likewise, God's love for His people is reflected in His fidelity, His unwavering commitment to the salvation of His people. Despite the fact that His people break the covenant, God remains steadfast in His love.

Also, fidelity not only reflects the fact that one endures in one's commitments, but as in marriage, fidelity includes the whole of one's life. It is a total and comprehensive giving of oneself to another, body and soul. In the marital images of Ephesians, it is precisely the redemptive gift of the whole Christ given in the one sacrifice of the Cross, that Christ, the Bridegroom, makes holy His bride so that she might receive Him. By the grace of Christ, the Bridegroom, the Church is able to give herself wholly to the reality of the New Covenant.

In the end, it is in and through Christ that all things are created and all things are saved. "He is before all things, and in him all things come together.... For in him all the fullness of God was pleased to dwell, and through him to reconcile to himself all things, whether on earth or in heaven, making peace by the blood of his cross" (Col. 17-20). By the cross, the whole of the created order is restored to the integrity of the good creation lost to sin. This includes the salvation and the restoration of human life in all of its dimensions.

4. Christ, Mary and the New Covenant

This language of the Bridegroom and Bride is biblical language that many Christians have heard time and time again. In fact, it is one of the dominant analogies for the relationship of Christ and the Church. Again, the use of marriage as an analogy for the covenant is more than a metaphor. This analogy says something essentially true about the nature of God's relationship to man. That is, through this bridal imagery, the scriptures reveal the intimate and personal nature of the New Covenant. And, as noted, since the covenantal structure not only describes the relationship of God and man, but the relationship of God to

---

[42]This will be taken up again in the next chapter.

the whole of the created order, this bridal/covenantal order must refer not only to the order of redemption, but to the nature of created reality itself.

One way of getting an insight into the meaning of the covenantal structure of redemption in Christ is to look at the role of Mary in the economy of salvation. Mary reveals the meaning of the human response to the divine offer of salvation, and therefore, the free human response to the New Covenant. Contained in her actions is the free response of the New Eve, the one who responds on behalf of the now fallen creation to the full offer of grace given in Christ.

Within much of contemporary theology, Mary's significance in the process of salvation has often been neglected. Even since the publication of *Lumen Gentium,* which again affirms the importance of Mary in the economy of salvation, many Catholic theologians have been less than enthusiastic in admitting the importance of Mary for understanding the faith. A result of this neglect of the significance of Mary by systematic theology is that the Marian doctrines and their relationship to the New Covenant have been often ignored.[43] Yet, her role in salvation history is not secondary or accidental, but essential, and any explanation of the faith that fails to include a discussion of the role of Mary is inadequate.

The doctrinal tradition concerning Mary, and the profound insights into the faith that these teachings indicate, has the capacity to deepen one's understanding of the order of redemption. If one cannot understand the role of Mary in salvation history, then one would have difficulty giving an adequate account of the freedom of the created order and the role that any human plays in the process of salvation. Likewise, it would be difficult to account for the biblical description of sin, freedom in Christ, and a final salvation of the whole created order.

Unlike most Protestants, Catholics understand Mary to have an essential role in the economy of salvation. Although Mary did not "cause" the incarnation, it is by the power of the Holy Spirit that she conceives. Yet in her role in salvation history she is not merely passive, for it is by means of her free acceptance that Jesus Christ, the Son of God, the second person of the Trinity, became incarnate. Her "fiat" is central to this economy, since she accepts on behalf of all humanity the free and complete offer of the grace of the New Covenant. Without her acceptance of this offer, the incarnation could not have happened, since God does not impose salvation on us, but freely offers it to His creation. And if, as has been noted, the New Covenant is the central event of all history, by means of which alone the intelligibility of all reality is given, then understanding the actions of Mary has an essential role to play in understanding the redemptive activity of Christ.

---

[43]There are theologians such as Henri de Lubac, Hans Urs von Balthasar, and Donald Keefe whose theologies reflect the significance of Mary in the economy of salvation.

The covenant, as a relationship requires the free action of two parties. For a covenant, like marriage, is a free agreement, consisting of an offer and a response. The offer of grace by Christ, then, cannot be imposed on another by Christ nor accepted by Christ, but requires another to accept what has been offered. The only alternative would be for the whole process of salvation to lapse into a monadic Christianity where all freedom is abolished and salvation is imposed. It has been noted that Mary's freedom was made possible in Christ. As all freedom, Mary's freedom has its source in the forgiveness of sin and the salvation accomplished in Christ. Therefore, Mary is not holy by her own means, but by the power of the Holy Spirit. The fact that the holiness of Mary is through the grace of Christ does not diminish her role in the economy of salvation. As holy, as sinless, it is her free acceptance on the behalf of the fallen creation that enables salvation to enter the world, a salvation, which as free, cannot be imposed on the fallen creation, just as it cannot be imposed on any free creature.

When many Christians hear of the holiness of Mary, they assume that she had to say yes to the offer of grace. But if this is the case, her agency would be reduced to mere passivity and diminish her significance in the order of redemption. Yet it is precisely in the "fiat" of Mary, by the free act of Mary, that the Immanuel enters into history. Through the "fiat" of Mary, the second Eve, the integrity lost to sin is once more restored, and now available in the Eucharistic life of the Church. Moreover, through her acceptance of God's offer of grace, the meaning of the feminine, the good creation and the redemptive order are revealed. Consequently, the role of Mary is important for understanding the Church, especially the sacramental and covenantal nature of salvation that she offers. Mary's role in the process of salvation affirms the sacramental nature of the New Covenant and the life of faith.

c. Faith and the Church

According to the Catholic tradition, if one is to understand the nature of faith, it is necessary to go beyond the individualistic interpretations of faith that have plagued Christianity during the modern era. Today, in the West, faith is often understood to be a matter of personal and private opinion. Yet, individual interpretations of the faith, though many are interesting and inspiring, always fall short of a complete interpretation of the faith. As individuals, we are sinners and never fully participate in the life of Christ while we are in the world. Our sinfulness prohibits us from receiving the fullness of the grace of Christ in any final sense. Limited by human sinfulness and by our nature, humans require "outside help."

Because of the limits imposed by human sinfulness, within the tradition, faith was understood to be an act with dimensions that transcended an individual Christian's act of faith. One way in which Catholics have expressed this larger dimension of the faith is by saying that faith is an ecclesial event. That is, within fallen creation, from the Ascension of Christ until the second coming of Christ, the Church mediates the faith to the individual believer through her preaching and in her sacramental life. Notice, it is the "faith of the Church" that becomes our faith. Only in the Church, the Body of Christ, are Christians brought to faith.

In the tradition, the Church is likened to a "mother" from whom the believer receives the faith.

> In proportion to our faith, the Church, this "family' into which baptism has introduced us, preserves the consciousness of our personal identity with this symbolic name. She furnishes us with the environment in which this consciousness can flourish. She maintains among us those things that are so endangered: respect for life and death, a sense of fidelity in love, the sacred character of the family; she maintains them only as a mother can. From birth to the grave, she envelops our life in her vast sacramentary structure.[44]

The Church is the womb in which the believer is given faith, and therefore, life. In a sense, then, the Church acts as a sacrament of Christ, mediating the fullness of the grace of Christ to the believer.

It needs to be understood that the Church is not like other human "institutions." She is more than a collection of believers who hold a set of beliefs, such as a fraternal organization or a political party of some sort. Rather, the Church is holy and "contains" the fullness of Christ. She is the Body of Christ, mediating Christ to believers in ways beyond the ability of any individual member or group of members. Her integrity comes from Christ, not from the lives of her members. This "integrity" and identity of the Church are seen in the ability of the Church to mediate Christ in ways that are unique. For example, since the faith is a great mystery, the mystery of God, no Christian can mediate that event. Christ, the divine subject of the Church's mediation, transcends the mediatory power of any individual or group of individuals. Yet, the Church is able to mediate the fullness of the faith. The Church is, like Mary, made holy by the blood of the cross so that she may respond fully to Christ, the full offer of redemption made to us concretely in the midst of fallen creation. In his graciousness, after his ascension Christ left us His "body," the Church, to mediate the fullness of

---

[44]Henri de Lubac, *The Motherhood of the Church* (San Francisco: Ignatius Press, 1982), p. 156.

the grace of His death and resurrection to all believers. The Church is His Bride, His Body, who, as made holy by the grace of Christ, responds to the offer of grace made to all humanity in and through the Cross.[45]

Because she is the Body of Christ and the Bride of Christ, the Church is made holy and given life by Christ. Her holiness and consequent authority is not her own creation, but given by Christ. As the Bride of Christ, His Body, the holiness of the Church is the holiness of Christ, since all that is salvific is given in Christ alone (Eph. 5:21ff). This is particularly evident in the Eucharist, where in the sacrifice of the Mass, the believers participate in the death and resurrection of Christ, the events by which they are saved and from which all things take their meaning. Here, the Church, as the Bride of Christ, participates in and mediates the New Covenant. In her role as mediator (like Mary), she responds to the offer of Christ, opening fallen creation to the larger dimensions and meaning of the grace of Christ. The Church's response to the Eucharistic celebration of the sacrifice of the Cross is one of praise. Her role is to respond to Christ, pointing to the role of Christ in creation and the economy of salvation history. In her life, the Church calls us to the fullness of the redemption offered in and through the mission of Christ, the bridegroom whose life and death frees us from sin and death.

Consequently, if the Church has this ability to mediate the grace of Christ, the sole reason for her existence, she has a holiness and consequent authority that exceeds any individual. The authority of the Church is not one that seeks to control people's lives, but to teach the faith and administer the sacraments. She is able to mediate grace, offer the holiness of Christ. She provides a context where the believer might come to faith, grow in faith, and find life in Christ. To recognize this sanctity does not usurp the freedom of the believer, but it is to say that Christ continues to be present in the midst of space and time, saving his people in and through the Church.[46]

The sanctity of the Church is precisely what Vatican II affirms as one of the central characteristics of the faith. In the document *Lumen Gentium*, the council affirmed the sacramental nature of the Church. There, it noted that the Church acts "something like a sacrament."[47] The Church, as she exists in history with

---

[45]Here, an analysis of Ephesians 5:21ff points to the relationship of Christ to the Church in terms of the marital relationship between the groom (Christ) and his bride (the Church). The Church is made holy by the blood of Christ so as to be free to "marry" Christ, thereby enter into a full communion of love.

[46]On the issues of legitimate authority and the difference between authority and power, today so readily confused, see Joyce Little, *The Church and the Culture War*, 23ff.

[47]*Lumen Gentium*, in Vatican Council II, ed. Austin Flannery (New York: Costello Publishing Co., 1988) para. 1.

her hierarchy, laity, and Marian character, mediates the grace of Christ. Insisting upon the holiness and the consequent sacramental nature of the Church, Vatican II even goes so far as to insist that the true Church "subsists" in the Roman Catholic Church.[48] Therefore, the Church is the great gift through which the believer is offered the redemption he seeks. Her essence is not a set of laws, but the free covenantal offer of grace that constitutes the heart of the New Covenant, which is concretely present in the sacramental representation of the sacrifice of the Cross given in the Eucharist. Either, one accepts her claims to authority, or rejects them; there is no other option.

Within Christianity today, one of the fundamental decisions that one must make is whether or not to accept this understanding of the Church. One must decide whether the Church is able to mediate the faith in this manner or she is not: i.e., either she is holy or she is not, either she is apostolic or she is not, etc. A view of the Church that emphasizes her holiness is for many difficult to accept. Today, modern consciousness formed by empiricism and the methods of the social sciences tends to separate the human from the divine, reducing the Church to one among many social institutions. At the same time, influenced by contemporary pluralism and individualism, faith is often relegated to one opinion among many. Or, many now tend to think of the Church as a kind of "democracy" whose beliefs ought to be determined by the majority. From another point of view, contemporary realism sees the Church as full of sinners; and if she is full of sinners, how can she mediate the grace of Christ in any definite manner?

More commonly, one hears of people accusing the Church of trying to mediate something beyond its authority, or claiming authority for itself that is beyond its grasp. Even more radical opponents of Catholicism accuse it of being an oppressor of others, using its power to exploit its members. For example, some feminists say that the Church is patriarchical, oppressing women. Liberation theologians say that it is aligned with the wealthy and powerful, oppressing the poor and powerless. On a more personal level, every Catholic usually has a complaint of some sort about the Church. They range from complaints about bad sermons, to severe nuns, to the Church's concern about money, to feelings of guilt, and a whole litany of other difficulties. Yet, most of these perceived and real difficulties do not diminish the holiness of the Church, they simply indicate that the Church is now in fallen creation. One also needs to be reminded that despite its failures, the Church and its members have continually bore witness to the grace of Christ in many of their deeds and sacraments.

In answer to such criticisms, the Catholic understanding of the faith has always been optimistic about the presence and continued redemptive activity of Christ in history. That is, despite sin, Roman Catholics hold that the Church

---

[48]Ibid., para. 8.

mediates the fullness of the grace of Christ in fallen creation. The redemptive grace of Christ is present to us here and now in the life of the Church.

The alternative to the Roman Catholic understanding of the faith is found in the Protestant emphasis on *sola fide*.[49] According to this interpretation of the faith, under the conditions of fallen creation there is no unambiguous mediation of the grace of Christ during the present time except the Bible. The Protestant interpretation of the faith rests on the two key ideas: one is saved by faith alone (*sola fide*), and the radical fallenness of creation. Within that tradition, these two ideas work in concert. Because of the radical fallenness of man, he depends solely on Christ for his redemption. In essence, all Christians would agree to this, but from the Catholic perspective the reformation understanding of the faith goes too far, minimalizing the role that the believer plays in the process of redemption. According to the Protestant tradition, because of sin man is completely passive in the process of redemption. No human action can be redemptive or participate in the redemptive activity of Christ. Those who hold the Protestant position argue that if human effort could in any way achieve or merit salvation, then Christ's redemptive death on the Cross would not be necessary. Consequently, all faith and grace are given *ab extra*. They are totally gratuitous, the gifts of Christ. All one can have is faith, which is the belief in the promise of Christ that if you believe, at the end of time you will be saved. Because of sin, the fullness of salvation that Christ brought into history in the incarnation is, since the Ascension, gone until the end of time when Christ returns again. The Church, as an institution existing in the fallen creation, is an eschatological community whose present authority is limited by sin. Therefore, during the present fallen history, there can be no definitive mediation of the redemption of Christ, including the Church.

Further differences between the Catholic and Protestant understanding of the faith can be seen in their differing views of the sacraments. Catholics and Protestants differ not only as to the number of sacraments, but also as to the very nature of the sacraments. Within Protestantism, there are various ways in which sacraments are understood, but in general they are thought to be an extension of the word. Moreover, since the world is fallen, a fallenness that even affects the Church, human symbols and rituals cannot mediate the fullness of the grace of Christ. For example, in the Protestant tradition, reconciliation is not a sacrament, in part because the Church is not thought to be able to mediate the forgiveness of sins here and now. That power belonged to Christ and he is gone from history. Likewise, marriage is not thought to be a sacrament. Marriage is understood to be part of the order of the good creation, thereby, it possesses a natural dignity and goodness, but it is not part of the order of redemption.[50] Be-

---

[49]Gerhard Ebeling, *Word and Faith*, (Philadelphia: Fortress Press, 1963), pp. 39ff.

[50]Walter Kasper, *Theology of Christian Marriage* , p. 33.

cause of sin, no human promise of love can be redemptive; therefore, marriage cannot be sacramental. Within this tradition, redemption is something to come, not present at this stage of history. The present time remains under the bondage of sin. The process of sanctification has not yet begun. There is only the promise of the future salvation given at the end of time.

Today, unfortunately, many Catholics do not share the optimism of their faith and tend towards the ecclesiology of the Reformation churches. They do not accept the teachings of the Church, claiming the Church to be wrong on this or that matter. Most of these criticisms of the Church are born of the implicit rejection of the Church's claims to holiness and her ability to mediate the divine life, which is the source of the authority of the Church. When an individual Christian claims the Church to be wrong and themselves to be correct on some issue, they are asserting that their insight into the faith has more authority than that of the Church. (It would seem that in accord with the virtue of prudence such claims should be rarely made.) Or that simply no authority at present is better than another, all are equally ambiguous or all equally good.

In contemporary Catholicism, there is a great deal of confusion about matters of faith, because more than ever there are various interpretations pressed upon the believers, many with ecclesiologies that depart from the tradition of the Church. Again, in this situation one enters into the realm of either/or decisions that one must make. For if the fundamental option within the life of faith is to believe or not to believe, a close, subsequent question concerns how one understands the faith. Either the Church has its origin in Christ and is dependent upon His redemptive activity and mediates His grace, or she is simply a human convention, the product of fallen human nature, with a minimal role in the redemptive process. Although the Church contains sinners, either she is holy, able to mediate the grace of Christ, and therefore, teach with genuine authority because she has been made holy by the blood of Christ, or she is not and can not do what she claims.

At the same time, how one answers this question will have significant consequences for the way in which one understands faith and the nature of marriage. For either marriage, as part of the life of faith, is an ecclesial event, opening one up to the larger process of salvation, participating in the fullness of the redemptive grace of Christ now operative in history, or marriage is merely a human promise, subject to all the ambiguities, mistrust and limits of fallen creation, and thereby, not salvific. Only in the former instance, marriage is thought to be a sacrament, capable of mediating the grace of Christ.

The best way to sort through this is to remember that the Church does not bear witness to herself but to the author of her life, Christ. She, like Mary, acts to mediate this grace, being transparent to the Son of God through whom salvation enters into the created order. One cannot by-pass the Church to encounter Christ, just as without the mediation of Mary, Christ could not enter into history. The mediation of the Church, especially in the sacraments, is central to the faith.

It is within the context of this mediatory role of the Church that the sacrament of marriage finds its meaning

Summary:

To understand the sacrament of marriage, one needs to see it in the light of the faith. Faith calls for a radical transformation of one's life that touches upon the very center of one's being. Because of its profound nature, faith must be comprehensive, giving answers to the questions concerning the whole of human existence. Christ is the comprehensive answer to fundamental questions. In Christ, all people are given answers to those significant questions about the mystery of the redemption and creation. For as the New Covenant, Christ is the one from whom the order of creation and the order of redemption take their meaning. And our faith is in the New Covenant, who is Christ.

Marriage, then, as an act of faith, needs to be understood in terms of the larger economy of salvation. This economy is, of course, centered on Christ and is distinguished from all other systems of belief by the salvation mediated in Christ. He reveals to us the Trinitarian nature of the Godhead. From this revelation one discovers that God is a personal God, whose essence is the relationship between the Father, Son, and Holy Spirit. The relationships within the Godhead are reflected in the created order where Christ is the one "through whom all things came to be" (Jn. 1:3). And as the New Covenant, he is sent by the Father to restore the fallen creation. It is into this creative and redemptive process, revealed in the fullness of the life of Christ, that the believer is called to participate.

This redemptive process is further summarized in Christ as the New Covenant. What is revealed is that both the order of redemption and the order of creation have their origin in Christ. Both come from the one grace of Christ and are covenantal. As a matter of fact, all of reality, including creation, needs to be understood in terms of the coming of Christ. For the New Covenant is a free offer of salvation made by the Son on behalf of the sinner. By His actions, the created order, now under the power of sin, is restored to the fullness for which it was intended. What was instituted in the beginning has its origin in the fullness of the New Covenant that is given in the historical event of the death and resurrection of Christ. This salvation is not imposed on the created order, but freely offered in Christ and accepted by Mary, as the representative of all humanity. She, freed from sin by the sacrifice of Christ, is able to accept the offer of redemption given in Christ. Christians, then, are called to act like Mary and accept the offer of Christ's grace now mediated to the believer primarily in the sacramental life of the Church.

What is of primary importance for understanding marriage is that it must be understood in terms of the larger system of salvation. In marriage, the couple is able to more completely participate in the economy of salvation, which includes in Christ, a unity of the order of redemption and the order of creation. In marriage, the tension between these two orders, which have their origin in the fall, is reconciled in and through the redemption death of Christ. In Christ, sin is overcome and the new creation in Christ, the conversion of our fallen nature, is brought to fulfillment in the New Covenant.

Suggested Readings:
The Catechism of the Catholic Church
Henri de Lubac, *The Christian Faith*
Donald Keefe, *Covenantal Theology*

Study Questions:
1. Why is the idea of a bodily resurrection so important? What does it tell one about the nature and extent of the redemption offered in Christ?

2. What does it mean to say that Christianity is an ecclesial religion? How does this affect the way in which the faith is understood and practiced?

3. What is the Trinity? What difference does it make to say that we believe in the Trinity?

4. What does it mean to say that Christ is the New Covenant? Why is this the central idea for understanding both the order of redemption and the order of creation?

5. Why is Mary so important for understanding the actions of Christ and meaning of the New Covenant? How does she reveal to us the meaning of the New Covenant?

Chapter III:
The Nature of the Sacraments

Throughout Christian history, the sacraments have played an important role in the life of faith. One finds the celebration of the sacraments to be an essential component in the life of the early Christian communities and they continue to be important to the life of the Church to this day. Yet despite the almost universal agreement as to their significance for the life of faith, at times the exact meaning and nature of the sacraments have been a matter of dispute. In the history of the Church there have always been attempts by certain Christians to "redefine" the sacraments in the light of what they consider to be the definitive aspects of the faith. The result of the Church's response to such heretical theologies was the development of a more complete doctrine of the sacraments.

Since the Reformation, the discussion of the sacraments has been controlled by the Protestant and Catholic interpretations of the sacraments. Within the Protestant tradition, the sacraments have for the most part been interpreted as an action at the service of the Word. In this view of the faith, the Bible is the primary means by which the redemptive activity of Christ is mediated in history. The sacraments are understood to be an extension of the faith now offered to the believer, *sola fide, sola scriptura.* That is, they are a means of proclaiming the content of the scripture. Consequently, the sacraments are circumscribed by the context of the scripture.

Contrary to the Protestant position, one of the identifiable traits of the Roman Catholic tradition has been the manner in which it has come to recognize the primacy of the seven sacraments in the life of faith. The reason for this is that Roman Catholics have understood the sacraments to be the primary means by which the grace of Christ is offered to the believer in the midst of fallen creation during the time of the Church. The sacraments bridge the gap between the Christ who lived two thousand years ago and the present. They are events through which one comes to participate in the redemptive events of the life of Christ. The grace that was ushered into history with the incarnation continues to be present to the believer through the sacraments. Consequently, the sacraments are the center of the life of faith and the faith needs to be interpreted in the light of this sacramental economy.

Faith, in the Catholic sense, is more than a psychological disposition, the expression of a feeling that one's relationship with God is well. Rather, faith is a sacramental reality, a relationship with Christ Himself, the mystery of salvation, a relationship that concerns all of the dimensions of human life, not simply the affective. Moreover, from a Christian perspective, this relationship between God and man is not only the center of the individual's life of faith, but also the center of the whole of human history and the foundation on which reality itself rests. The sacraments provide the means by which the believer comes to understand and participate in the redemptive activity of Christ at the heart of reality.[51] They are the gift of Christ to the Church.

a. Christ and the Sacraments

As with all things within the economy of salvation, in order to understand the sacraments, one must turn to Christ. In the most profound sense, Christ is the foundational sacrament, the key to understanding any theory of the sacraments. As the New Covenant, He is the one through whom the promise of salvation is completed and fulfilled. Here, in the individual life of a man, God reveals himself by entering the created order in such a way that the complete union of God and man is accomplished. This revelation on the part of God is free gift of the triune God. In and through Christ all things are created and redeemed. In the present stage of salvation history, though creation is good, it is now under the power of sin. Only in Christ is sin overcome, creation fulfilled, and the reign of truth established. In Christ, salvation history reaches its fulfillment, and that which was foreshadowed in the Old Testament becomes complete. Salvation history is now fulfilled, although the realization of the present fullness awaits its eschatological fulfillment in the second coming of Christ. During the present, Christians are living in the time of Church. It is a time of the proclamation of the good news of redemption and the time of the realization of the redemption offered in Christ.

As a "sacrament," Christ is the visible sign of invisible grace. But unlike signs that point beyond themselves to something else, Christ is what He represents. He is the redeemer, the Son of God. There is nothing beyond Him. He is the perfect and complete revelation of God. He contains and *is* what He symbolizes.

Just as the Christ can be said to be a sacrament, the Catholic tradition has also contended that the Church also, acts as a sacrament. As the Body of Christ, the Church mediates the grace of Christ in history. As noted, Christianity is an ecclesial religion, since the believer comes to faith always in the context of the life of the Church. This does not mean necessarily that a person cannot be drawn to the faith of Christ without belonging to a particular church, but it does mean that the Church, like Mary, has an integral role in the process of salvation, including the salvation of each individual.

In the Roman Catholic tradition, the Church is understood to be more than simply the collection of individual believers. This "more" that the Church "con-

---

[51]*Catechism*, 774.

tains" is Christ, who is present to the Church continually as the "Head" of His Body and the Bridegroom of the Church, His Bride. The Church, as the sacrament of Christ, is the concrete presence in history of the continued offer of salvation given in Christ himself. All that is achieved in and through Christ is mediated by the Church. She is the Body of Christ, the Bride of Christ.

These images, the Body of Christ and the Bride of Christ, reveal the Church's unity with Christ and the consequent nature of that unity. The unity of the Church with Christ is founded upon the grace of Christ from whom all grace and salvation comes. As the Body of Christ, the Church is directed by Christ and receives her life from Christ, her Head. As the Bride of Christ, the Church's holiness is not derived from her own efforts, but she is made holy by the blood of Christ and sustained in her holiness by that one sacrifice which she continually offers in the sacrifice of the Mass. This unity with Christ, a perfect covenantal unity initiated and sustained by Christ, is the sole source of her holiness and consequent authority. There is no other basis for it. Because of this union with Christ her head, the Church is holy in a manner not diminished by her existence in the world. Her visible form in the world, although within fallen creation, is not overcome by sin. On the contrary, since the Church is holy, she is therefore able to mediate the grace of Christ in a definitive manner in history. Yet apart from the grace of Christ, the Church would lose her integrity within the fallen created order. She would become like any other human institution. But on account of her union with Christ, she has an authority that no individual believer has since the individual believers always remain under the effects of sin during the present age. Within the present, however, the Church functions like a sacrament, communicating the *fullness* of the grace of Christ in a manner that is unique in fallen creation. The Church is the concrete historical locus where the grace of Christ is given to the faithful.

Roman Catholics understand the relationship between the Church and the sacraments to be essential to the life of the faith. On the one hand, the Church is the place where sacramental worship is located in fallen history. Not only is it the duty of the Church to protect and promote her sacramental worship, but also her existence has a liturgical function at its very center: she responds on the part of humanity to the grace of Christ offered in the New Covenant. This response, the *sacrificium laudis*, is most evident in the Eucharist, the sacrament of the New Covenant. On the other hand, the sacraments are the concrete locus of the presence of Christ in the Church and, therefore, the source of the Church's life. As the source of the life of the Church, the sacraments have the priority within the Church. One might go so far as to say that in order to understand the Church one needs to understand it in the light of the sacramental economy.

Recent Church documents reaffirm the belief that the sacraments are the source and summit of the life of the Church. This means that in order to understand the Church, one must realize that the sacraments are the a priori *cause* of the Church. The sacraments are not the creation of the Church simply expressing an individual or communal experience of God. Neither the Church nor any human agency creates the sacraments. As instituted by Christ, the sacraments have an order and structure that transcends any human construct.[52] Like the Church, the sacraments are a gift from God, instituted by Christ. The sacraments represent the concrete offer of the presence of Christ in history. They are the means by which the recipients come to participate in the life of Christ, and are therefore, the means of sanctification where both the individual and the Church, as the Body of Christ, are made holy. One might say that in the sacraments it is as if one were standing before the Cross of Christ, looking Him in the eye and being offered salvation. In the sacraments, one participates in the historical event by which and through which one is saved.

This understanding of the sacraments may sound somewhat dramatic in an age when religious piety is often reduced to an inner experience of God; but a sacramental faith has the character of an event in which one encounters Christ, the Savior. Remember that salvation occurs by means of the death and resurrection of Christ. Those events are not mere show or drama that point to a salvation that takes place apart from them. Rather, the tradition contends that Christ's death and resurrection are essential to the order of creation and redemption, and these events alone are salvific. In this sacramental economy, the heart of the faith is not a *thing,* but a person, the Word made flesh. The sacraments connect us with those events by which we are saved, and at the same time, bring us into unity with the one who saves. They are the means by which we come to participate in the reality of life in Christ in all of its levels and dimensions. They incorporate the believer into the larger dimensions of redemption, placing the believer in a relationship to the very terms of their existence, terms that lie well beyond the power of human activity. From this perspective, the sacraments do not only have an instrumental function, uniting the believer and God, but like the truths that they mediate, the sacraments are great mysteries, revealing and mediating the whole dispensation of grace. As such, they need to be given to man, offered to him, since he can never construct or appropriate this reality or meaning through his own efforts.

Perhaps the best analogy for understanding the sacraments would be found in human relationships. One of the most unfortunate aspects of contemporary culture is that we are too busy to spend time with people. We are always working or running off in different directions trying to "get things done." Yet, the most profound dimensions of our life take place in human relations. Why is this? This is because in these relationships the truth of reality and about us as human beings is revealed. These relationships are so important because they engage the

---

[52]For instance, when Pope John Paul II insists that the Church cannot ordain women, he is assuming that the sacramental order is not the product of human convention, but part of an extension of the order of redemption initiated in the Incarnation. This is an order that is beyond human control.

person on the most profound levels of human life. For example, in the love of one person for another, the whole person is placed at the disposal of another. In a like manner, the sacraments are also comprehensive acts. They are personal acts, acts that engage the whole person, calling each of the recipients into the mystery of God. By means of personal encounter mediated by the sacraments, the believer comes to know and love Jesus better. It is this personal relationship with this personal God that gives Christian faith its unique comprehensive and foundational character.

But while the relationship with God is a personal act, it is not a private act, a mere internal change. It is an event. Note that in human relationships there is always what one might call a history. People who become good friends have spent time together, doing things, sharing experiences. Through these actions a person comes to participate in the life of another. Notice how skeptical we are of people who say they are in love only after knowing another person for a short time. We usually exhort them to take time to get to know the other person. One would argue that one cannot simply will that a deep relationship happen. A person needs to participate in the life of another for love to develop. The same can be said of the act of faith. One comes to love God only over time by participating in His life, sharing in those events through which He offers us His love and life.

Because of the essential importance of the events of Christ's life, the role of the sacraments in the economy of salvation is a necessary one. That is, one should not think of the sacraments as something merely "added on" to the faith or one option among many that a believer can simply choose. Rather, they are essential to the order of faith, since through the reception of the sacraments the believer participates in the events through which one is able to grow more deeply in the mysteries of creation and redemption. It is true that the Church recognizes that grace is given apart from the sacraments, but it is never given apart from the Cross and resurrection of Christ. Yet, even recognizing that grace is given apart from the formal reception of the sacraments, within the Catholic tradition, primacy has always been given to the sacramental worship of the Church. Even extra-sacramental grace is always understood in terms of the sacramental life of the Church. For instance, one can come to faith but never be baptized: e.g., a person dies before they have the chance to receive the sacrament. In those instances the faith of the person is described in terms of baptism *in voto*, by desire. Thus, even when the sacramental action has not taken place, that sacramental action remains the norm for understanding the faith. During the time of the Church, the sacraments are the central encounters with Christ and all other encounters are defined by them and in particular by the Eucharist.

As an essential component of the process by which the sacraments define the life of the faith of the individual believer, the sacraments incorporate the believer into the orders of creation and redemption. Within the sacraments there is an essential link between faith and the created order and the order of redemption. In the Christian tradition, the exact nature of the relationship between redemption and creation has been a matter of continual dispute. But essentially, Christians hold that the order of redemption and the order of creation coincide. It is the good creation, now fallen, that is redeemed. In the sacraments, the believer is called to participate in the redemptive activity of Christ in its full dimensions and the scope of that redemptive activity extends beyond the life of the believer to the larger order of creation. This is particularly evident in the Eucharistic worship of the Church.

The Eucharist, the sacrament of the New Covenant, offers the individual recipient the fullness of grace as given in the Cross. It offers the believer an encounter with Christ through which he is saved. The sacraments move the individuals beyond a personal holiness to a participation in the triune life to which each human being is called. Sacraments, then, can never be understood as simply accidental to the life of faith. Rather, the sacraments have both a definitive and necessary role in the process of salvation.

In addition to the fact that the sacraments are necessary in the economy of salvation, they are also great gifts that *inform* the recipient and the Church in the great mystery of salvation given in Christ. The faith of the believer and the Church reflects this sacramental foundation. The sacraments call the believer into this mystery of God's love for man. Thus, the sacraments, at one and the same time, open up the believer to the great mystery of redemption that is given in Christ, and they concretely offer to the individual, in the midst of their lives, the grace by which and through which they are brought closer to God. It is only within the sacramental life of the Church that these two different emphases are brought to fulfillment.

Before going on to discuss sacramental theory more directly, it might be helpful to reflect upon the nature of worship in general.

b. Worship and the Sacraments

Within human history, one of the central human experiences is religious worship. There are lots of different theories as to why worship is so basic to human life. Some argue that the most basic human experience is the desire to fulfill our daily physical needs. But at the same time human beings are well aware that all of our desires are not completely fulfilled by physical goods. Humans look for a larger meaning and purpose in life. This leads to the search for transcendent meaning and security within a cosmos that is often experienced as hostile to man. This search for the meaning of human life is often said to begin with the man's experience of his own finitude and the desire to find some solution to the problems of finitude. Attempts to answer those questions have led to a variety of religious expressions ranging from animism, to polytheism, to monotheism.

In the animistic view of the cosmos, the world is believed to be alive, filled with a variety of forces and powers. Religious life, which encompassed the whole of existence, was in part learning about those spiritual powers that animated the universe and learning to live in harmony with them. In polytheism, there were gods or divinities of some kind directly responsible for the different aspects of life. Prayers and sacrifices were offered to the gods, so that the gods, usually identified with forces of nature, would protect and benefit those who paid tribute to them. All such animistic and pantheistic religions were dualisms. They held that there is fundamental antagonism at the center of reality between good and evil, order and chaos, finite and the infinite, matter and form, the One perfect unity of eternal divine being and the many. What was real was found in the realm of the eternal, transcending the limits of finite existence. Anything caught up with or identified with matter was bound to be evil and oppressive. Thus, unlike the Christian view of the created order, where God creates and enters into history in such a way as to become man, in most ancient religions human beings and the gods are forever separated, the mortals never become immortal. In such religions, worship is understood to be the only means through which man is able to participate in reality, the realm of the gods.

In these cultures one did not separate religion from the rest of life. As a matter of fact, in most cultures something had to be religious for it to have reality. That is, to have reality, each thing that existed needed to have its origin in or be sustained by the realm of the gods. It was the divine realm alone that was real. It alone had power and endured, everything else passed away. If something fell outside the parameters of religion that meant that it lacked reality, that it did not have its origin in the eternal. In the worship of these religions, the adherents tried to escape the temporal world since no answer to the problems of existence could be found within the finite order. The realm of the gods was the source of order and power that stood against the ever-present forces of chaos. In the ancient mind, chaos was non-being. It lacked order; therefore, it lacked reality. Creation happened when the divine power was imposed upon chaos. Human life, as all things, found its purpose, meaning, and reality in and through the human participation in the divine realm, the realm of order. To find reality, one needed to transcend the finite.

Within these religions, worship is more than simply a means of finding individual meaning or security; worship is the center of all of life and essential to life. Worship is the *a priori* where people not only pray to the divine or encounter ultimate reality, but worship is thought to order and define human existence. It was presupposed that realm of the divine or the transcendent possessed an intelligibility that informed all that participated in that divine realm. Worship was the means by which human beings entered into that ultimate reality that transcends man, where human beings entered into a realm that was beyond their control. Man did not create this divine realm, nor does he control it, yet through worship, he is able to enter into it. Not only was worship a means of entering

into the divine, but it was also the means by which the worshiper came to understand and appropriate the meaning of life. "That which is created through this
meeting is nothing less than all reality which the community or assembly needs
in order to live. This includes the natural, historical and the spiritual realities
among which, of course, the ancients did not distinguish."[53] Worship not only
bridges the gap between the eternal and finite, but the very order of worship
embodies and reflects the divine order so that one becomes immersed in the
mysteries of the religion simply in the rite itself. Worship is the center of life,
sustaining, ordering, and fulfilling it.

Like all forms of worship, the sacraments are meant to unite the finite creature with the eternal, the real, the true, and the divine. What is unique about the
sacramental worship of the Church is that its object is Christ. This means that
Christians do not worship forces of nature, or some eternal being that stands
apart from the finite order, rather, the believer worships a personal God who acts
to save us not *from* history, but *in history*. This is the unique character of worship within the Judeo-Christian tradition. It is expressed definitively in the biblical idea of the covenant.

Within the biblical tradition the covenantal structure is established by God
in the beginning and pervades both the created order and the order of redemption. One might say that the whole order of grace is a covenantal order. This
covenantal order is centered in the relationship between man and God. In the
Old Testament, God calls the people of Israel into existence and acts to save
them. The actions of God in history reveal the meaning of their faith. The very
existence of Judaism depends upon the call of God and their response to His
offer. Jewish faith and worship are ordered according to this historical covenantal revelation of God to His people. The covenant, then, determines the whole
meaning of their existence and orders all aspects of existence for the people of
Israel. They are fundamentally a religious people whose existence is dependent
upon the fidelity of God to the covenant.

It is not surprising, then, that the worship of the people of Israel was centered upon those events that came to define the nature of their faith and their
existence. These events are not accidental to history, to be repeated or someday
replaced by others. What this means is that in those particular events God acted
definitively, uniquely and irreversibly to establish His people. For example, it
was the Exodus event, from the birth of Moses, the plagues, the exodus from
Egypt, the giving of the Law at Sinai, the wandering in the desert, to the cross-
ing into the Promised Land, that molded the Jews into a people. They came to
realize who God is and what it meant to believe in Him. They took on an identity from those events and those events came to form the center of their worship.

---

[53]Sigmund Mowinkel, *Religion and Cult*, trans. J.F.X. Sheehan (Milwaukee: Marquette University Press, 1981), p. 108.

One of the interesting facets of the Jewish understanding of faith and worship was the concrete historical nature of their worship. In their worship, they celebrated those events that formed them into a people. By means of their liturgical actions they once again entered into the covenant and became God's chosen people. Notice that according to Judaism, it was not proper or adequate to think about the faith or God in some abstract manner. Rather, they saw God's actions as historical and their religion as concrete. Consequently, their worship was not a mere memory of what God had done, but an actual participation in the salvific events. In worship, the events of salvation history are made actual for each subsequent generation; these events retain their significance for believers of all generations. "They [events] were actual for each subsequent generation; and not just in the sense of presenting the imagination with a vivid present picture of past events - no, it was only the community assembled for a festival that by recitation and ritual brought Israel in the full sense of the word into being: in her own person she really and truly entered into the historic situation to which the festival in question was related."[54] The event character of their worship gave the Jews a unique identity and concretized that identity in the life of the people.

Just as the worship of Israel was rooted in the definitive events of its history, in the same way the sacraments are acts of worship whereby the believer comes to participate in those events by which the faithful are saved. Christianity shares with Judaism a historical view of the world that accepts the revelation of God in history. But unless the sacraments are simply the same worship as that of the Old Testament, something new must have happened that distinguishes the Old Covenant from the New.

What is "new" is the coming of Christ. This revelation does not replace the past, but brings the past to completion and anticipates the future. Unlike the Old Testament, the sacramental worship of the Church is not informed by a series of historical events across the ages, but by the Christ-event, the life, death and resurrection of Jesus Christ. What is new is that in the life of this single man, history is fulfilled, the New Covenant is given, and the redemption of the whole of the created order is completed. In Christ, the whole of the created order finds its meaning and purpose, and the fallen creation finds its redemption. The sacraments, then, are focused on the life of this man who opens up fallen history to the life of grace now offered in His person.

This understanding of the sacraments is consistent with the New Testament term for sacrament, *mysterion*, "the term Paul used in referring to the hidden plan according to which God in His eternal good-pleasure intended to save, re-

---

[54]Gerhard von Rad, *Old Testament Theology*, trans. D.M.G. Stalker, vol. II (New York: Harper & Row, Publishers, 1965), p. 104.

new and unite all things in Christ (Eph. 1:9; 3:3-9)."[55] In the sacraments, the believer enters into this unfolding of the plan of salvation given in the life of Christ. It is here that sin is overcome and the offer of salvation is extended.

The definitive character of the revelation given in Christ is in one sense what makes the revelation different from that of the Old Covenant, where the definitive revelation of God is awaited. Moreover, the revelation in the New Covenant is given in the concrete life of a man, Jesus of Nazareth, through whose love we are saved. Both of these dimensions, the definitive nature of the revelation and the personal concrete nature of the sacramental worship are unique to Christian worship, a worship that finds its full expression in the cross of Christ.

The Cross is considered by Christians to be the center of reality. So that if one wishes to understand Christianity, one must begin and end with the Cross. The Cross is the focal point of the redemptive activity of Christ, the event in which the true nature and meaning of Jesus' mission are made evident. For in this one event, seemingly contradictory to everything that the world expected, Christ showed the depth of His love by dying on the cross, overcoming sin once and for all. In this sacrifice, the perfect sacrifice of Christ in perfect obedience to the Father, the New Covenant is established, the source of life and redemption. The Cross is the sole source of salvation, there is no other.

What is significant here is that the Cross is a historical event, which in conjunction with the Resurrection (also a historical event), reveals the whole meaning of the creation and its redemption in Christ. All the sacraments take their meaning from this event, communicating different dimensions of the complete redemption earned for us by Christ.

The sacraments, as founded upon the one act by which the faithful are saved, reflect the very event character of the source of their life. Like the cross, they are "events." Or, better, they are *representations* of the one event through which we are saved. In Baptism, we are baptized into the death and resurrection of Christ. In the Eucharist, we receive the Body and Blood of Christ. Moreover, the Mass is a sacrifice, a participation in the one and final sacrifice of the Cross, the perfect sacrifice in which Christ is both victim and priest (Hebrews 7:26-28). In the liturgy, Christ "principally makes His own paschal mystery present."[56] In each sacrament, the sacramental representation reflects the unique character of the paschal mystery, an act of complete love by the Son for the world.

The New Covenant cannot be separated from the revelation of God through Christ. In fact, he is the New Covenant. As noted, this revelation is definitive

---

[55]Jared Wicks, "The Sacraments: A Catechism for Today," in *The Sacraments: Readings in Contemporary Sacramental Theology* ed. by Taylor (Alba House: New York, 1981), p. 2.

[56]*Catechism*, 1085.

and unique since it is the full revelation of God. The sacraments, therefore, take their meaning from this definitive revelation in Christ. But the sacraments do not merely mediate a grace given in that event, but the sacraments themselves have an "event character." That is, the sacraments themselves have been informed by the historical nature of the revelation. The sacraments mediate more than an internal experience of God; rather, the sacraments, are acts by which we are made contemporary with the redemptive acts of Christ. As the *Catechism* explains:

> His Paschal mystery is a real event that occurred in our history, but it is unique: all other historical events happen once, and then they pass away, swallowed up in the past. The Paschal mystery of Christ, by contrast, cannot remain only in the past, because by his death he destroyed death and all that Christ is - all that he did and suffered for all men - participates in the divine eternity, and so transcends all times while being present in them all. The events of the Cross and Resurrection abides and draws everything toward life.[57]

Because of the event character of the sacraments, the faith of the believer can never be an abstraction. It does not retreat from history into some mythical time, but it is founded upon "what has happened." Such a faith is concrete. Such a faith alone is a historical faith.

If one begins with such an understanding of the sacraments, they can never appear to be unnecessary or simply an addition to the many "requirements" of the faith. Instead, they need to be recognized for the great gift that they really are. They are given to us by Christ so that those who come after Him will be able to participate in the redemption offered in and by the Cross. The sacramental actions extend the redemptive acts of Christ across time and into our present. Because of their ability to do this, the sacraments are the most profound and concrete of all human acts. In them, the believer is brought to the core of human existence and offered the grace necessary for all that is good and holy. To reject such an offer is a serious issue.

It was important to begin this chapter by placing the sacraments within the larger context of the life and redemption offered by Christ. This helps one to see the place of the sacraments in the larger economy of God's grace given in and through Christ. One discovers that the sacraments are not a later addition to the life of faith, nor the construct of the early Church; rather, just as the Eucharist is

---

[57]*Catechism*, 1085.

the summit of the life of the Church, the sacraments become the center of life in fallen creation, reflecting the covenantal structure of the grace of Christ offered to us in the New Covenant. They reflect the tension between the Christ who is at once concretely incarnate in fallen history, and the one who is at the same transcendent, not to be identified with anything in fallen history. This is the eschatological tension of the salvation offered in Christ. He is ever-present, continuously redeeming His people in the midst of fallen creation, but at the same time transcending fallen creation, not by escaping from it, but by converting it. His presence in history reveals the sacramental nature of reality. The seven sacraments reflect the sacramental nature of reality itself.

c. Teachings about the Sacraments

In the Roman Catholic tradition, the seven sacraments are understood as the gifts of Christ given to the Church so that the redemptive activity that began in the life of Christ can continue in the Church. In and through the sacraments, the conversion of the Christians becomes concrete since in the reception of the sacraments the believer becomes more and more deeply immersed in the mystery of salvation. As noted, the mystery into which the sacraments initiate the believer is the mystery of the New Covenant.

The significance of the sacraments within the history of the Church was clearly understood by most Christians from the very beginning. From the early accounts of the Church in the New Testament and the Church Fathers, it was assumed that the sacraments were essential to the process of coming to faith and salvation. Noticeably, throughout history there were some who disputed the need for the sacraments, but most Christians understood that they were constitutive of the life of faith. Yet, from time to time, there were great debates about the precise meaning of these sacraments, and out of these conflicts came some of the teachings concerning the sacraments that we have today. One of the changes that took place in the context of these debates was that there was a shift away from understanding the sacraments in the larger process of salvation history to a more direct concern for how the sacraments work and what were their effects in the lives of the believers. This shift was the result of the questions that arose out of controversy. For example, during the fourth century there was a challenge to the orthodox faith from the Donatists. In short, the Donatists believed that if one gave up one's faith during persecution, the effects of baptism were lost to the one who apostasized and upon a re-conversion or repentance, the person needed to be rebaptized. This, of course, raised the question about the nature of baptism and as to whether or not sin can overcome the grace of Christ and thereby destroy the sacrament. The response to the Donatists was that the sacramental grace remains despite sin (at least the sacramental character given in the sacrament), so a sinner need not be rebaptized when he reenters the

Church. Of course, it remains true that the one who receives the sacraments can reject the effects of the sacraments and the corresponding personal grace. But there are dimensions to some of the sacraments that do not require the explicit acceptance by the believer and are not contingent upon their response. In the case of baptism, it meant that one needed not be rebaptized after a serious sin, although penance was required.

Over time, the Church's teachings on the sacraments have developed and this process continues today. What these teachings represent are the discerned and revealed truths about the mystery of Christ and the process of redemption during the time of the Church. The Church and the sacraments are great gifts of God that lead the believer into this mystery. In the end, the Church does not "make" the sacraments, but through the revelation given in Christ and by her participation in the liturgical life, she is able to discern the proper use and meaning of the sacraments.

1. An Outward Sign

Within the tradition, the sacraments are described in a number of important ways. In most cases, they are understood to be *signs* that *effect or signify* something. The Greek word for sacrament, *mysterion,* was translated into Latin using two terms. The first term *sacramentum* refers to the visible sign of the deeper reality. The second term used was *mysterium.*[58] This was the deeper reality to which the sacramental sign referred. The *mysterium* referred to the mystery of God and the plan of God as it unfolded in creation and the process of redemption.

One common definition of the sacraments is that they are visible signs of an invisible grace. What the relationship between the sign and the effects of the sacraments is, and what kinds of effects these sacraments bring about, have been a matter of discussion. Yet, the need for a visible sign (*sacramentum tantum*) and the fact that they do bring about an effect (*res tantum)* or effects, has seldom been disputed.

The importance of signs can be explained in two ways. First, because human beings are physical creatures they need visible signs. It is not enough to simply imagine the redemptive activity of Christ or reduce that activity to some form of "inner" experience, the signs make that activity concrete. The visible character of the sacraments makes the grace of Christ available to the believers concretely in their lives. Second, the signs are not a secondary addition to the sacrament; they cannot be discarded or replaced by something else since they are constitutive of the sacramental economy. Each individual sacramental sign signifies the redemptive activity of Christ. They are not simply a reminder, but

---

[58]*Catechism,* 774.

make it possible for the believer to participate in the redemptive acts of Christ. Moreover, the physical signs point to and reflects the importance of physical reality in the plan of redemption, a truth affirmed in the bodily resurrection. This means that the physical world can mediate the divine, as indicated by the incarnation. In Christ, the true sacramental meaning of all creation is reveled.

Sacraments are visible signs, and as signs they cannot be separated from the event in which they have their origin or from the effects that they bring about. So, unlike some interpretations of the sacramental symbols that define symbols as mere signs that point to a reality that lies beyond them, leaving a separation between the visible sign and the reality signified, within the Roman Catholic understanding of the sacraments, there is no so such separation. In the sacramental action, something really happens. The Church points to this when she teaches that the sacraments work *ex opere operato*. For instance, in baptism, one is freed from sin, enters into the life of the Church, and now stands before God in a new way. This is accomplished through the sacramental action; i.e., the pouring of the water, anointing, etc. Noticeably, the recipient did not accomplish this, but by the power of Christ those who are baptized into the death and resurrection of Christ now live a new life. Likewise, in the Eucharist, one of the effects is that the bread and wine become the body and blood of Christ. Neither the priest nor the congregation "cause" this to happen. By stating that the sacraments work *ex opere operato*, the Church is saying that grace is offered in the sacramental action to us "by virtue of the saving work of Christ."[59] It is precisely this relationship between the sign, the sacramental action, and the effect that is the unique identifying mark of the sacrament, and at the same time, the mystery of the sacrament. The unity between the sign and the effect is sustained by the power of Christ through the working of the Holy Spirit. That is the guarantee of the sacraments.

The key to understanding the relationship of the sign to the reality signified is the concrete presence of Christ in history. That is, just as Christ became incarnate in the world, bringing salvation, so too, the sacraments continue to mediate the grace of Christ in a concrete historical manner. The man, Jesus of Nazareth, was the Christ. One no longer needs to hope that God will be near; rather, in Christ, He has entered into history. He is really here and present. In the same way that Jesus was visible in history as the fullness of redemption, the sacraments mediate the redemption of Christ when and where the sacramental actions take place. The physical signs, then, are essential to the sacraments as historical actions.

The Christian faith requires an engagement with the real historical, resurrected Christ, since it is through the acts of Christ that salvation is accomplished. There is no communion with God not mediated by the historical life of Christ;

---

[59]*Catechism*, 1128.

thus, faith can never be abstracted from the particular events in which God acts to save us.[60] If one is to admit that there is a means of salvation apart from Christ, one would then render the events of His life insignificant, or at least, limit the significance of His life to one possible means to salvation among many. But because of the essential connection between salvation and history, not only should the sacrament be understood in terms of the events of Christ's life, but they too must be understood as events. The sacraments are like events in that they are something that happen in one's life, and as all events, they define the life of the one who participates in them.

The teaching of the Church that best articulates this truth about the event-character of the faith is the belief that the sacraments act *ex opere operato*. That is, by the doing of the work, by the act itself, the effects of the sacrament are communicated. Here, the sacramental grace or effect is not thought to be the result of the faith of the believer or the congregation, but as all grace, it is the result of the redemptive activity of Christ. The believer can never be the cause of grace, or even merit the grace of Christ by any of his actions. Grace is always a gift, given *ab extra*. And even though the believer needs it, grace lies beyond the believer, given solely in and through the activity of Christ. The sacraments, then, reflect the covenantal order of creation and redemption, since every sacramental action relies totally upon the actions of Christ through which He freely offers salvation to those who will accept it. In the sacraments, the believers come to participate in the actions of Christ through which grace is offered and by which they are saved.

2. Cause and Effect

The Church not only teaches that sacraments are signs, but she also teaches that these signs are effective, "they contain the grace they signify."[61] This unity of sign and the signified is affirmed by the Council of Trent as constitutive of the Catholic understanding of the sacramental economy. The sacraments, then, are not solely reminders of a past event or promises of a future redemption; they mediate, here and now, the very grace by which we are saved. Unlike the

---

[60]In many instances today, people understand religious faith to be basically mystical. That is, it moves towards the direct encounter with the divine. Within such encounters, the self is usually annihilated and a union of sorts is achieved with the transcendent being. Such spirituality is not essential to Christianity. In Christianity, it is in and through the historical mediation of the love of Christ that one enters into the divine life. The sacraments mediate that encounter.

[61]Bernard Leeming, *The Principles of Sacramental Theology* (Westminster, MD: Newman Press, 1956), p. 95.

Catholic tradition, most of the Protestant interpretations of the sacraments place an emphasis, not upon an "objective" presence within the sacrament, but upon the personal increase and deepening of one's faith. This deepening of the faith, as understood within the Protestant tradition, is no doubt important and a real possible effect of the sacrament, but it has the tendency to empty the sacramental sign of its unique and definitive significance. If some other sign can bring one to faith, in what ways are the sacraments normative?

Within the Catholic tradition, perhaps the most common understanding of the Church's teaching concerning the effects of the sacraments is that they are understood to be "God's instrument for conferral of grace on the soul of the recipient."[62] The common effect of the sacraments is grace; i.e. the personal sanctification of the individual. The typical understanding is that the sacraments sanctify the soul of the believer, making the recipient holier, "bringing the believer closer to God." It is the ability to confer specific grace on the believer that has been the identifying mark of the sacraments.

As noted in the previous section, since all salvation is given in Christ, the sanctification of the believer takes place through the participation in those definitive events by which we are saved. This is the heart of the sacramental economy. Yet, even though the sacraments reference the same events, the effects of this participation seem to vary from sacrament to sacrament. In an effort to describe the different effects of the various sacraments, some theologians explain that the individual sacraments mirror the different stages in life.[63] That is, each of the sacraments is focused on helping believers at different stages in their lives. The sacraments make God's grace available throughout the whole of human life from birth to death. Other theologians argue that the diverse sacraments reflect the different aspects of the ministry of Christ. They would argue that the different sacraments tend to focus upon a particular redemptive action of Christ and mediate that activity to the believer. In each case, the individual is offered a grace consistent with the sacrament.

The difficulty that this creates is that if there are a variety of graces given at different times, or reflecting the redemptive activities of Christ, does this not mean that grace is somehow fragmented? One might respond that the number of sacraments indicates the various needs of man in fallen creation. And despite the fact that humans seek a totality and comprehensive unity in Christ, man approaches this slowly and in "parts" throughout the whole of his life. Corresponding to that type of "development," each sacrament appeals to the particular needs appropriate to the individual, while at the same time, as only the love of

---

[62]Toshiyuki Miyakawa, "Ecclesial Meaning of the *Res et Sacramentum*," Theological Studies Vol. 31, October 1967, p.389.

[63]J.D. Crichton, "The Sacraments and Human Life," in *The Sacraments: Readings in Contemporary Sacramental Theology* ed. by Taylor (Alba House: New York, 1981), pp 31ff.

God can, the sacraments draw man more deeply into the complete and total mystery that is the love of God. In the end, it is all one process unified by the saving love of God, but as developing within history, this grace needs to unfold over time in the concrete lives of people. Redemption takes place in the particular acts of individuals over the whole of their lives.

In fact, the effects of the sacrament must mirror or conform to the only real grace given in Christ *ex nihilo*. What this means is that the grace of Christ is the free grace of the free creation, a creation rooted in Christ and offered to us now in the sacraments. The sacraments are not some means to an end that will pass away, but they are constitutive of the life of faith, essentially in unity with the sacramental nature of the Church and the very sacramentality of reality as created in Christ. The sacraments share a fundamental unity, a common task, a common structure that made it possible, from the earliest times, for them to be recognized as "instituted by Christ." Yet, despite the unity of the sacraments in Christ, they each communicate His grace to the believer in different ways. Moreover, not only in the sacraments are there different means or actualizations of the one redemptive act of Christ in the life of the believer, but also as worship, they have an ecclesial dimension.

It is important to realize that the sacraments are gifts through which the believer is offered God's grace. This means, first, that the recipient always stands before God in need of redemption. The believer can neither earn nor merit the grace of God. As distanced from God under the power of the fall, man is unable in any way to "merit" the grace of Christ, so that even the most minimal response to Christ's offer of grace, requires the prior presence of the grace of Christ. This may sound as if everything is dependent upon Christ, and of course this is the case, for He alone makes the gift of salvation possible. Because of original sin, man stands in need of the forgiveness that only God can give.[64] Nevertheless, redemption can never be imposed upon the individual. In the same way that one can never be forced to believe, grace can never be forced upon anyone. The free acceptance of grace on the part of the believer reflects the covenantal nature of the act of faith, where the "effect" of the sacrament is to be

---

[64]The sense that one is radically dependent upon the grace of Christ is the Christian experience most notably recorded in the theology of St. Augustine. Because of the radical effects of sin, humans are in need of a redemption that comes from outside themselves. As a result of the fall, human beings are impotent in establishing a relationship to God. If left to their own devices, they are prone towards sin. They can only be freed from this sin in and through the help of God, who alone can forgive sin. The Cross, then, becomes the center of all salvation.

Against this position is the heresy of Pelagianism, which held that humans are neutral and sin only after they reach the age of consent. Here there is only personal sin, and because of their standing before God, the place of Christ and His death on the Cross is of less significance. In fact, they can, theoretically, attain eternal life apart from the grace of Christ.

drawn into the life Christ. In the sacramental action, the participants are offered the grace of Christ. The believer requires the grace of Christ (*gratia operans*) so that one can freely accept His grace (*gratia cooperans*). The sacraments, then, work in such a way as to not only offer grace, but also enable the believer to accept that offer of grace.

This understanding of faith, as being a free act, reflects a view of the human person that sees human life as being formed by free human decisions and actions. In the exercise of their freedom, each human being becomes a certain type of person in and through their choices. From a Christian perspective, in the life of each believer all their actions represent either the acceptance of the offer of God's grace, thereby preserving the image of God in them, choosing sainthood, or the rejection of that grace, sinning, choosing to be something else. This is the meaning behind all human actions.

Although the act of faith is essentially a personal act, at the same time faith can never be reduced to the experience of the believer. Many people today tend to describe the sacraments as simply expressions of our faith. But such an understanding of the sacraments certainly falls short of the Catholic view of the sacraments. This is particularly evident when the sacraments are described as an action in which one participates in the events by which one is saved. The sacraments, because of their link to Christ, have an objective character that transcends the believer's faith. Also, the Catholic Church teaches that there are certain sacramental effects that are not dependent upon the faith of the believer in the sense that they remain even if the recipient commits a grave sin or gives up his or her faith.

Perhaps the key to understanding the "objective" nature of the effects of the sacrament is to say that they work *ex opere operato*. It has already been noted that to say that the sacraments work *ex opere operato* is to say that grace is present by the "doing of the deed." Also, to say that the sacraments work *ex opere operato* is to affirm the event character and the effective nature of the sacramental actions. In each sacramental action, effects occur which correspond to the particular sacrament. But the effects are not simply the change in the soul of the believer. Rather, in each sacrament, one of the particular effects of the sacrament transcends the individual faith of the believer. Within the tradition, this was referred to as the *res et sacramentum,* that is "a thing or reality and a sacrament." It designates an effect of the rite which is different from grace, the *res tantum*, the effect of the sacrament in the soul of the believer.[65] As a res, it is an effect of the sacramental sacramentum tantum and at the same time it is the sign of another grace. For example, in the Eucharist, the *res et sacramentum* is that the bread and wine become the Body and Blood of Christ. This is possible through the grace of Christ by the power of the Holy Spirit whose promise is

---

[65]Leeming, *The Principles of Sacramental Theology,* p. 251.

that when the Eucharistic acts are done, certain effects occur. Here, the sign and the signified are unified. The Body and Blood are both the effect of the sacrament as well as the sacrament of Christ. This presence transcends the sanctification of the individual. for Christ is said to be "present" after the consecration.

As in the case of the Eucharist, the other sacraments also have the *res et sacramentum*. And, just as in the case of the Eucharist, in the other sacraments the *res et sacramentum* does not simply refer to the presence of Christ in the soul of the believer (although there certainly is the possibility of such a presence), but like the bread and wine that really become the Body and Blood of Christ, there is a corresponding sacramental effect that transcends the faith of the individual believer. Often, this objective effect is understood in terms of the Church.[66] That is, the sacraments are causes of the Church. It is precisely this sacramental realism that affirms and shapes the unique concrete and historical nature of the faith as found in Roman Catholicism.

The objective character of the sacraments is affirmed in different ways in different sacraments. For example, Baptism and Holy Orders give a sacramental *character* to the recipient of the sacrament. This means that the reception of the sacrament causes an ontological change in the recipient. By means of the participation in these sacraments, a definitive change occurs in the soul of the participant, since the believer's very existence rests upon his relationship with Christ, and in the sacraments that relationship is now changed.

This understanding of the sacraments mirrors the covenantal order of creation revealed in the Christ-event. In this account, there is no "natural" reality; "neutral" or "objective," standing apart from God, but reality in all its dimensions is essentially rooted in the Trinitarian life of God. Just as in Christ the order of creation and the order of redemption come together, participation in the sacramental life *affects* a new manner of participation in the reality of the New Covenant. This participation in the grace of Christ is not contrary to the created order, but completes it, restoring the order lost to sin. In a number of the sacraments, this effected change is thought to be a substantial change, which, despite sin, cannot be undone. Even in marriage, where no sacramental character is said to be given, one effect of the sacrament is a bond that cannot be broken. It is a bond that exists apart from the feelings of the individual at any particular moment. It is founded upon the New Covenant, redemptive love of Christ for His Church.

Within the Christian tradition, there have been extensive debates about the meaning of the sacraments. Many of those debates have centered around a discussion of the objective nature of the sacraments. It is around the Eucharist, more than any other, that the most extensive discussion of this objective charac-

---

[66]*Catechism*, 1097. "In the *Liturgy of the New Covenant* every liturgical action, especially the celebration of the Eucharist and the sacraments, is an encounter between Christ and the Church."

ter of sacramental grace has taken place. At the heart of the theological debate surrounding the Eucharist are issues such as the relationship of the bread and the wine to the body and blood, the problem of location, and whether or not the Mass is a sacrifice. In particular, though, it is the question of the "real presence" that has dominated the theological discussion of the Eucharist.

The Catholic position has been that the words of consecration, "This is my Body," are to be taken literally and to insist that Christ is present on the altar. Terms such as transubstantiation and *ex opere operato* have been used to indicate the nature of this "real presence." Such terms are helpful in preserving the concrete historical nature of the sacramental presence, a historicity in continuity with the incarnate and risen Christ. In the Catholic tradition, faith is not something simply in the mind of the believer, but has a concrete presence, like the incarnation itself. Only as concrete and historical, the faith becomes the means by which one enters into the truth of existence. This truth is sacramental, not simply affective.

The concreteness of the faith and sacramental mediation of that faith can be understood in two ways. First, it is concrete in the sense that as a participation in the truth of all reality, it is the foundation of human life. There is no other foundation upon which one can base one's life. The concreteness here means the concreteness of living in the truth. The only other alternative is to live with some other understanding of the world at the center of one's life. Apart from the truth, there is only falsehood and misconception. An existence founded upon something other than the truth cannot be concrete. Second, it is concrete in the sense of being historical. The truth of existence is given in space and time, mediated by Christ and the Church, in particular historical events. In the revelation of Christ, these two ways of understanding "concreteness" come together. It is this insistence upon the sacramental concreteness that, more than anything else, is the distinctive character of the Catholic theology of the sacraments.

Still, there are some difficulties speaking of an objective presence of Christ or to objectify the effects of the sacrament as "something being there" or as "getting something." This does not mean that the teachings about an objective presence need to be discarded; they affirm a very important dimension of the sacramental economy. But, it is also helpful to look at the sacramental actions and the effects of the sacraments in terms of not only what one "gets", but to consider what they *do* for us.

In the *Catechism of the Catholic Church*, the sacraments are described as "liturgical actions." What they mediate is not a static unity with Christ, but they unite God and man in the dynamic redemptive activity of Christ. Perhaps the best example is to once again use the example of the Eucharist. Catholics have always taught that the bread and wine become the Body and Blood of Christ. At the same time, however, the Mass is also a sacrifice. To say that the Mass is a sacrifice means that it is not the mere remembrance of the Cross of Christ. Nor is it another sacrifice in addition to the Cross. It is a representation of the one sacrifice by which we are saved, the death and resurrection of Christ. Since this is the New Covenant, the source of all life and grace, the death and resurrection is not only the center of the New Creation, but of the whole of the created order, which has its existence in and through the Christ, the Word, "through whom all things came to be" (Jn. 1:3). Consequently, it is only by a participation in the *acts* of Christ that the redemption of the world takes place. It is then, in the sacramental action, that we come to share in those acts of Christ by which we are saved.

d. The Sacramental Economy and the Church

It has already been noted that the sacraments are not caused by the faith of the believers, but that they are the product of the love of Christ, a gift to the believers through which they are continually offered the grace given in the life, death and resurrection of Christ. The sacraments mediate the "real" historical and concrete presence of Christ in history. In the Catholic tradition, this "objective character" is described by the terms *ex opere operato* and *res et sacramentum*. They describe the relationship of the sign and the signified, in which what is signified is present in the sign. By emphasizing this aspect of the sacrament the Church points to an effect of the sacrament that cannot simply be reduced to affective changes in the faith of the believer. Rather, they explain this "objective character" not only as something done to the believer, or the sacramental sings, but also in terms of the Church. That is, the sacraments also have an ecclesial effect. This ecclesial effect is centered upon the New Covenant, the one Flesh union of Christ and His Church.

It was noted that the Church is not the cause of the sacraments but the sacraments are prior to the Church, issuing from her "intrinsic structure." The sacraments, then, are not only a means of grace for the individual believer, but they are also the source of the life of the Church. The worship of the Church, as all Christian worship, has its source in the one sacrifice of the Cross of Christ.[67] There is no other sacrifice by which the created order is redeemed. In each sacrament, not only is the individual life of the believer built up, but the Church, the Bride of Christ, is made holy by the blood of Christ. This is the New Covenant, the very source of the life of the Church.

The New Covenant places at the center of the order of creation and redemption the one flesh unity of the Second Adam and the Second Eve. This covenantal unity is the source of all life and grace. Within the Roman Catholic tradition, the Eucharist is understood to be the continuous concrete presence of the New Covenant, the one event of redemption, the sacrifice of the Cross. Consequently, the sacramental economy, in particular the Eucharist, is not accidental to the

---

[67]Miyakawa, "Ecclesial Meaning of the *Res et Sacramentum*," p. 395.

history, but integrates history in the New Covenant. For as the participation in that event, the Eucharistic sacrifice orders all things to that truth. Likewise, the Church finds its source and completion in the Eucharistic worship made possible by Christ. In the sacrifice of the Mass, the New Covenant, the Church is united with Christ. She becomes His body. In this sacramental unity, the Church herself is made holy and comes to possess a sacramental quality so that she is free to respond to and participate in the one sacrifice of the cross. The concrete source of the unity and continuity of salvation history in the Church is offered in the sacrifice of Christ.

In the continued celebration of this sacrament, the Church finds the source of its life, the cause of its existence. The sacramental action gives the Church life in that in the Eucharist she is made holy and united with Christ. This union finds its origin in the one sacrifice of Christ. As covenantal, the offer of grace in the sacrifice is free and requires the free response of the Church. This response to the offer of grace on the part of the Church is a response that transcends the response of any individual Christian. Because the Church is made holy by the blood of the Cross, she is free to accept the fullness of the offer of grace. Through the covenantal unity with Christ as His Bride, the Church receives the holiness that is the source of her authority and integrity. It is a holiness and integrity that is complete in that she has been washed clean by the blood of Christ.

During the present time of the Church, the Eucharist, as the New Covenant, is the representation of the Cross by which the Church is continually made holy. It is by means of the sacramental life, particularly the celebration of the Eucharist, that the believer comes to participate in worship of the Church, the *sacrificium laudis*, the response of the Church to the one sacrifice by which we are saved. Such a complete encounter cannot be achieved by an individual mediation; yet, each individual is called to participate in the full revelation of Christ in the sacramental life of the Church.

Historically, the Church has always affirmed that in the sacraments there is an effect that transcends the faith of the individual. It has traditionally been taught that not only is the forgiveness of sins given in Baptism, not only is original sin washed away, and not only does one receive some of the gifts of the Spirit, but the recipient enters into the life of the Church. That is, the baptized person now stands in a new relationship to Christ, but it is a relationship that must be understood in terms of the life of the Church. Again, this relationship is best defined in the light of the Eucharistic worship of the Church, for the Eucharist is the summit of the Christian life. To participate in the one sacrifice by which we are saved in the sacramental economy is a liturgical act, and therefore ecclesial. In the different sacraments, then, the believer is called to participate more deeply in the one sacrifice of Christ, and at the same time, the believer comes to participate more fully in the life of the Church, which is His Body. As His Body the Church is "the mother" in whose womb all are brought to the faith and nurtured in the one true faith. One cannot separate the faith of the individual from the faith of the Church. Thus, in Confirmation, Holy Orders, even Marriage and the Sacrament of the Sick, the believer comes to a more complete fullness of faith, a better understanding of our vocation as Christians, and a deeper love of God. As will be pointed out in the next chapter, this is the context in which marriage needs to be understood.

It is within the framework of this sacramental objectivity that some of the lasting effects of the sacraments can be understood. Only in this ecclesial context can the *res et sacramentum* dimension of the sacrament take on its full meaning, for the individual faith cannot sustain these sacramental effects. The effects rely upon the offer of grace given in Christ and the mediation of that grace by the Church. The effects are more than "things" that can be lost or discarded. These effects reflect the fidelity of God to His people. Today, just as in biblical times, the people forsake God, sin and lose their way, but God remains faithful. The New People of God, the Church has been made holy by the blood of Christ, so that now she can stand before God, in manner different from those prior to Christ. Like Mary, she remains faithful, a fidelity which individual Christians do not possess, but in which we share as we enter into the life of the Church. Therefore, we are marked; we stand before God called to further holiness in and out of season. In the life of the faith we enter the Church, this Eucharistic reality, and the salvation of each person is never apart from the life of the Church who in her freedom, integrity, and holiness, alone can respond completely to the one sacrifice of Christ. Within the Church, the believer comes to take on an identity as a Christian and comes to understand his or her vocation within Christian life.

e. The Eschatological Nature of the Sacraments

To say that the sacraments have an eschatological dimension is to say that the sacraments are concerned not only about the past and present, but also about the last things. In the cross of Christ, the full revelation of the Triune God is given; there can be no fuller revelation of God. Likewise, in Christ, the final redemption of the world is given; both sin and death are destroyed. Thus, what is to come is already realized in the person of Jesus Christ. Notice, He is raised from the dead, an eschatological event that even the saints, those who have died in Christ, now await. In the description of the sacraments given so far, one sees that they are linked to the New Covenant, mediating the grace of the one sacrifice of Christ. The sacraments are redemptive in that they mediate the grace of Christ, which is definitive of all human history, revealing the true meaning of history, including the future.

The eschatological dimension of Christianity reflects the tension between the completion of salvation accomplished in Christ and the final realization of that grace associated with the end of time and the world to come. This tension is born of hope and faith that salvation has occurred, or will shortly occur, and is tempered by human experience of the continued existence of sin in the world. Human life is torn between the experience of sin and the promise of salvation in Christ.

An image in Christian thought that represents this eschatological tension is the image of the Church triumphant.[68] The triumphant Church reflects the optimism that by His death and resurrection, Christ has conquered sin and death. This image depicts the Church as already victorious over sin and death. The fullness of life is now present in the Church that is present in the world. It is precisely this eschatological image, much like the image of the Kingdom of God found in the gospels, that expresses the hope that the grace of Christ has and will win out and the heavens and the earth are already being recreated in Christ.

This tension between the grace of Christ given in the past and now present, and the complete realization of that grace yet to come, is an essential component to the Christian faith. In baptism, we enter the Church, a Church that as the Bride of Christ is holy, able to mediate the grace of Christ in history, here and now. The Church is not simply an empty sign that promises a grace that is to come only in the future, but she is holy, like Mary, and able to freely respond to the full revelation of God, thereby able to mediate that grace in history. Still, the Church awaits the return of the Bridegroom, at which time that which began in Christ will be brought to completion.

As noted, the eschatological tension is based on the experience that despite the fact that Christ has come, sin remains and the economy of salvation is not complete. It is just this experience of the world as sinful, and the suffering that corresponds to that experience of the fallenness of the created order that leads one to believe that the process of salvation is not complete. Sin remains real. Yet, this experience of sin should not undermine real hope in the final triumph of Christ's grace. The evidence of this final victory is given in the forgiveness of sins and the final triumph of the resurrection of Christ.[69]

---

[68]It is an image that is often misunderstood today, many saying that it represents an idealistic view of the Church, a Church that refuses to get her "hands dirty" since it does not belong to the world. In many instances, people have accused those who hold this image of the Church of a failure of charity, refusing to recognize the reality of sin and oppression in the world, and refusing to aid those in need, often siding with the oppressors rather than with the victims. But this seems to be a rather limited way of looking at this image.

[69]Many theologians today assert that the bodily resurrection did not literally happen. Rather, they contend that the resurrection was the expression of the faith experience of the early Christian community. Yet, most traditional Christians have believed that it is a historical reality. It is the event of the final triumph over sin and death. That the resurrection was a historical event is critical for understanding the faith. I would agree with St. Paul, without the bodily resurrection one would have to rethink the whole meaning of Christianity. (Cf. I Cor. 15).

Another way to look at the eschatological dimension of the faith is to view it in terms of salvation history. In the history of salvation, the truth and the definitive meaning of all things is given in Christ. He is the savior of the world. Within the history of salvation, the time of the Old Testament was brought to completion in Christ, who fulfills the promises made to the people of Israel. At present, we find ourselves in the time of the Church, where the New Covenant is sacramentally present in the sacrifice of the Mass. This is not an empty time awaiting salvation at the end, but the grace that Christ promised is here and now operative. It is alive in the proclamation of the Church and the sacramental celebration of the death and resurrection of Christ. In those events, Christ is really made present in the world and those who participate in that faith and those events of salvation really become closer to God. In this present period of salvation history, the time of the Church, we await the final coming of the Lord, the Lord who is present to us in and through His Church.

The sacraments, like the Church, take their meaning from the fullness of the revelation of Christ. In one sense, they are eschatological since they help strengthen the faith of the believers so that they are able to remain faithful despite sin and suffering. This is evidenced in the sacrament of the sick, where the person who is ill is strengthened so that he might remain faithful and thereby share in the future resurrection in Christ. On the other hand, the sacraments are eschatological in that the fullness of grace, which transcends fallen creation, is now present in fallen creation, and at the same time, continues to extend beyond that historical present to a future fullness. One could say that the sacraments introduce into the world something that transcends fallen creation, while at the same time, they restore creation to its original order. A good example of this is found in marriage. In marriage, the two people freely enter into a community of love and give themselves to each other permanently. How can this be? How can two people give themselves to each other for the rest of their lives knowing the difficulties that they must face? They can do that because despite sin in the sacrament of marriage the couple participates in the New Covenant. Like the covenant between Christ and His Church, a covenant whose full unity is realized in history, marriage is too the concrete realization of the love of God in the concrete lives of the two people. This permanency is made possible by their participation in the New Covenant. In this way the sacraments not only await an end, a transcendent order to which they bear witness, but are the locus of the realization of the fullness that we all seek in the present. As such, they are the real locus of Christian hope in the present age.

Summary:

One way to understand the sacraments is to look at what they do. In the sacramental action, the believers are invited to participate in the covenant by which they are saved. This means that in and through the sacraments, they are called to enter into the New Covenant, the very heart and center of all reality. As noted earlier, not only is the order of redemption described in terms the New Covenant, founded in the death and resurrection of Christ, but it was also argued that the whole structure of reality is covenantal. That is, all things come from Christ, the historical locus of creation and redemption.

That means that reality cannot be reduced to some abstract set of ideas or mere material existence, but has its origin in a historical event, the Christ-event. The Christ-event is the historical prius of all things. In this event, His incarnation, death and resurrection, the meaning and purpose of reality itself is given. As the New Covenant, Christ does not establish an order other than that which comes to be through His act of creation. He is the source of reality itself as the New Covenant. It is in Him and through Him that all things come to be and that all things are saved. This means that since Christ is the Son sent by the Father, in the Christ-event we enter into the very Trinitarian life of God, an interpersonal and free relationship between the three divine persons. In this revelation, the truth about the real nature of creation is revealed in God's love.

This understanding of God reveals the interpersonal nature of reality. This sounds strange to those of us who usually think of "reality" as either physical reality or in terms of one of its positivistic variations. The Christian tradition, likewise, affirms that reality cannot be reduced to some "spiritual realm" apart from the world to which one goes after breaking free from the world either through spiritual enlightenment or death. Rather, the faith affirms that reality is sacramental. Like the revelation given in Christ, this interpretation of Christianity is comprehensive, showing how the whole of reality in all of its physical and spiritual dimensions are included in the activity of Christ, activity that encompasses both the orders of creation and redemption. That is, in and through Christ, all things have their being, and through Him all of creation finds its redemption.

The place where the comprehensive nature of the activity of Christ is revealed is in the Cross and resurrection. In His mission from the Father, the Son mediates between the created order and the order of redemption. Creation is through the love of the Father for His Son. The Word that issues forth from the Father is the Word through whom all things come to be. Yet, it is a free creation, one that is contingent upon God. He sends His Son into the world to save it, to bring it to completion. Such freedom reflects the personal nature of God, who does not put "natural forces" or "physical things" at the center of reality, but places Himself at the core of all things.

The interpersonal nature of God and creation is further affirmed by the Christian belief that God is a being who is not only capable of love, but who *is* love. All things are created out of that love and called to participate in that love. This love is definitively offered to us in the person of Christ. This personal relationship to Christ is the heart of the offer of salvation, where the whole of creation finds its locus. The sacraments are the means by which we come to participate in that love.

Just as the Christ-event is comprehensive in nature, so too the sacraments are comprehensive, drawing the recipient more deeply into the salvation given by Christ. In the day-to-day life of the believer, sacraments may appear to be only a "part" of the life of faith, appearing to many to be something that one can take or leave. But in truth, they are essential to the life of faith. They are locus of the continued historical presence of Christ, a salvation that includes the whole of reality.

This comprehensive nature of the sacraments is especially evident in the Eucharist. There is nothing in the Christ-event that is not given or offered in the sacrifice of the Mass. The Eucharist is the sacramental representation of the New Covenant, the One Flesh unity of the Second Adam and the Second Eve, an event which is none other than the sacrifice of the cross. There is no grace or reality apart from this; it is the source of all life and holiness. The sacraments, then, are comprehensive in that they are a participation in the very acts of salvation by which one is saved. There is nowhere else to turn.

This comprehensive character of the Eucharistic worship also means that in this sacrament, the unity of history is to be found. As the real presence of the Body and Blood of Christ, as the mediation of the one sacrifice by which we are saved, the Eucharist mediates that very fullness which we seek in Christ. It is precisely in the Eucharistic worship of the Church that the sacrifice of Christ is represented in history as the very source and term of its existence. In the Eucharistic worship, one finds the truth, unity and continuity of all history. It is the center of history.

In the sacraments, because of this historical presence, the faith of the believer is opened up to the larger process of salvation history. That is, not only do the sacraments call an individual to holiness, but the believer is also called to participate in the history of salvation, a history whose unity and intelligibility are found in the Eucharist. At the same time, such an act of faith can only be understood in terms of its relationship to the Church, the locus of this Eucharistic worship.

One might wish to stop at this point and ask what this all means. Most Christians believe that religion is a "part of life." Most would admit that it is an important part, but still only a part of one's larger life. It has been suggested here that faith is not a part of life, but the center of life. Moreover, faith is actually comprehensive, including all dimensions of life. There is no dimension of human life that is outside the realm of faith. If one were skeptical about this, one might ask, what are the limits of faith? Or, are there not limits to the biblical view of the world that need to be respected? Or, better, what parts of human life are unaffected by faith? But it is precisely the comprehensive nature of the actions of Christ and the salvation of the New Covenant that reveal the comprehensive nature of the sacramental life, and consequently the meaning of the life of faith. For as these events are comprehensive and definitive, so are the sacraments.

In the end, there is no mere nature, no natural order with an integrity of its own apart from the grace of Christ. There is no "pure nature" that needs to be converted. There is, no doubt, a need for conversion, but the only conversion is from the sinfulness of fallen creation to the fullness of the life in the New Covenant. It is precisely this message that is at the heart of the New Testament message. It is faith in Christ that redeems one from sin. This theological perspective places the economy of salvation at the heart of reality. This alone is the truth.

Our role in the sacramental economy of salvation should model the lives of Christ and Mary. Like Christ, who because His humanity was in perfect union with His divinity, the human was not destroyed but raised up, the believer must stand in unity with Christ, a unity in which the whole of our lives as creatures before God is affirmed. Thus, just as the whole Christ is raised and not just his spirit, the believer is likewise saved. With the whole of his life, the believer should likewise strive for union with Christ. In this, one should follow the example of Mary, whose act of faith included the giving of her whole self to Christ. There is no aspect of Mary's life that is not drawn into the salvific mystery of the New Covenant. From her *fiat* to her assumption, she stands faithful and fully committed to the acts of redemption in a way that is both exemplary and yet instructive of the truly comprehensive nature of the Christian faith.

At this point, the teaching that "outside the Church there is no salvation" can begin to make sense. This does not mean that the grace of Christ does not work outside the visible structure of the Church. What it does mean is that there is only one economy of salvation, an economy that is historically present and fulfilled in the Eucharistic worship of the Church, which is the source of the historical continuity of this salvation in history. The New Covenant, the One Flesh union of the Second Adam and the Second Eve, the union of Christ and His Church, is alone the free act of God's love that forms the created order in the act of creation, and in the same act, redeems fallen creation. In Christ, the whole of the created order, past, present, and future, finds its meaning. As a participation in the life of Christ, the sacraments take one into the heart of this economy.

The effects of the sacraments, although they vary from sacrament to sacrament, find their unity in the cross of Christ. Thus, the sacraments lead one more deeply into the mystery that is Christ. But this is more than simply conveying "something," a kind of objectification of grace. It might be better to say that the "objective nature" of the sacraments is the personal act whereby God acts on the behalf of the believer to save him. This makes the salvation less of a private event whereby the believer receives something in his soul, than an event, like all human events, that molds one's life in all of its dimensions. These sacramental actions are unique in that the sacraments shape one's life in unity with the life of Christ, the center of reality.

Suggested Readings:

Catechism of the Catholic Church
Jared Wicks, S.J., "The Sacraments: A Catechism for Today"
Donald Keefe, S.J., *Toward a Renewal Of Sacramental Theology*
Henri de Lubac, *The Christian Faith*

Study Questions:

1.   What is the nature of a sacrament? How can it best be understood in the light of the salvation history?

2.   What does it mean to say that the sacraments must be understood in terms of the Christ? Why is the Cross of Christ the center of His revelation?

3.   What does it mean to say that the whole of reality given in Christ is sacramental? What does one learn about the nature of the sacraments from Mary?

4.   What does it mean to say that the sacraments have an eschatological dimension? In what ways does that reflect the true nature of the faith?

5.   What does it mean to say that the sacraments are events or actions? What does this reveal about the concrete nature of the sacraments and the way in which they are redemptive?

Chapter IV:
Marriage as a Sacrament

One of the identifying marks of the Roman Catholic teaching on marriage is the belief that marriage is a sacrament. If one has been raised within the Catholic tradition, to hear someone say that marriage is a sacrament might sound like a tautology, but many Christians outside of Roman Catholicism do not believe that it is a sacrament. As a matter of fact, within the various Protestant traditions marriage is not understood to be a sacrament. In those Christian churches, marriage is thought to be a holy and blessed estate, reflecting the order of the good creation; yet, most of these Christians do not believe that marriage was instituted by Christ as a sacrament. To be sure these Christians recognize the goods of marriage, but of themselves these goods are not redemptive. Another way to say this is to say that for most Christians, marriage is not thought to be salvific since it is simply a human act. In this tradition, marriage was understood to be a promise, a human promise, a human oath, which, like all other human commitments in fallen creation, is subject to the limits of sinful creation. As affected by sin, the promises made in a marriage are subject to the changes and limits of the sinners who enter into such promises. Therefore, such promises may not last (divorce is possible) and, since they are human promises they cannot mediate the redemption of Christ in a definitive manner. That is, they are not sacramental.

Within the Roman Catholic tradition, on the other hand, marriage is understood to be a sacrament because it is understood to be redemptive. As a matter of fact, one might argue that this would seem the only real reason to get married: so that one might be saved. It is only too obvious that many of the "old" social reasons for marriage have disappeared. This is especially true today when such things as extra-marital sex and children outside of marriage are fairly commonplace and, if not the ideal forms of behavior, they are at least not publicly condemned. Yet, Roman Catholics have held that more is at stake in marriage than simply what is articulated by social theorists and cultural trends. They hold that, ultimately, the whole of one's life and existence finds itself at issue in marriage. Indeed, marriage is really about the salvation of those people who marry. The Church teaches that the love of a husband and wife is a means by which one enters more fully into the mystery of the New Covenant by which and through

which one is saved.[70] In and through their marriage, a couple comes to participate in the love of God.

To say that marriage is sacramental makes a great deal of sense since what
is at stake in marriage is so fundamental. Of course, this is apparent from the
very nature of marriage itself, for what makes it so fundamental is that it encompasses the whole person, the spiritual as well as the physical. Moreover, the
husband and wife are engaged in a way of life that defines their lives. Such a
relationship is so basic to human living that it is bound to touch upon the very
meaning and purpose of human existence. Therefore, it is bound to be a religious event.

Among the sacraments, marriage is unique. First, it is not simply an event
that takes place in a Church on a certain day. The ceremony is the beginning of
the process of marriage, which endures throughout the whole of one's life. This
is not to say that during the rite, the couple does not become married. Like the
other sacraments, it works *ex opere operato*. By taking the vows, the marriage
does take place at a specific place, at a specific time. But it is not simply a rite
with only immediate effects (most sacraments contain both dimensions: immediate effects and the long-term effects of growth in faith). Rather, like a covenant, it begins and is established at a certain point in time, but at the same time,
it is a continuous human act lived out in the very concreteness of everyday life.
In this "everydayness," as the love between the man and woman grow, they enter more deeply into the life and love of God.

Second, marriage is an act that is directly rooted in the order of creation. It
is a sacrament that was established at the very beginning in the act of creation.
Therefore, one might say that marriage is a "natural" sacrament that is universally part of the order of creation and redemption. As already noted, being
"natural" here does not mean that it is "ungraced." Since all things are created in
Christ, there can be nothing outside of the grace of Christ. Thus creation, from
the very beginning, is graced and therefore marriage, as established in the very
beginning, is a graced relationship and ordered according to the New Covenant.
So, to say that marriage is "natural" means that it has its foundation in the order
established in the act of creation. It is a means of participating in the love of
God through which the creature comes to image and worship the Triune God
who is both the source and goal of human life.

As a sacrament, and therefore redemptive, marriage does not deal with simply one aspect of life, nor are the sacraments simply an addition to a profane or
secular life; rather, marriage is religious in the sense that it is both comprehen-

---

[70]The contemporary acceptance of other alternatives to marriage tends to show a
lack of understanding of the dynamics of human sexuality. To accept an alternative "lifestyle," one would have to trivialize human sexuality, reducing it to the common and necessary, rather than understanding it as a free act aimed at the redemption of the whole
person.

sive and profound. In the sacrament of marriage, the spouses participate in both the order of redemption and the order of creation that have their origin and purpose in the New Covenant, which is the one flesh union of Christ, the second Adam, with the Church, the second Eve. In the New Covenant, the whole created order is brought to completion. It is the sacramental participation in this New Covenant that reveals the exact sacramental nature of marriage.

Within the economy of salvation, marriage has a special meaning. For among the sacraments, apart from the Eucharist, marriage most explicitly and concretely links the order of redemption to the order of creation. At the heart of this assertion are certain presuppositions about the nature of man, as created male and female, and the corresponding meaning of human sexuality.

a. Marriage and the Order of Creation

In the creation story, man is created in the image and likeness of God, male and female. "Then God said, 'Let us make man in our image, after our likeness'; . . . So God created man in his own image, in the image of God he created him; male and female he created them" (Gen. 1:26-27). According to this account, man is created as the crown of creation, alone among all creatures, imaging God in His very existence. And, as part of the order of the good creation, sexual differentiation was thought to be good. As a matter of fact, one of the most significant insights in the Judeo-Christian tradition is that the human body and the whole of its physical existence, as created by God, is good. According to the Genesis account, man images God as male and female. They are to be "fruitful and multiply and fill the earth." But this is more than a mere biological joining, since from the beginning, the two "become one flesh" (Gen. 2:24). In the joining of the two, they take on a new identity, an identity that can only be understood in terms of the covenantal fidelity between God and His people.

As part of the original good creation, human sexuality, as the whole created order, is ordered to the service of God. From the beginning the union of the man and wife, where they became "one flesh," was understood to be order to God. This "one flesh" union was constituted by the total gift of self, both body and soul. It is ordered to the nuptial union of the New Covenant. Human sexuality is likewise ordered to this fullness of the New Covenant. It is not contrary to salvation, but a means by which we come to serve God.

This attitude towards sexuality may seem strange in the modern age, so full of talk about sexuality, its use and meaning, or lack of meaning. Within the Judeo-Christian tradition, sexuality is part of the order and mystery of the good creation. It has a meaning that cannot be reduced to social or psychological theories, as so many theorists try to do today. Recently, an acquaintance told me that if one measures the influence of an intellectual in terms of the contemporary use

of the ideas and vocabulary introduced by that particular thinker, then the man
who would be considered most influential today would be Sigmund Freud. This
is certainly a disturbing thought when one considers the adequacy and accuracy
of his views of the human person and human sexuality. For his account of human life is to reduce all aspects of human existence to several essential components, to "flatten man," making him more understandable and, possibly, more
manageable. Freud's philosophy, although is a reduction of human life to only a
few of its components, is interesting in the sense that he sees the importance of
human sexuality. The emphasis upon the importance of human sexuality is
something that a Christian might agree with, although for very different reasons.

To say that marriage is a sacrament is to indicate that human sexuality is a
great mystery through which one enters into the mystery of redemption. In the
Genesis account of the creation of man, for instance, the text indicates that we
image God not simply as spiritual, rational or free beings, but as beings who find
fulfillment in the love of God and love of neighbor, including marriage. One
way to articulate this is to say that we image God in our ability to love as interpersonal creatures.

Of all the human actions that encompass the varied dimensions of human
life, the act of love is unique. From the Christian perspective, love is not a mere
affection, nor an abstraction, but includes who we are as beings created by God,
including our sexuality. In marital love the whole of human life is involved.
Real love calls for the dying to oneself for the good of another. It requires that
one give oneself directly to another. It calls upon the person to empty oneself so
that one might be filled by the love of another and the love of God.

One way that the Christian might speak of the encompassing nature of human love is to speak of the sacramentality of human sexuality. This means that
human sexuality is "so rich in intelligibility that it can never be exhausted by an
individual or group."[71] The biblical accounts express this richness in the description of man as imaging God as male and female. Remember, to be likened to
God is an awesome thing; therefore, to promote human sexuality to that level,
signifies its importance. Yet, notice that the biblical accounts not only signify
the importance of human sexuality, but understand it to have a particular meaning.

Such efforts to interpret human sexuality are commonplace in every era of
human history. But in most cases, unlike today, these interpretations usually try
to preserve the importance of human sexuality, pointing to its power and mystery. In most ancient civilizations, sexuality was linked to fertility. Many of
these societies understood human fertility as part of the cycle of biological fertility that permeated nature. This cycle was profound and mysterious, usually sub-

---

[71]The work in this section reflects the influence of the thought of Joseph Murphy,
S.J., who taught at Marquette University in the 1980's.

ject to the power of some god who bestowed fertility. Yet, even within these cultures, fertility was more than simply producing something or reproduction, as one might call it today. In these societies, sexual fertility had a cultic function. It was thought to be so powerful that through sexuality, one was able to enter into the realm of the divine. Human sexuality was understood to mirror the archetypal fertility of the gods.

In some of these ancient societies, and in some philosophies even today, the model for human sexuality was androgyny. According to this philosophy, the perfect creature was both male and female. Sexual differentiation was evil, the product of a fall, splitting man into male and female, leaving them separate yet both striving towards each other in search of completeness. From this view of sexuality, it is not good to be either male or female; both are partial, fragmented modes of existence constitutive of human existence in fallen creation.

Unlike many of their neighboring nations, the Jews did not make fertility into a goddess, nor accept androgyny as the norm for human sexuality. Contrary to what many of their polytheistic neighbors believed, what seemed to be important to the Jews was not so much fertility as fidelity. Although it is true that fertility is important in the Judeo-Christian tradition, its significance is linked to the New Covenant which views it in terms of its relationship to God. It was through the faithful love of a man and a woman that the true meaning and depth of human sexuality was revealed. In their fidelity they imaged God.

It is precisely because of the richness of human sexuality that moderate men and women have always pointed to its importance in human life and tried to guard it. For example, in most cultures, men and women were taught the virtue of modesty. This was not simply prudishness or being "old fashioned," but it reflected a sense of mystery about the power of human sexuality and that one ought to handle this power cautiously. Likewise, many other traditional social conventions were enacted by society to guard this special mystery. As moral virtue helped the individual control the passion, social structures were put in place to order the passions to their proper ends: e.g., courtship. Today, however, neither the virtues nor the social structures are thought to be important. For instance, one often encounters efforts to trivialize sex, leading one to think that one can be "casual" in one's use of human sexuality. Some even argue that sex can be a form of recreation, that extra-marital affairs might be good for one's marriage, or even that a "variety" of sexual experiences are good for a person. But such efforts fail to be convincing and only tend to undermine human integrity. In the end, through one's sexuality, one gives oneself to another in the most intimate way one can as a bodily being. Can one simply be casual about sexuality because one wants to? Or does sexuality have a meaning that transcends such simplistic and relativistic answers?

Contrary to those theories that trivialize human sexuality or accept the model of androgyny, the Church's teaching that marriage is a sacrament rests upon the belief that human sexuality is "good." This was affirmed in the Genesis account and again affirmed by the discussion of the dignity of marriage given in the scriptural accounts of the covenant. Noticeably, marriage and sexuality are not things that need to be overcome so that one might become holy or enter into unity with God. Furthermore, sexuality is not a deprivation, but a means to the fullness of life through the marital exercise of that sexuality. This fullness is contingent upon a sexual complementarity. That is, it is male and female, and this is the basis for the one flesh unity of marriage. Marriage, then, the love between husband and wife, is a means of imaging God. In this imaging, the male and female become what they are through the act of giving of themselves unconditionally to each other in the sacrament of marriage.

On account of its profound nature Christians hold that sexuality is sacred: it is constitutive of who we are as creatures created in the image and likeness of God, since it is a means by which the believers participate in the order of redemption. Thus, the common accusation that Christians are against sex is not accurate. The gospel does not state that sexual intercourse or sexuality is sinful. Rather, it has always affirmed the goodness of sex and procreation by pointing to its redemptive significance and by pointing to the good of procreation. But the Christian tradition is quick to condemn abuses of sexuality such as adultery, rape, incest, homosexuality, lust, fornication and artificial contraception. This condemnation of certain forms of sexuality does not rest upon the belief that sexuality itself is sinful, but that the abuses and misuses of sexuality are serious offences against a fundamental human good.

One way to put this is to say that it is in and through our sexuality that we serve God. For at the heart of the Christian understanding of existence is the belief that human life is a gift, created in and through Christ, and ordered to the triune love of God. As a gift, our lives have a fundamental dependence upon God. Yet human dependence upon God does not mean that human life is simply part of a "determined" or necessary natural order without freedom, but that man is free not despite the fact that he comes from God, but because of it. Within the covenantal order of reality, man is not a mere extension of the power of God. He is a free person able to accept his existence or to reject it. Man is free when he responds to the love of God and lives in that truth.

At the same time, to say that human life is a gift means that human life, which is essentially free, is not in any final sense subject to human authority and human power. Rather, human freedom transcends any earthly authority, since its origin and end are beyond any worldly philosophy or institution. One can submit to legitimate authorities in this world, but such submission must be free, and always remains contingent, since those earthly things are limited and will always "pass away." Since human life is radically dependent upon God, it has a transcendent dimension that is substantially good and free since it comes from the love of God. Consequently, man stands before God in the totality of his being which comes from God. No other authority can make the same kind of claim on man. And this complete claim on man includes human maleness or femaleness,

since it is with the whole of one's existence that the believer is called to respond
to God.

Perhaps the best way the Scripture describes this is to say that it is in our
maleness or femaleness that man images God. In such a view of the person, the
integrity of the human body and the unity of body and soul are assumed. This
might best be expressed by saying "we are our bodies." Quite simply, humans
are created as bodily creatures. When they attempt to abstract from their bodies,
such attempts are dehumanizing, reflecting an inadequate understanding of what
it means to be human. Usually, when such abstractions are applied to human
sexuality, they undermine the significance of being male and female, attempting
to point beyond the body to a more basic unity prior to our sexuality. But according to the scriptures, man does not image God as "human beings," but as
male and female. That is, man does not image God because he has a soul, but
with the whole of his being, including his body.[72]

This unity of body and soul and the importance of body in the economy of
salvation is evidenced in the bodily resurrection. Note that Christ does not leave
His body behind, but the whole Christ is raised from the dead. There is an empty
tomb. He appears to the apostles and the body is His, the one that died on the
cross. Likewise, it is a tenet of the Christian faith that at the end, those who are
to be saved will undergo a bodily resurrection. They will have a glorified body;
something the believer can only get a glimpse of in the post resurrection accounts of the risen Lord in the gospels. Yet, the inclusion of the body in the
order of redemption is consistent with the idea that the whole of the created order is significant, since it is part of the good created order, created in Christ, and
therefore is to be saved. As part of the good creation given in and through
Christ, the physical world, although fallen and under the effects of sin, awaits
the redemption given in and through Christ. In His redemptive activity, Christ
comes to restore the world, including the body. So that when man is called to
redemption, a participation in the life of the triune God, man is redeemed in and
through his bodily existence, as male and female, for it is in the whole of his
being, including his sexuality, that man images God.

Traditionally, when one used to say that man imaged God, this imaging was
usually described in terms of some part or dimension of the human person as
being like God. That is, this imaging was described in terms of particular ontological characteristics or in terms of a particular human capacity. For example, it
was said that because man had a soul, or was rational, that he imaged God. Others argue that, imaging of God was associated with those dimensions of the human person or characteristics that could be best described as "relational." That
is, man is a being who knows and loves. In each instance, human beings tran-

---

[72]Keefe, *Covenantal Theology*, 483ff, 502.

scend themselves, finding their completion in knowing and loving God.[73] Consequently, imaging God, then, has to do not only with having a particular "characteristic," but also with the relationships that flow from the characteristics. The best way to say this is that imaging God has to do with man's actions by means of which the believer is opened to the depth of God's grace at work in the order of creation; i.e., in the love of God and neighbor. In such a view of faith, imaging God cannot be construed as an escape from the body or the limits of creation, but as an encounter with God in the covenantal order of that creation.

By means of man's participation in this covenantal order, an order described as marital and free, human beings image God. Notice that this participation is understood here not to be an escape from the concrete, but the opposite. It is precisely in the concrete covenantal and historical life of man, that he images the concrete and historical covenant. Man does this through his participation in the New Covenant where he enters into the triune love of God. The imaging of God, then, as covenantal, is marital, reflecting the one flesh union of Christ and the Church. For in the second Adam and second Eve, the primordial covenant of the good creation is established, in one and same act creating and redeeming fallen creation from sin. This is the foundation of the whole order of reality, and therefore, the concrete basis of faith.

If faith is to be described as marital and covenantal, then virtues such as love, fidelity, trust, and hope will be at the center of history. Within this worldview, love of God and neighbor are not simply "nice" things to do, but the central acts of human life; they alone place one at the heart of reality. But despite the importance of love and human relationships in life, this is often overlooked today.

In contemporary society, there is a great emphasis upon function and productivity in human life. How one succeeds in those areas becomes the primary means by which human life is judged. On the one hand, most people would claim that family and friends are more important than success, professions, and money. On the other hand, many in the United States do not hesitate to leave their families, work long hours, and even move to a distant land in order to further their professional careers. At present, most Americans are divided between their beliefs and their actions. Most claim to have the correct priorities, placing people first, but do they really live that way? Is not the present orientation of culture and the philosophies underlying our culture problematic for anyone trying to live a Christian life?

---

[73]*Catechism*, 355ff.

Because of sin, the true meaning of man as the image of God is often distorted by any particular culture. Yet today, beyond personal sin and the limits of culture to articulate the true meaning of human life, some aspects of or culture embody "anti-Christian" interpretation of the human sexuality and human life. Because of this cultural pressure, our understanding of the meaning of human sexuality has also been distorted, so that the universal truth available to all men in the created order is now lost and in need of restoration. It is precisely in the redemptive activity of Christ, a historical revelation, that the full meaning of the order of creation is once again established. Here, human sexuality takes on its proper meaning in the light of the New Covenant. For it is here that the truth of human sexuality and its role in the order of redemption is revealed. It is precisely to this truth that Christians need to bear witness in the present age.

b. Marriage and Salvation History

It often seems awkward today to try to convince Christians that the true meaning of human sexuality is revealed in the process of salvation history recorded in Scripture. After all, many people today presuppose that modern man has a much more complete knowledge of sexuality than people in the past and so people today are certainly more "advanced" in those areas than people in previous eras. But in the face of such claim, Christians hold that the truth about human life is given in Christ, the New Covenant, and that this truth is comprehensive. It is the truth of the whole of reality, including human sexuality. Consequently, the claims made to the truth by any culture or age need to be judged against the truths of the faith.

As Christians can testify, following the truth contained in the biblical message is difficult and demanding, often conflicting with modern interpretations of human life, yet, it is the truth and holds the only promise for living a "good" life. For the truth is given, not in some abstract psychological or philosophical theory, but in the revelation of God which culminates in Jesus Christ, who is the way, the truth, and the life (Jn. 14:6). To understand the nature of this truth, one needs to look at what the scriptures say about it. Only in this context can one come to understand the meaning and purpose of the sacrament of marriage.

1. The Old Covenant

When reading the scriptures, one is not hard pressed to find allusions to marriage. As a matter of fact, marriage is frequently used as an analogy for understanding the biblical revelation. The particular appropriateness of this analogy reflects the structure of the biblical revelation itself. At the center of the old covenant stands the covenantal relationship between the Lord God of Israel and His people. In the Old Covenant, God entered into history establishing a relationship with "a people" who become the means by which His plan unfolds in history. This covenant orders the life of the people to the truth of God and the world. As a covenant, this plan is not imposed from the outside, but is offered freely to His people, who by accepting His offer, become His people. It is precisely this free offer of grace and the acceptance of that offer that constitutes the covenant.

In the Old Testament, the analogy of marriage is used to describe the relationship between God and His people. By using this analogy, one not only comes to know something about man's relationship to God, but correspondingly, one learns something about marriage by the relationship between the Lord and His people of Israel. Through the use of marriage as an analogy for the covenant, one comes to better understand the nature and meaning of marriage.

Upon examination, the Old Testament reveals a kind of "development" in its understanding of the meaning of marriage. There are two ways of approaching this development. First, one way to understand the Jewish meaning of marriage is to compare their idea of marriage to the understanding of marriage held by their pagan neighbors. Second, there is a development within Judaism itself concerning the meaning and the nature of human sexuality and marriage. The first of these developments reflects a new understanding of God and the meaning of creation. The second represents a better understanding of marriage in the light of the covenant.

As opposed to the neighboring religions with their emphasis upon nature and fertility, the Jews understood that there was only one God who created all things. The Jews came to understand that this God was not a nature deity who exercised a power limited to a force of nature, but He was a free and sovereign God in whom they could put their trust.[74] He was the God of history, a personal God, who acted purposefully in a just manner and out of love for His people. He was a God who was faithful to His people, and they in turn, placed their trust in Him. It was this experience of the God of the covenant that became the basis for their understanding of marriage.

---

[74]Edward Schillebeeckx, O.P, *Marriage: Secular Reality and Saving Mystery*, trans. by N.D. Smith (London: Sheed and Ward, 1965), pp. 75ff.

Although not a ritual performed at the temple, the Jews understood early that marriage reflected the order of the good creation. Marriage was a gift of creation that followed a basic order ordained to the worship of the true God. By being married, one not only physically built up the people of God (through pro-creation), but came to understand more deeply the meaning of fidelity to the covenant which formed the foundation of their existence as the people of God. It was understood that marriage, as the covenant, placed one at the heart of the created order and at the heart of the historical covenant between Israel and her Lord. Since the God of Israel was the creator and the one who acted in history to establish the covenant, both the order of creation and redemption refer to the same truth, the truth in which the liturgical order, particularly marriage, participates.

The theme of the nuptial nature of the covenant is quite common in the prophetic writings. The relationship between God and His people of Israel is likened to a marriage. Israel is supposed to be the faithful spouse who responds to the offer of God's love. The Lord is the husband who offers salvation to His wife, Israel. In the writings of the prophets Isaiah and Jeremiah, the infidelities of the people are likened to adultery. The people are described as acting like a harlot, forsaking the worship of the one true God for other false gods. As all sin in the Old Testament, this infidelity is connected with idolatry. Instead of worshipping the one true God, the people put another god or something else in the place of God. Nevertheless, despite their sin, the covenant remains; it is sustained by God who is ever faithful so that the infidelity of the people does not destroy the covenant. It is true that the Jews suffer because of their infidelity, but as Isaiah proclaims, God is faithful, saving a remnant, not letting his people die out (Is. 40-66).

A constant theme in the prophetic literature is the theme of fidelity. Again and again, God calls His people to be faithful to the covenant. This fidelity is not subservience to the whim of a despotic god, as their neighbors were subservient to the caprice of their gods. It was the free response of the people to the offer of God's favor, reflecting the free order of the covenant between God and His people. It was from this covenant that the Jews took their meaning. The Jews were God's people; they had no other identity. Consequently, fidelity was considered to the primary virtue that one should have towards the world. Without this fidelity to the covenant, the Jews would fade into history. This is evidenced by the prophetic texts.

In the book of Hosea, the theme of fidelity finds one its most profound expression. In the story, Hosea remains faithful to his spouse, Gomer, who has been unfaithful to him. Despite the public humiliation and cultural pressures to forsake his wife- if not kill her, Hosea, like God, remains faithful to his spouse despite her sins and calls her back to fidelity. From this story, one learns that the covenant can never be destroyed in any final sense, for their God is not a fickle god of nature, but a steadfast God, a personal deity who has chosen them as His

people. The covenant is not an afterthought, an addition to an already complete
world, but it is an extension of an order already present from the beginning.
Nevertheless, the people of Israel are constantly unfaithful, placing their love
and trust in something other than God. But despite their sin, God remains faithful to His covenant. It is by His love and by His authority that the covenant remains.

It is likewise, within the light of the covenant, that the meaning of creation
becomes evident. Creation is not prior to the covenant, but the product of the
God's covenantal offer of grace. Marriage and the whole of creation reflect this
covenantal structure. On the ontological level the covenant is prior to creation.
"This covenant of love is the theme of all God's saving activity and the deepest
meaning of creation.... The community of marriage, as a gift of creation from
the God of the covenant, was a first draft of the finished picture of grace, God's
covenant with man."[75] Yet, under the Old Law, this historical revelation does
not reach its fullness and which is revealed in the New Covenant. The final and
definitive meaning of the covenant and marriage is given in Christ.

2. New Covenant

In order to reach the understanding of the sacrament of marriage that Catholics have today, something new "has to have happened" beyond what was believed about marriage under the Old Covenant. What this something "new" is,
no doubt, stands in continuity with what has been revealed in the Old Covenant,
but it needs to be "more." Perhaps the best way to talk about this is not as if
something is now added that was missing before, or that something has entirely
replaced what was there before, but that the covenant given in the Old Testament now reaches its fulfillment in the revelation of Christ, true God and true
man, since in Christ, the grace promised for the redemption of all the created
order is accomplished. In Christ, the covenantal order is brought to completion.
It is an order that is fundamentally historical, yet, not subject to the fallen creation and able to break the bonds of sin, which now hold fallen creation in bondage.

This process of liberation from sin is not simply a move from the old to new
in such a way that the old is replaced by the new, but the process of redemption
that is at work here is a restoration of that which has been lost to sin. This restoration has its assurances in the cross and resurrection of Christ. For in and
through the grace of Christ sin is overcome once and for all. Under his authority,
the reign of grace enters into its last phase of salvation history, the time of the
Church.

---

[75]Ibid., p. 111.

Within the life of the Church, the definitive expression of the New Testament's understanding of the effects of this "newness," as accomplished by Christ, is found in the sacramental life of the Church. An example of how this works itself out in the life of faith is evident in the Church's understanding of marriage. Divorce, which was accepted under the Old Law, is no longer possible. Now "anyone who divorces his spouse and marries another, commits adultery" (Mt. 5:31ff). This change in the understanding of marriage is possible because something new has "happened. There is a new grace now present, the definitive grace of the New Covenant that enables marriage to endure despite sin.

This "newness" that is revealed in the Incarnation has its roots not only in the Old Covenant, which serves as a preparation for the New, but also in the order of creation itself. For Christ is the Son, sent by the Father, creating, bringing all dimensions of reality into existence, and at the same time, redeeming it in and through His Cross. There is only one grace, the grace given in and through the Cross of Christ. This means, then, that the grace of the New Covenant is prior to the creation, anticipating it as well as shaping and forming it. As shaped by the grace of Christ, creation has the nuptial character of the New Covenant, and this order that is manifest in the order of creation finds a clear expression in the sacrament of marriage.

In order to understand the sacramental nature of marriage in its relationship to the New Covenant, it is best to see marriage as it affirms and exists in relationship to the economy of salvation, an economy that is essentially Christocentric. As focused on Christ, who is the one true covenant, the economy of salvation is covenantal and nuptial. Within this nuptial order, marriage is understood in terms of the relationship of the Bridegroom and the Bride, the relationship between Christ and his Church, which stands at the heart of this order. This covenantal unity is that of the incarnate Son who acts in history to save His people. In Christ, the creative and redemptive orders find their unity. Again, this is not to say that only an aspect or a dimension of reality finds their meaning in Christ, but all of reality has its origin in the New Covenant. The "one flesh" unity of the second Adam and the second Eve, is the very heart of reality, a reality in which one participates in the sacrament of marriage.[76] What this means is that marriage has a reality that is rooted in the very structure of the way things are, it is rooted in the order of creation. It is not the construct of society, but reflects the truth of existence. It is not only a moral choice, but part of the very ontological order of creation itself.

To say that this economy is rooted in Christ is to say that it is substantially historical, since the prius and source of all things is given in Christ whose incarnation, death, resurrection, and ascension are historical events that form the revelation. The one true Lord of history reveals himself in history at the same

---

[76]Ibid., p. 171.

time redeeming that very history from the sin of the first Adam and Eve. But the priority of this historical revelation is not simply as the culmination of history, that is, simply as the end towards which all things move; rather, this priority is metaphysical, revealing the source and very nature of the created order, an order, which like the revelation itself, is covenantal. Marriage, as instituted in the good creation, also has this covenantal order.

Under the New Covenant, marriage is restored to the integrity for which it was intended (now lost to sin) by the redemptive activity of Christ. During the present age, the New Covenant is concretely present in the Eucharistic worship of the Church. It is the reality from which and towards which the life of the faith is oriented, the reality in which marriage participates and from which marriage takes its meaning.

i. Bridegroom and Bride

The one text in the New Testament that best reveals the nature of marriage under the New Covenant is the one found in Ephesians 5. In this text, the relationship between Christ and his Church is compared to that of marriage. Unlike the Old Covenant that never reached completion, the New Covenant is freely established by the definitive and final redemptive activity of Christ. According to Ephesians, all things are brought to completion in Christ. (Eph. 1: 10) Yet, what reveals the true nature of this restoration of all things in Christ is the relationship of Christ to His Church. From this text, one not only learns something about the Church, but in the light of the relationship of Christ to His Church, one comes to understand the true nature of marriage.

In his Ephesians, Paul is concerned with understanding the Church in God's unfolding plan of salvation. In this plan, Christ is the central figure through whose sacrifice we are united to Him in faith, a work of His hands, not our own. The goal of this redemptive activity by Christ is to unite all men in faith and to unite the whole created order under His Lordship. "For he has made known to us in all wisdom and insight the mystery of his will, according to his purpose which he set forth in Christ as a plan for the fullness of time, to unite all things in him, things in heaven and things on earth" (Eph. 1:9-10). In this plan, the Father gives dominion to the Son, restoring all things to their proper order. "... and he has put all things under his feet and has made him the head over all things for the church, which is his body, the fullness of him who fills all in all" (Eph. 1:22-23). This unity of all things in the plan of God is not externally imposed on man or creation, but it is the order that befits the creation from the beginning. During the present age, it is a unity that is offered to the whole created order in and through the Church. The Church, in this analogy, is the "body of Christ," the fullness of Christ whose role in the present is to mediate the grace of Christ in fallen creation. It is precisely this presence that denotes the difference between the time of the Old Covenant and the time of the New.

Perhaps the most famous passage concerning the present stage of the economy of salvation is found in Ephesians 5:21ff, where the nature of the relationship of Christ to the Church is compared to the male\female, husband\wife relationship. Many who read this passage today believe it to be demeaning of women, since it states that wives should be submissive to their husbands. This is only the case if the submission of the wife to the husband is a matter of power: i.e., of the husband having some controlling power over his spouse. But that is not an adequate explanation of the text. For the Christian, the ordering force in the world is not sheer coercive power, but the demands of love. People who do things in charity are not attempting to control others through power, but freely give of themselves to another in love. In much the same manner as the Church is called upon to submit to the Lord, wives are called to submit their husbands. As a covenantal relationship, this can only be the free submission of the Church by the Church. Within this free covenantal relationship, the Church, now made holy like Mary through the cross of Christ, is free to respond to the fullness of grace, offered in and through Christ. The very life of the Church is dependent upon Christ, who calls her into existence. In Christ, the Church is freely offered the salvation which is the very goal of her life. It is her responsibility to respond to that offer of grace. But the very offer and the ability to respond are made possible by the grace of Christ, since it is only by the one sacrifice of the cross that the Church is made holy. Out of love, Christ died for her at the same time cleansing her and freeing her to respond fully to His love. He loves the Church as His own body, giving Himself up for her so that she might have life. The result of this covenantal act of love is the one flesh unity of Christ and His Church, the unity of the New Covenant.

What is significant here is that now, within fallen history, the integrity and restoration of the New Covenant is concretely present in the life of the Church. She is made holy by the one who can restore her to holiness, by the very one to whom the Church owes her existence. The Church, like any Christian, has her identity in her mission and vocation in the service of Christ. There is no other source for her identity. It does not come from her members, for she is more than simply the summary of her members. Moreover, she is like Mary, whose holiness is never focused on her own self, but was always directed toward and transparent to the call of God. As holy, the Church, like Mary, is a kind of a sacrament. That is, the Church is a visible sign of invisible grace, mediating that redeeming grace in fallen history. She is the extension of the New Covenant in history, the fullness of life in fallen creation.

Just as all the sacraments must be understood in terms of the New Covenant but this is especially true of marriage. When this covenantal analogy is transferred to marriage, the Bride, then, stands in unity with the Groom, who is the source of her existence, identity, and authority. Within this context, it is particularly obvious that marriage is not some natural state to which a blessing is added, but that in the love of the husband and wife for each other, they enter into the very redemptive reality toward which the whole of the created order strains. The mutual submission of husband and wife in love forms the man and woman in that self-sacrificial love which alone makes us human and frees man from all that prohibits him from the fullness of grace for which human life is intended. In marriage the self sacrificial love, which is the heart of the bridal relationship between Christ and His Church, is made concrete in human life. In this love, the believers achieve the unity, wholeness, and integrity for which they were intended in the order of creation.

ii. Marriage and the Eucharist

To understand the particular nature of the dynamic relationship between marriage and the relationship between Christ and his Church, it is necessary to look at the Church as the context in which, during the present time, the sacrament of marriage finds its meaning. Despite the fact that marriage is a very personal act that is administered by the couple to each other, it is not a private act. Marriage is an ecclesial event, not to be separated from the life of the Church whose life reflects the nuptial order of grace.

> The entire Christian life bears the mark of the spousal love of Christ and the Church. Already, Baptism, the entry into the People of God, is a nuptial mystery; it is so to speak the nuptial bath, which precedes the wedding feast, the Eucharist. Christian marriage in its turn becomes an efficacious sign, the sacrament of the covenant of Christ and the Church. Since it signifies and communicates grace, marriage between baptized persons is a true sacrament of the New Covenant.[77]

Within the Catholic tradition, the sacraments are understood in terms of the covenantal love of Christ for His Church. In baptism, one enters into the faith by being baptized into the death and resurrection of Christ and the believer is freed to enter into a relationship with Christ. In this sacrament, one acquires a "new being," now standing in a new relationship to Christ, participating in the New Covenant offered in the life of the Church. Baptism is essential, since through it the Christian is freed by the grace of Christ to enter into full participation in the

---

[77]Catechism, 1617.

life of the Church. It prepares one for marriage by freeing the recipient to re-spond to the nuptial order of the good creation now offered to the believer in the love of one's spouse. This was the original order of the good creation which has been damaged by sin, but restored in Christ. But if marriage is an ecclesial event, not only must it be understood in terms of baptism, through which one enters the Church, it also needs to be understood in terms of the Eucharist, the source and center of the life of faith.

In the Catholic tradition, the Eucharist is the apex of ecclesial life. It is the fullest expression of the Christian faith in fallen history during the time of the Church. It is the font from which the life of the Church flows. The reason that the life of faith finds its fullest expression in the Mass is that in the sacrifice of the Mass, the Church born of the Cross of Christ, finds its complete concrete expression. The Mass is the true representation of the Cross of Christ. It is a participation in the one definitive act of redemptive love in history, the sole means by which sin is overcome. It is by this sacrifice that we are saved, and it is precisely that sacrifice which is represented in the sacrifice of the Mass.

> In the Eucharist the memorial of the New Covenant is realized, the New Covenant in which Christ has united himself forever to the Church, his beloved Bride for whom he gave himself up. It is therefore fitting that spouses should seal their consent to give themselves to each other through the offering of their own lives by uniting it to the offering of Christ for his Church made present in the Eucharistic sacrifice, and by receiving the Eucharist so that, communicating in the same Body and the same Blood, they may form but "one body" in Christ.[78]

The link between the marriage ceremony and the Eucharist is more than co-incidental. One does not simply "add" the Mass to the marriage ceremony to thank God for the good things that He has given us. Rather, marriage, as the whole of Christian life, is defined by the sacrifice of the cross and moves toward the unity given in the one perfect sacrifice of Christ. One way to indicate the profound nature of marriage is to say that in marriage we come to participate in the one sacrifice of the Cross, the source of the new creation, the center of salva-tion history. Apart from the Cross, there is no salvation, there is no truth, there is no integrity in fallen history. As the representation of the sacrifice of the death and resurrection of Christ, the Eucharist is the source of unity in fallen creation, a unity that is ordered according to the New Covenant, the free offer of

---

[78]*Catechism*, 1621.

grace to a free people. Essentially, it is in the freedom and integrity of the New Covenant that marriage finds it's meaning.

Like the other sacraments, the sacrament of marriage works *ex opere operato*. That is, like the Eucharist, in which the bread and wine become the body and blood of Christ, marriage also has an objective character that extends beyond the individual experience and faith of the believer. This simply means that salvation and salvation history did not originate with the believer or the believer's experience. It has its source in a reality which the married person does not create; rather it is something beyond the person that he or she freely enters. I am not married because I feel like it nor do I define marriage according to my own desires, although personal free participation is essential. Marriage is a sacramental reality that extends beyond my personal feelings, just as the bread and wine are not the body of Christ because I believe it to be, but because it simply is changed by the sacramental action. As in the other sacraments, in marriage, it is the redemptive activity of Christ that provides the objective character and order for marriage. So that although a man and woman freely enter in marriage, the marriage bond is sustained not by their will, but by the grace of Christ, whose authority, unlike our own, cannot be undermined by sin. Through marriage, the spouses are drawn into the unity and integrity of the New Creation given in Christ.

The insistence upon the real objective nature of the sacraments asserts the presence of the redemption in Christ in history here and now, not simply as the promise of something yet to come. That objective presence must be historical as defined by the incarnation. The objective character of the sacrament of marriage is the bond, the *res et sacramentum*. But the bond is not a mere "thing," but as a historical sacramental reality it has the character of an event. Perhaps of all the sacraments, marriage, in one sense, is most easily understood to be an event. The marriage bond, as a relationship and participation in the New Covenant, is an action which orders human life at it very foundation. Like all of the sacraments, the event character of marriage is determined by its participation in the redemptive events of the life of Christ. Christ alone saves, and only by participating in those events is one saved. Yet, marriage has an event character that distinguishes it somewhat from many of the other occasional sacramental acts.

The unique event character of marriage is found in its very structure. In the concrete day-to-day living out of the one sacrifice of Christ by means of the mutual love of man and wife, the married couple enters more deeply into the salvation offered by Christ. Within this sacramental economy, the husband and wife are initiated more deeply into the love of God in all the dimensions of married life. In marriage, the couple partakes of the spousal love of the New Covenant, into the mystery of the nuptial relationship between Christ and His Church. The bond, although freely entered into by the couple, is the bond of New Covenant given by Christ. Only in Christ is such redemptive love possible.

In its most fundamental sense, the *event-character* of marriage is a participation in the New Covenant, the one sacrifice of Christ, whose one flesh unity with His Church stands at the center of reality. The concrete act of marriage places one at the heart of reality. That is, when one enters into this covenant, the marriage is not over, but continues to grow throughout the life of the husband and wife, just as the Jews grew in faith and love of God in their obedience to the Old Covenant through their individual acts of faith. So too, in marriage, through the individual acts of one's married life, the husband and wife affirm and deepen their love for each other, thereby participating more completely in the love of God. Ironically, it is often times through the mundane events and actions in one's life that one lives more deeply into this reality. Although the sacrament of marriage is sustained by the grace of God, who offers us life in the New Covenant, and not by our own efforts, it is in and through the particular acts of love over the course of one's married life that the believer enters more deeply into the sustaining mystery of Christ's grace. Only in such freedom, sustained by the love of Christ, can one choose to love another for the whole of one's life.

Such a bond, as that found in marriage, cannot be imposed. The marriage act requires the free consent of the individual recipients who marry each other. In marriage, one participates through one's life as husband and wife, as sexual beings, in the New Covenant

c. Marriage - Sign and Effect

Like the other six sacraments, one of the effects of marriage is that by the power of the Holy Spirit, the participant is incorporated more completely into the life of Christ, a life that is at once Trinitarian and covenantal. This participation is not only the end of marriage, but the goal and purpose of human life itself. The unique character of marriage is that in and through the love of husband and wife, the married couple comes to share in the truth about man given in creation and in the great mystery of our redemption. Through the love of one man for one woman, as sexual creatures, married people receive grace.

Like each of the other sacraments, marriage is concerned with a certain stage in human life. Marriage (and Holy orders) is a sacrament that defines one's adult vocation within the life of the Church. But what is distinctive of its character as a "vocation" is its claim that the nuptial relationship can mediate the redemption of Christ. Marriage, then, as a sacrament, not only is a positive response to the love of God, but also in a most profound manner reveals the very sacramental nature of the created order. In the concreteness of our existence as creatures, the grace of Christ is operative, redeeming the believer in this most profoundly "natural" event of the union of a man and woman. And though under the present conditions of fallen creation the true ends and meaning of marriage often appear to be lost, in Christian marriage the truth about marriage and the truth of our beings as sexual creatures is revealed.   Marriage is a sign that mediates God's grace.

In the traditional description of the different components of the sacrament of marriage, the sign, the *sacramentum tantum*, is the rite itself. In this rite, there are two essential components. First, in marriage, the man and the woman freely give themselves to each other. The two people commit themselves to loving the other for the whole of their lives. It is the most intimate gift possible, that of one person to another, a gift that cannot be determined by any external forces. In this important decision, the believers affirm their being before Christ and His Church, and allow themselves to be formed in and by the love of Christ. By their free gift of themselves to each other, they are the ministers of the sacrament, not the priest.

One of the most difficult things about marriage for most people to believe today is that although marriage is the result of a free decision on the part of the believer, it is not a human creation. For in marriage, the believers enter into the mystery of salvation given by Christ in creation. The couple does not control it or define it, neither does the Church nor society. It is beyond any human authority; consequently, one cannot divorce or put an end to a marriage. It is by the decision of the individual believers that they alone can enter into marriage. In this act, they come to take on a new and irrevocable identity in Christ.

Second, the free gift of self that is at the heart of marriage must also be a total gift of self. According to the tradition, one way to say this is to say that marriage needs to be consummated. In the conjugal act, the total self-donation of one believer to another is completed. It represents total union of the spouses, one with the other. The relationship between a man and a woman in marriage, then, can never be simply a "spiritual" union, abstracted from the living of their whole lives together. Since it must include the whole self, it needs to be physical. On the other hand, it cannot be simply a physical giving. Conjugal love represents a total giving.

It was assumed by the tradition that sexual intercourse is the most intimate physical expression of one bodily creature to another; one could not be more physically intimate. That is why the casual use of sex: e.g., a one-night stand, was always thought to be sinful and destructive. Since sexual intercourse was such an intimate expression of one's self, how could one simply have sex with anyone who came along? It was not simply the worry of pregnancy that was the main concern, but the problem of a violation of intimacy. Such limited sexual experssion was thought to be a grave violation of human integrity. If we are our bodies, we cannot give ourselves casually to another, since every human act affects the whole person. Such a casual use of human sexuality denies the true the meaning of conjugal love.

On the other hand, by its proper use, sexual intercourse reveals the totality and intimacy of the love of a man and woman. In this act, loving spouses partake of the goodness of creation, giving themselves totally, revealing themselves to each other, and growing in love for each other.[79] As the total gift of the themselves, the love of the spouses is symbolic of the permanence of Christ's love for His Church, imaging the triune love of God, the unity of the New Covenant, which is sustained by the unchanging love of Christ.

In marriage, the baptized Christians give themselves freely to one another. Because of their baptism, the man and woman are freed by the grace of Christ to participate in the New Covenant. They now stand in a new relationship with Christ through whom they are saved. In the tradition, the Church has always distinguished between sacramental and non-sacramental marriage. Sacramental marriage required that the believers be baptized in order to enter into marriage. This does not mean that the marriage of non-Christians is insignificant, for by their participation in the order of creation, the marriage of non-believers is significant. Non-sacramental marriage indicates a basic recognition of the order of creation and the place of male and female within that order. But presently, under the effects of sin, non-sacramental marriage lacks the redemptive significance of the New Covenant. Bound by original sin, the couple is not free to make an irrevocable commitment that is alone made possible by one's participation in the grace of Christ through baptism. In a positive sense, non-sacramental marriages point beyond themselves to a fullness that is given in the New Covenant. But the presence of faith, which has its initial concrete expression in baptism, is essential to a sacramental marriage because in baptism, the freedom of the grace given in Christ is given to the recipient. As baptized into the death and resurrection of Christ, the believer now participates in the events by which the believer is saved. The way in which the tradition has articulated the objective concrete effect of baptism is to say that in baptism, one receives an indelible character; one undergoes an ontological change in which that which was damaged by sin is now renewed. The effects of baptism, standing in the light of God's grace, freed from original sin and a member of the Church of believers, enable one to freely enter into the redemptive mystery of Christ given in marriage.

The effects of marriage, like many of the sacraments, is the reception of grace. The sacramental sign, the profession of love between the couple, mediates that grace. In the reception of the grace, *res tantum,* the faith of the believer is deepened. Although the individual is affected by grace, as the couple enters into the nuptial mystery of the New Covenant, it is always given in relationship to the other. The love of God is always communal or interpersonal. It unites people in truth and love. Grace itself, as the love of God, is an interpersonal act, the self-sacrificial love that is at the heart of the New Covenant. Marriage is a sign of this love and makes that love concrete.

---

[79]This theme will be examined later in chapter 6 when discussing the meaning of the body according to Pope John Paul II.

The unique nature of the effects of marriage is to be found in the *res et sacramentum*, which is the bond between the husband and the wife. This term refers to both the symbolic reality and the effect of the sacrament. The *res et sacramentum* is at once the product of the sign, the vows taken, and the consummation of the marriage, the two become "one flesh." This bond between the husband and the wife is a fundamental good achieved in marriage. It is an effect, a *res* of the sacrament. At the same time, as a sacramental sign, this bond points beyond itself as a sign or sacrament of the relationship between Christ and His Church. So that one can say that in this bond, the love between the husband and wife, they image the relationship between Christ and His Church. It is precisely in this imagery that one can come to understand the grace received in marriage, the grace of the New Covenant that images and participates in the love of Christ for His Church.

1. The Indissolubility of Marriage

Perhaps the best way to discuss the sacramental nature of marriage and the bond that constitutes the *res et sacramentum* is to look at it from the perspective of the indissolubility of marriage. In the Roman Catholic tradition, the teaching that marriage is a sacrament is inextricably linked with the notion that marriage is indissoluble. In marriage, something irrevocable happens. Here, the one flesh unity of the New Covenant established in creation is realized in a special way in the life of the believer.

Edward Schillebeeckx identifies two ways in which this indissolubility has been articulated in the history of the Church. He describes the first description of the marriage vows, belonging to the New Testament and patristic period, as what he called a *moral obligation* to indissolubility.[80] This meant that the marriage vow should not be broken because when one entered into marriage one took an oath that obligated one to live in such a way that the vows *not* be broken. According to the culture of the time, oaths were taken very seriously. These oaths defined one's identity. Schillebeeckx notes that within this understanding of marriage, there was never the sense that when a marriage failed because the husband and/or wife did not live as they should, that the marriage could end. Already in this early period, it was assumed that marriage vows were inviolable and could not even be destroyed by sin. Yet, in this early understanding of marriage, the emphasis was not on an ontological bond, but on the obligations undertaken in marriage. Failure to meet those obligations did not "undo" the marital bond. Rather, the emphasis was to live in such a way that the marriage, this central commitment in one's life, be continuously nurtured and preserved.

---

[80]Schillebeeckx, *Marriage*, vol. II, pp 210ff.

The second way in which Schillibeeckx describes the indissolubility of marriage was articulated in the theology of the twelfth and thirteenth centuries. The theology of this period began to articulate marriage in terms of an ontological bond. This bond, as a participation in the covenantal relationship between Christ and his Church, was founded upon the grace of Christ which cannot be destroyed, even by sin. In sacramental marriage the very being of the man and woman changed as they entered this relationship. They now came to stand in a new relationship to God, a relationship that revealed the true meaning of human sexuality. And because of this participation in the redemptive grace of Christ, the marriage vows cannot be overcome by sin. In this theology of marriage, the marital bond is more than moral; it is rooted in the economy of salvation. The emphasis is placed upon the objective nature of the sacrament which cannot be destroyed since it is sustained in the love of Christ.[81]

Within the Christian tradition, although divorce was permitted under the Old Law, it was not thought that indissolubility was something new added to marriage after the coming of Christ, but it was thought to reflect the very nature of the marriage covenant itself. All adequate definitions of marriage point to this dimension of permanency. It is an essential and identifying characteristic of marriage which defines the particularly unique character of marriage, something missing from what today is often called domestic partnership, or a relationship with a "significant other." It signifies that if one is to give oneself to another in a total manner, this includes the whole of one's life, including one's future. Perhaps one definition of marriage that best underscores the essential nature of the indissolubility of marriage is to define marriage as a "free, permanent, exclusive heterosexual relationship."[82]

According to this definition, the individual gives oneself to another freely in marriage. Since it is a total giving, it can never be forced upon anyone. Only a person who is free can open up the depths of their being to another. Such a relationship, in which two people reveal themselves to each other, the intimacy can only develop over time. This self-revelation to another is the medium in which one grows as a human being and the foundation of permanence in marriage. Such self-revelation is difficult today.

Notice that in our contemporary culture there is a conflict between the understandings of freedom described in the sacrament of marriage and that found in popular culture. Almost universally, today people define freedom in terms of "doing what one wants to do." This is often understood to stand in contradiction to the making of commitments, especially marriage. In some instances, a person might contend that he or she wants to make a commitment to another. Yet, even

---

[81]Schillebeeckx, *Marriage*, vol. II, 212-213.

[82]For this definition I am indebted to Fr. Joseph Murphy, S.J.

in those instances such a decision is thought to be no better than that of the person who refuses any commitment or chooses something trivial. In most cases, this popular understanding of freedom requires that one keep one's options open. If one is to live a really free life, there can be no external authority to which one can submit, no particular obligations. Yet, if one follows this logic, and if keeping one's options open is the essence of real freedom, then any commitment is impossible and so are the freeing benefits of loving and being loved.[83]

It was noted earlier that in one of his writings G.K. Chesterton points out that the greatest adventure in life takes place in the family.[84] Within marriage and family, the most profound levels of human life are shaped; i.e., one learns to love, one learns morality, etc. In this familial relationship, the most important aspects of human living take place. But such a position is hard to understand today when most people are told to be individuals and do whatever they desire. This individualism permeates much of our cultural life. Look at the number of words that use "self": self-esteem, self-awareness, self-fulfillment, etc. Take for example the importance that people place upon careers. Today, people spend all sorts of time acquiring professional degrees and working long hours "to make something of themselves." Yet, most people change careers (not simply jobs) six or seven times. If they are so important, why are people changing them? Against this, Chesterton contends that what is really important in life takes place in the relationship between people in the private sphere, where the demands of the public square no longer control one's life (unlike the market place with all of its rules). In these relationships, especially that of the family, each member learns to be really human, they learn to love and to be virtuous and to be holy. These are the most important things in life. In these loving relationships, the love of God and neighbor, the person is at stake. By being "good" at these things, one is free. For only when one has this integrity that is born of real commitments can one live a fully human life, something that a career in itself cannot give to anyone.

Against the modern understanding of freedom, the Christian position has always contended that real freedom is doing the will of the Father through Christ. Within this intellectual framework, the loss of freedom is not the result of submitting to the will of God, rather, real human slavery is due to sin, submitting oneself to something other than the one true God. To be free, then, is to be utterly dependent upon the one who can free us from our sins, to live in the

---

[83]See Monica Miller, *Sexuality and Authority in the Catholic Church* (Scranton: The University of Scranton Press), 1995. In the text, she indicates that the most significant refusal of human responsibility and obligation to another is abortion. The mother rids herself of her child.

[84]G.K. Chesterton, *Brave New Family*, pp. 23ff.

truth. Only in the life of faith is the sinful world, which is closed in upon itself, opened. In faith, as in any loving relationship, when one enters into it the individuals are drawn beyond themselves, called to be more than what they were. Think, for example, of people in love, or children in a loving family. In each instance, the lovers and the children mature in innumerable ways. Through the love that they receive, they call the others to greater love and to greater maturity. Note the difference between children who come from a loving home and those who do not. Those from a loving home are generally more secure, have greater integrity and maturity than those who do not come from such homes. The difference is that they have learned to love and trust. Human integrity is the result of interpersonal commitment. This is essential to understanding what practically happens in marriage. In marriage, one comes to grow in the love of God and the grace of God, a process that takes place by means of the love of husband and wife for each other.

Like God's love, the permanence of marital love provides a context in which one can grow. Unlike the many today who say that human growth comes from a variety of human experiences, a Christian might answer that real growth comes from commitment. To dedicate one's life to God, to serve others over the years is believed to bring about a greater ability to love, a more profound wisdom, and a more complete integrity of life than simply experiencing a variety of things. Only in the life of commitment is there real freedom.

One of the things that commitment presupposes is that it takes time to learn to love another. One needs to know the other and then to offer love and be offered love, a love that moves towards a total giving of oneself. And such wholeness or completeness requires that one be there for another. How can you give yourself completely if you hardly know the other person? Or if the other person will not be there tomorrow? Thus, to say that marriage is the total giving of oneself to another is also to affirm its indissolubility. As temporal beings, humans must give themselves across time. This really means that if a man and woman give themselves to each other in a complete manner, which is the nature of the marital bond, that giving includes not only who they are in the present, but also their futures. To give another one's future is not only to give oneself as one now is, but also to give all that one can be.

In this promise of one's future there is, of course, a risk. One may become ill, or impoverished, or undergo any number of large or small changes. But apart from death, nothing can end this total gift of oneself to another. Once made, this commitment simply cannot be undone. Such a relationship takes one to the heart of human life since the most profound dimensions of one's life are at stake in this love.

The Catholic tradition understands marriage as the call to love in the complete and total manner that Christ loves his Church. Since this love touches upon the most profound dimensions of human life, such love cannot be but rooted in the grace of Christ. This grace is not external to the marital relationship itself.

Rather, the relationship between the man and the woman is the participation in the very reality of the New Covenant; a covenant sustained by the grace of Christ, the one and the same love that sustains a Christian marriage.

i. Exclusivity

In addition to understanding marriage in terms of permanence, it is important that the marriage be *exclusive*. That is, the spouse promises to love the other across all time and "across all space." The one spouse chooses another unique person to love as a spouse from among the many possible people one could choose to live with. It is true that an individual could marry any number of other people and live a happy life with them. Yet, in marriage, one chooses a particular person. This means that marital love is a unique kind of love that cannot be repeated or replaced with the substitution of another person. Notice that attempts to replace the other, as in the case of adultery, are ruinous to a marriage.

Much like permanence, exclusivity provides an opportunity for one to grow in love in ways that multiple partners could not. It presupposes that I cannot give myself completely to a variety of partners. By being faithful to one particular person, there are possibilities for growth and love that multiple partners could never make possible. This reflects the idea that the human person and the mystery of God's love are so "deep" that it takes the whole of one's life to "live into them." That is, to grow in the multiple dimensions of the love of another, one requires not only time, but also a specific person to love.

In addition, to say that marriage requires only one partner is to say that it is a historical event. That is, one often hears love spoken of as some abstract emotion. People say that they love all people. But you can only really love particular human beings. In and through this love the life of the one who loves is made concrete and given form. Love is an act that shapes us as human beings, grounding us in the love of God.

An example of the sort of abstract way of thinking that leads away from real love was the movement calling for "open marriages." The proponents of these relationships argue that sexuality should not be exclusive, but inclusive. The defenders of open marriage say that to avoid the sterility of a marriage that was closed in upon itself, it would be healthier if the couple had a variety of experiences with other people and that they would bring those experiences into the marriage. Their marriage would greatly be enriched from these external sources, including intimate relationships with others. This, of course, included having friends of the opposite sex and even sexual encounters with these "friends." Yet, the movement really did not work because it failed to realize that what was really interesting was not the fads or passions of the external world, not the mere variety of human experiences, but the uniqueness and possibilities of the relationship between the two married people. In the end, open marriage was boring, shallow and destructive.

Rather than focusing on how the external world and the variety of external experiences can help to shape marriage, it would be better to say that what strengthens marriage does not flow from the external world into the marriage, rather, it is precisely the opposite. What strengthens the muddled world is what flows from religious commitments, especially marriage, into the external world. For the world at large is a world that is full of confusion and various passions. To belong too closely to it is bound to lead one astray amid the confusion of those competing passions. Think of the people who commit adultery, they do it because they are seduced by one of the passions existing in the world. Such seductions are destructive of what is true. As a matter of fact, they refuse what is true and what is good.

Such temptations have always existed. In addition, there are, of course, other temptations that seduce individuals away from their marital intimacy, e.g., jobs, social concerns, etc. These passions, as challenges to marital life, promise that one can find human fulfillment by pursuing such passions. But in the face of such temptations, the Christian teachings on marriage hold that by giving oneself totally to a person, not a series of persons or some object, that one is called to a growth and depth of love that cannot be found anywhere else. In effect, only in a self-sacrificial love, such as this marital love, can the rejection of those forces and passions that enslave one to immaturity and superficiality be overcome. Exclusivity, then, is not a hindrance, but is an essential condition for marital love, and consequently, an essential component of the indissolubility of marriage.

ii. Heterosexuality

A second component of the definition of marriage that reinforces the permanence of marriage is that marriage is a heterosexual relationship. That is, marriage is a unique kind of relationship, or perhaps a better term is commitment. It is more than a friendship, although it certainly does include that dimension of love. Rather, it is a relationship that is essentially male and female. This means two things. First, as sexual beings, there is a complementarity between male and female that cannot be replaced by any other sexual relationship. Unlike many interpretations of the marital relationship that see it as the product of a purely cultural interpretation of human sexuality that can vary from age to age, as for instance those who argue for homosexual marriages, the Christian position presupposes that men and women are definitively different. These differences are not divisive, but are constitutive of human life as beings created in the image of God. Within the context of the love of God, Christians realize that as sexual and bodily beings, men and women signify and represent different aspects of the nuptial structure of the New Covenant. According to the biblical accounts, the New Covenant, which is the source of the order of creation and redemption, is understood in terms of the love of Christ for His Church, the relationship between Christ and Mary, the New Adam and New Eve. During the present time, the reciprocity between the sexes is a participation in the One Flesh union of the Eucharistic worship of the Church, the historical locus of the New Covenant. All other psychological or social interpretations of human sexuality fall short, failing to realize the depth and significance of the sexual differences.

Second, the genital complementarity is not unimportant. Many people today hold an androgynous or unisex theory of human sexuality. Such theories tend to abstract from the sexual differences, seeing humans as primarily "persons" rather than as men and women. Within such theories, genital differences have no or only accidental significance. For example, some would argue that as long as people love and respect each other, the forms of genital exchange do not matter. This approach to human sexuality is not uncommon today. In universities, this theory is evident in many of the politically correct movements such as gender studies. The gay marriage movement in contemporary culture also reflects the diminished significance of the sexes. Once the significance of those differences is negated, most ideologues promote the fact that all of the different possible modes of genital exchange are equally legitimate: e.g., homosexuality, etc. In such instances, there appear to be no norms by which to judge sexual behavior.

The Church, on the other hand, has held that it is precisely through the union of husband and wife, as man and woman, in the conjugal act that the true and unique character of marital love finds its expression. In this union, the one flesh unity of the New Covenant, now symbolized in the marital act, the husband and wife are drawn more deeply into the love of God. On account of the fact that human sexuality is understood in terms of the New Covenant, the Church refuses to hold that the conjugal act can be reduced to a mere genital exchange. The conjugal act always signifies something deeper and more profound. In the conjugal act, the husband and wife give themselves to each other in the most intimate manner possible for bodily creatures. And the act of conjugal love, as all true love, overflows beyond itself and brings about new life. Such life, children, reveal to us what the purpose and meaning of married life are all about. Children are not incidental to marriage; they draw the parents beyond themselves into the mystery of human life. They affirm our faith in the future, reflecting the overflowing and the deepening of the love of husband and wife. The procreation is not an accidental addition to human sexuality, but linked to its very purpose and fullness.

Some would argue that it is precisely in the link between the marital love and procreation that this nuptial love mirrors the Trinitarian life of God. Just as the Father's love for the Son sends the Spirit, the love of husband and wife brings about new life. Consequently, the sexual complementarity of male and female necessarily includes the procreative dimension. In this process, human sexuality is deepened: one moves from being man and woman to husband and wife, finally to being father and mother. Each step is a further realization of the mystery of human sexuality. In each case, one is drawn more completely into the mystery of Christ.

It is precisely in the conjugal act, the sexual union between husband and wife, that the true meaning of marriage is revealed. Notably, it is in this bodily giving that a fundamental unity is achieved. Yet, the marital unity cannot simply be achieved through sexual intercourse, and at the same time, it cannot be separated from it. In the end, it is only within the complete gift of self that the true meaning and purpose of sexuality is revealed. And this complete gift of self is a participation in the truth of human existence as revealed in the New Covenant.

2. The Goods of Marriage

It should be briefly noted that within the Roman Catholic tradition, one of the primary ways of articulating the importance of marriage has been by stating the three "goods of marriage." These goods refer to the observed good or benefits or blessings that are associated with marriage. In many ways, they represent a "practical" Christian description of the value of marriage. Nonetheless, they indicate the effects of the sacrament of marriage. It was St. Augustine who pointed to the three benefits that are at the heart of married life.[85]

The first good of marriage is children. The importance of children and the good that they are is often lost on the modern world. One need only look at what people say about children today and how they treat children to get the "real" picture. In many instances, children are "put off" until the married couples' careers are well under way or until they are "financially secure." In such instances, whether one has children or not often becomes simply the product of economic calculation. One often hears people say, "How can you afford to have children?" On those occasions, children are often depicted as a drain on the economic resources of the family, possibly requiring the adult having to sacrifice some comfort for the child. From this perspective, children are spoken of in a negative fashion.[86]

This attitude towards children is quite different from the past, when children were considered to be economic resources. In many societies where gathering, herding or agriculture was the economic mainstay, children were thought of as assets. In some capacity or another, they worked from youth, bringing some

---

[85]John Hugo, *St. Augustine on Nature, Sex and Marriage* (Chicago: Scepter, 1969), 106ff.

[86]In the not too recent past, children had an economic function in the family. This was especially true when most businesses were family businesses or family farms. This is the first age in history when such an economic value is no longer there. Instead, today they are simply thought to be drains on one's economic resources.

economic benefit to the family, and caring for their parents in their old age. Today, however, in our seemingly ever-growing urban culture, most often children
are seen as an expense. If one begins from an economic perspective, one will
probably not see children for the good they are. There is no doubt that economics should be seriously considered when deciding to have children. But in most
instances in the West, the "cost" of the children does not impoverish the family
(especially in a culture as wealthy as ours), but it might deprive them of certain
comforts such as new cars or vacations.

The modern attitude towards children that see them as a tax upon one's resources is precisely the opposite attitude that the Church has held. According to
the Church, children are a primary good of marriage life. "Marriage and conjugal love are by their nature ordained toward the begetting and educating of children."[87] This assessment is based on the recognition that children are a fundamental good and their worth is not derived from anything that the culture or the
parents ascribe to the child. They are a good in and of themselves. Their very
life is a gift from God that needs to be protected and fostered. It is a good that
needs to be received and nourished. Furthermore, married adults have an obligation to bring children into the world and to raise them. In this act, they fulfill
the promise and possibility of their marriage vows.

According to the Church, children are a gift from God that parents are to
humbly receive and care for. As a good, they are not simply an option or a
choice peripheral or accidental to the married life. One of the confusions that the
use of artificial contraception has caused in people's understanding of sexuality
is that they now separate sex and procreation. Women are able to chemically
control procreation. By means of artificial contraception, women are now said
to be freed from the burden of pregnancy. As a result, many people are of the
impression and argue that children are an option, something that one can simply
add on to a marriage. Some married couples even argue that one can have just a
good of a marriage without having children. It is simply a matter of preference.

Against this attitude towards children, the Church contends that children are
a good that married couples have an *obligation* to pursue. The Church is, of
course, well aware that there might be serious circumstances under which one
might put off having children, but warns that such an act must only be undertaken for serious reasons, because children are a great gift and an essential component to married life.[88] A real part of adult maturity and responsibility is to
bring children into the world and educate them. This is evidenced by the holy
men and women who have done this throughout the ages.

---

[87]"The Church in the Modern World," *The Documents of Vatican II*, 50.

[88]See the encyclical *Humanae Vitae*. Even in such instances the Church insists that
this can only be done by moral means.

Consistent with the redemptive nature of love, the self-sacrificial love that causes the good of children also feeds back into the marriage, informing the life of the mother and father. In their responsibility as mothers and fathers, parents grow in a better understanding of the meaning of their lives as sexual beings. In marriage, women become wives and then mothers, in each instance actualizing dimensions of their femininity, moving towards greater fulfillment. Likewise, the man, in becoming husband and father, grows in realizing the depth of his sexuality. In both cases, bringing children into the world informs the life of the mother and father, calling them more deeply to the self-sacrificial love of Christ and therefore to a more complete human life.

The second good of marriage is the *bond* of love between the husband and wife. The basis of this bond is the total gift of self in love, including the sexual unity between husband and wife. The Christian understanding of marriage pre-supposes that there is a complementarity between the sexes which leads to mari-tal love. In this love a man and woman give themselves to each other in a unique manner, including the conjugal act. From this view, sexual intercourse is a "part" of marriage, but in marriage conjugal love finds its completeness and becomes redemptive. The bond, then, which results from the love of the couple as they participate in the redemptive grace of Christ, is not an abstraction, but the gift of the whole person to one another. This union defines the life of the man and the woman. It is in this complementarity and the gift of self of a man to a woman in marriage that man, as created as male and female, images God most clearly.

It is important to understand that sexuality is not simply a neutral force that one can choose to use in any number of "neutral" ways, but a powerful force and passion in human life. This is all too painfully obvious in our day when the un-restricted use of sexuality is often destructive, resulting in and from the exploit-ing of others as the objects of one's passion. The Christian tradition has always understood this danger and tried to guard against its work. Marriage was thought to be the remedy for concupiscence, where the proper use of sexuality was established issuing forth in a charity leading to holiness.[89] The bond of mar-riage, then, also serves a social good; it stands for the right order of human sexuality against those forces of human sexuality that are destructive and frag-menting. It was precisely this bond, this giving to each other, that came to define the bond and redemptive nature of conjugal love.

The third good of marriage is fidelity, the faithfulness of the husband and the wife. Marriage, as lived out faithfully, provides a context which frees one from the threats of infidelity, providing a context for the growth of the couple and their children in love. Fidelity, then, helps to free the couple so that they can contemplate the higher things in life, providing a fertile ground for faith to grow.

---

[89]Hugo, *St. Augustine on Nature, Sex and Marriage.*, p. 118ff.

As a human virtue, fidelity is more than external circumstances limiting the behavior of the person, nor is it a matter of subservience. Rather, it is a virtue that becomes part of the life and character of the spouses. Human fidelity is analogous to the gift of faith that one receives from God. Like one's religious faith, fidelity to another person must be rooted in the truth. Real fidelity cannot be based on mere affection or the passions alone. Nor can fidelity be an arrangement based on power. If human relationships are based on power, then control of the other becomes the basis for the relationship. But this is not the basis for genuine human fidelity. One can only really give oneself to another if the relationship is based on the true vision of man revealed in Christ. Here, fidelity is an act of will that becomes reinforced by habituation. Again, it requires that one live in the truth. To give oneself to another on some other basis outside the truth given in Christ is false and ultimately destructive. But if one's commitment to another is based in truth, the gift of self need not be episodic nor a matter of power, but contain the seeds of enduring love. In the faithfulness of this spousal love, the man and woman are shaped more deeply in the infinite love of God, who never abandons those He loves.

These three goods are not thought to be just aspects of marriage, but goods that are consistent with the order of marriage. Consequently, one is obligated to pursue them and foster them in marriage. One must be faithfully bound to the one that one loves. And one must be open to the gift of children.

d. Marriage as a Vocation

Yet another way of describing the meaning of marriage as a sacrament is to understand it as a Christian vocation. That is, marriage is not simply a "right," something that one should be able to do as a matter of justice. Rather, it is a gift to which one is called. It is a way of serving God. Often in the Catholic tradition the idea of vocation has been narrowed to mean simply those who become priests or enter religious life. But marriage is the vocation of the majority of Christians, a vocation that is not without significance.

The idea of marriage as a vocation is founded upon what was said at the beginning of this chapter. That is, marriage is fundamentally a religious act. For in this sacrament, the believer freely enters more deeply into the process of redemption. In marriage, then, the believer "assumes his place" in the service of God. This service has two primary foci: the love of the spouse and the begetting of children. In each of these acts, the husband and wife are incorporated into the mission of Christ through whose redemptive activity all things are saved. It is Christ's mission that alone is universal and comprehensive in nature, and it alone provides the context for every Christian vocation. Marriage, understood within this larger mission, is a means in which the gospel is preached to the world.

In marriage, the process of evangelization takes place through the love of the spouses for each other. They continue to evangelize each other in much the same way that the early Christians, living with their pagan spouses, would continually bear witness to the truth of Christ before their spouses. As Christians, spouses have the obligation to assist each other in achieving holiness. In one sense, the mission of every Christian is to help others in their quest for salvation. Here, love of God and love of neighbor come together. In fact, that is what the true love of neighbor is really about: the salvation of their souls. In a special way, spouses who have professed their love for one another have an obligation to one another, exhorting the other to holiness. For if marital love is to touch upon the whole of another's life, touching the most profound depths of one's spouse, that love cannot but be redemptive.

Inevitably, the mission of the married people overflows into the family, which is a direct consequence of their married love, and into the community, the Church. If you know people who are truly in love, it is obvious that their love overflows their relationship. Despite all of the limits and difficulties of loving another, real love is not closed in upon itself. For instance, when two people fall in love, they are often preoccupied with each other. But at a certain point their love opens them up to those around them, including others, helping them, enriching the lives of those they touch. On the other hand, there are instances in which a relationship closes in upon itself, usually resulting in great instability and tension. The nature of real love is such that it always calls those involved to transcend themselves. Real love is self-sacrificial. It requires that one give oneself to another, even to the point of dying so that another might live.

This description of love may sound strange in an age where self-assertiveness and self-fulfillment are held up as essential goals for successful living; yet, Christians claim that it is not in pursuing personal goals or careers or any other worldly accomplishment that one finds life. Rather, the Christian message proclaims that one only finds life in self-sacrificial love, dying to oneself so that one might live. Of course, this is the message of the Gospel and the example of Christ, who through His own suffering and death was able to bring about the salvation of the world. It is only in losing one's life that one receives life.

The manner in which this love between husband and wife manifests itself most obviously and uniquely is in procreation. Again, children are not only a natural or accidental product of the conjugal union, but a fundamental good toward which marriage should move. They symbolize the generous love, the self-donation, of the husband for the wife and the wife for the husband. Children reflect the true nature and demands of marital love. The total giving of oneself that began in marriage now extends itself to the love of one's children. In and through their children, parents extend the mission of Christ. Through their family life, they bear witness to the true richness of the gospel.

The begetting and education of children, through which husbands and wives are brought more completely into the love of God, is a great responsibility and mission that demands much of the parents. Yet, if you were to ask parents if they would die for their children, most would not hesitate to say yes. Fortunately, most parents are not asked to do this; instead, throughout the years, they freely take on the trials and difficulties of parenthood. For people of good sense, children are recognized as great gifts that need to be nurtured, educated, and protected. In doing this, the parents bear witness to the very truth and nature of marital love.

There are other ways in which the love of the married couple overflows into the community, nourishing it. Marital love and family are obviously the basis for much of the stability in social life. The responsibility of married couples for the community begins with the love of their children. They are obligated to raise and educate their children to be moral, mature human beings. But the communal dimensions of marriage and family transcend a mere focus on their own children. Secured in the love of the one for the other, husband and wife should seek opportunities to exercise charitable acts. This is particularly true as they practice their faith. Real love is said to grow, and as its grows, it directly affects the lives of others.

It is within the Church that marriage and family should find themselves especially at home. The leaders of the Church, understanding the many difficulties that face family life today, must act boldly to defend it and decisively to support it. The Church should be a font from which the family receives support and a haven where it finds protection. This support should, first of all, be primarily through the prayer life of the Church, especially the Eucharist, which is the source of the Church's faith and therefore life. The worship of the Church should be a source of unity for the family, binding them to each other and uniting them to the larger community. Of course, the other side of this is that if a family fails to practice its faith and to participate in the worship of the Church, that family is in grave danger, for such a family loses its focus as to its meaning and ultimate purpose. As already noted, apart from faith there are many dangers.

Today, the family has been described as the *domestic church*. This phrase reveals the particularly important religious mission of family life. It is the context in which the love of man and woman for each other overflows into the love of their children. The family should become a "school" for that love. It is here that the education of those individuals who will mold and shape the world through their actions is accomplished. It is in the sacrament of marriage that Christ is present, bringing not only new life into existence, but through the marital love of the couple, the New Covenant becomes concretely present in history. It is in the family that Christian parents actualize their vocation in the education and formation of their children in the faith. It is here that the work of God is concretely begun, work that moves the couple out into the community, witnessing to the redemptive love of Christ.

Summary:

To say that marriage is a sacrament means that it is fundamentally a religious act despite the fact that there are legal, sociological, and psychological dimensions to marriage. In the end, all non-theological explanations are inadequate since the real purpose and meaning of marriage is to bring one closer to Christ. As a participation in the New Covenant given in and through Christ, marriage takes one to the very heart of reality. Marriage, then, as a sacrament informed by the New Covenant, reflects the Christocentric nature of reality. Marriage derives its meaning from a view of the world that sees that all things come from Christ, and in and through Christ they are brought to completion. Participation in marriage results in the ordering and structuring of life according to the New Covenant.

Against some contemporary trends that argue that marriage needs to be redefined in terms of recent social changes, the Christian believes that the real significance of marriage is revealed in the economy of salvation. That is, one must look to the revelation of Christ to understand the meaning of being male and female. So that in the life of faith, the believer not only comes to know Christ, but at the same time discovers the truth about man as created in the image of God, male and female.

Within the life of the individual believer, through baptism the Christian enters into the life of faith. The baptized Christian now stands before God in a new way. This new participation in the grace of Christ is redemptive. In this covenantal relationship, salvation comes from God, and the promise of salvation is sustained by God, not by human effort. In the same way in marriage, the free creatures made in the image and likeness of God, men - as male and female - are called to freely respond to the offer of grace that is mediated by the love of one's spouse. In the intimate love between the husband and wife, they participate in the salvific activity of Christ by which they are saved. The unique part of marriage is that through another person's love, the spouses are brought more deeply into the love of Christ. Through the conjugal act and corresponding commitment, husband and wife give themselves to each other in a unique and irreplaceable manner. In the vows, they promise to give themselves totally to the other, forever. This total giving as the free, permanent, exclusive and heterosexual relationship means that in and through human sexuality the husband and wife come to participate more completely in the love of God. Being male and female, then, is not simply good as part of the good creation, but as "good," it is the means through which we worship God. One might say that human sexuality is sacramental.

In the end, against most of the pressures of society and its reinterpretation of marriage, the reason for marriage is not self-fulfillment, but the service of God. In self-sacrificial love, one believer gives himself to another in such a way that it fulfills their individual human lives. In the giving of oneself to another, one comes to grow in the love of God, who demands that all the faithful follow the way of the cross, giving their lives so that they might live. In marriage, the spouses serve God by their love of each other, calling each other to the fullness of life given in Christ. At the same time, the love of the spouses should overflow their relationship into the community. This is most evident in the begetting and rearing of children. Children are not an option in marriage; rather, they are a good to be sought. In our love of children, the self-sacrificial love of the parents moves beyond themselves in begetting children and educating them. The family becomes the "seminary' for the formation of the young, strengthening both the Church and the community.

Suggested Readings:

The Catechism of the Catholic Church
Edward Schillebeeckx, *Marriage: Secular Reality and Saving Mystery.*
John Hugo, *St. Augustine on Nature, Sex and Marriage.*

Study Questions:

1. What does permanency reveal about the nature of the sacrament of marriage?

2. How would one explain to another that marriage is really a sacrament and not just a "natural" thing?

3. What does procreation reveal to a husband and wife about the meaning of marriage?

4. In what ways is marriage best understood in terms of the Eucharist? In what ways are they alike?

5. What are the effects of the sacrament of marriage? How is indissolubility intimately tied to those effects?

Chapter V:
Human Sexuality as the Basis for Marriage

If marriage can be described as a sacrament and defined as a permanent, exclusive, heterosexual, and free relationship open to the procreation of new life, then it is fundamentally a sexual relationship. As a matter of fact, one important way to understand the exact nature of marriage is by examining the meaning and purpose of human sexuality as it is understood within the Judeo-Christian tradition. Within this tradition, marriage is understood to be the fullest form of sexual expression. It is the goal of all sexuality and the end toward which sexual expression moves. Today, many people are aware of competing views that hold that other forms of human sexuality are as equally valid; e.g., the debate as to whether homosexual marriage ought to become lawful. Yet, the Catholic doctrinal tradition has always held up marriage as the most complete expression of human sexuality, and that sexuality is ordered toward that expression. To believe otherwise would certainly be to jeopardize the normative nature of heterosexual marriage and the sacramentality of marriage.

In the Christian tradition, the meaning of human sexuality is derived from the revelation, the truth of existence given in Christ. Since human life is a gift which has its origins in God, it is from this source that human life receives its order, purpose and meaning. Therefore, the Christian response to any attack on the unique nature of marriage has always been based on two premises. The first point of defense has always been that human sexuality is sacramental. It reveals a depth that transcends any simply biological, social or psychological analysis, and that living out the male/female complementarity of human sexuality finds its most complete expression in marriage. This means that man images God in and according to the order in which he was created. This imaging of God includes human sexuality, since it is in and through our bodily existence as sexual beings, we are called to serve God. According to the tradition, this physical complementarity was ordered to marriage in which the "two become one flesh." In marriage, the believers image God, a God who, as trinitarian, is a personal deity, a God whose very nature is love. Therefore to image God means that the believer participates in the trinitarian love and life. Thus, if human sexuality becomes a means through which the husband and wife participate in the love of God, then sexuality is sacramental. It is redemptive, leading beyond itself to the deeper love of God.

Second, other forms of sexual expression, then, are judged in terms of the fullness reached in marriage. They need to be understood not only for what they do, but also for what they do not do.

a. The Biblical Interpretation of Human Sexuality

The Christian understanding of human sexuality has played a significant role in the development of the cultures of the world, especially in the West. Even though there have been numerous debates among Christians as to the exact meaning of the biblical teachings concerning human sexuality, the biblical principles have, up until recently, influenced the understanding of human sexuality in American culture. Of course today, that biblical understanding of human sexuality is being challenged and in many instances being replaced. More than ever in the West, many are interpreting the meaning of human sexuality from some other perspective than the Judeo-Christian biblical tradition, usually approaching it and interpreting it within some secular intellectual framework. This "new" context for understanding human sexuality is framed by the numerous ideologies and psychological theories that influence the way people think about sexuality. Because of their different presuppositions about reality and human life, they naturally come to other conclusions about the purpose and meaning of human sexuality. In many instances, the theories are openly contradictory to the understanding of sexuality found in Christianity. At best, most of these theories lend to the general confusion about human sexuality that is so prevalent today.

According to many of the contemporary approaches to sexuality, the meaning of human sexuality is left to the choice of the individual, each choosing to express his or her sexuality in the manner he or she prefers; i.e., choosing a particular lifestyle that befits his or her opinions about human sexuality. The premise behind many such theories is that sexuality is just a part of human life. As "part" of life, it is subject to the free choices of the person, as individuals decide how to live their lives. Sexuality, as subject to the will of the individual, is thought to be open to human control and manipulation in all of its facets.[90]

At the same time, many contemporary theories describe human sexuality as primarily instinctual, as part of the forces of nature, and consequently, an impersonal force determined by drives within human beings. Since, humans have little or no control over human sexuality, men and women are subject to these natural forces which need to be fulfilled. Thus, it is often argued that one needs sexual activity of some sort to have a "healthy" sex life. But even though the forces are instinctual and natural, they can be manipulated in any number of ways, and it is up to the individual to determine the best way to actualize that usage.

Unlike the preceding argument, where human sexuality is thought to be a matter of preference and usage according to human freedom, most arguments for homosexuality are a little different. These explanations presuppose that the natural human sex drive is not open to the free manipulation of the individual, but

---

[90]Later, this will be discussed in terms of partial sexuality or the separatist understanding of sexuality.

that one's sexuality provides one with a specific orientation. Unlike the first argument that focuses on human freedom to use one's sexuality, here, freedom is thought to be subservient to a basic orientation, which is beyond the mere preference of the individual.[91] Nevertheless, both arguments understand human sexuality to contain sexual variations that are condemned by traditional Judeo-Christian teachings.

These interpretations of sexuality depict attempts to articulate the meaning of human sexuality from a secular perspective. It is not surprising that such theories continually occur in history since the effort to articulate the meaning and purpose of human sexuality is a continual struggle for human beings. This is due to the fact that human sexuality is more than mere sex, sex reduced to mere biological instinct. Rather, as a human act, human sexuality encompasses the whole person and is therefore linked to the ineffable mystery of human life. For humans are a real mystery, a mystery whose being can never be reduced to conceptual categories but whose meaning can only be revealed in the interpersonal actions of God.

In response to such secular theories of human sexuality, the Judeo-Christian tradition has always been careful to defend the idea that there is a certain universal order and meaning given in human sexuality from the very beginning. There is a created order established by God. Then God said: "Let us make man in our image, after our likeness.... God created man in his image; in the divine image he created him; male and female" (Gen. 1:26-17).

Of all the creatures, man alone is made to image God. He has a special place in the order of the good creation. Since man is created in the image of God, male and female, human sexuality has an important role in creation. This is evidenced in the two stories of creation. In the first creation story, man is created in the image and likeness of God, male and female. In the second story, Adam searches for one like himself; in the end, God creates the woman for man. Adam, realizing the likeness of the woman, says, "This at last is bone of my bone, and flesh of my flesh" (Gen. 2:23). At the same time that this nuptial order is affirmed, the biblical revelation has always insisted upon the reality of human freedom as essential to understanding human life and human action. Man is called to unity with God. He is also free to reject that order and unity.

In the first creation story, man is the crown of creation, the one who has dominion over the rest of creation. Human beings, created in the image of God, consequently have an authority and purpose that the rest of the creatures lack. In

---

[91] An important question that needs to be considered is the cause of homosexuality. If congenital or genetic, one might argue that it is not a matter of preference but a compulsion of some sort. It still leaves the question of whether or not "nature" is open to a variety of orders or whether homosexuality is a disorder. Also, there is still widespread evidence that the cause of homosexuality is social and psychological. This raises the question of the freedom of the homosexual on another level.

the second creation story, Adam likewise has a place of prominence. He participates with God in the ordering of creation. He names things. What is most noticeable in both instances is that man is not simply different because of certain
attributes, such as intellect or will, but what is unique about man is that he
stands in relationship to God. He is the creature who is capable of responding in
faith and love to God's offer of grace. This relationship is crucial, since it is the
basis upon which man and his place in the universe is understood. Man's relationship to God stands at the very heart of reality, a reality that needs to be
freely accepted by man.

The importance of the relationship between man and God is not only evidenced in the story of creation, but also in the story of the fall from grace. In the
story of the fall, it is precisely this relationship, this proximity to God, that is
lost. Prior to the fall, God walks in the garden. That is, He is close to man, and
man stands in relationship to God. The fall places a distance between man and
God. They no longer stand in the immediate light of God and they experience
shame. And, in the end they are driven from the garden. The loss is devastating.
Man is no longer close to God, but separated from God, yet still desiring that
unity now lost to sin. The resulting alienation is punishment for that sin, the effect that characterizes man's state in fallen creation.

Understanding, then, the meaning and purpose of human life requires that
one see it in terms of the purpose of human life, its unity with God from which
humanity is now alienated. There is no other purpose or meaning that can be
found within the created order that gives adequate expression to human life. To
substitute this for this relationship with another is simply a form of idolatry,
necessarily leading to the destruction of man. This is precisely the meaning of
the fall. It means to choose something other than God and elevate it to the place
of God, as central in one's life. Of course, such a choice is fundamentally irra-
tional. It is to choose death rather than life, to choose lies rather than truth, to
choose evil rather than good. The biblical account reveals that this is the case.
Once one rejects God as the center of one's life sin and disorder enter the world.

This whole process of creation, the creation of man and the fall, points to
the fundamentally covenantal order of the good creation. It places man's relationship with God not simply at the center of an individual's life, although it is,
but also at the heart of reality. Out of love, God calls man into existence, an
existence that finds its completion and fulfillment in the unity of God and man.
Man is called not only in the depth of his being, but with the whole of his being
to a unity with God. Included in his response to the call of God is not only his
soul or some "spiritual" dimension, but the whole of human life. Human life in
all of its dimensions needs to be understood in the light of its vocation and goal.
To try to come to grips with any dimension of human life apart from this covenantal structure will end in some kind of reductionism, the failure to see man in
all of his dignity, and the consequent dehumanization of man.

If this is the case, that all of human life must be understood in terms of the covenant, then this is the context in which human sexuality needs to be understood. That human sexuality has a role to play in this order is clear from the start. As a matter of fact, what is striking in the creation accounts is the importance that is given to human sexuality. In the first Genesis account, man is created in the image and likeness of God, male and female. Notice it is not simply that man or human beings image God, but that they do so as male and female. Accordingly, the woman leaves her father and mother and joins with a man, and the two become one flesh. In this marital unity, not only is the sacramental nature of being male and female symbolic in some abstract sense, but also it now becomes concrete. The redemptive nature of human sexuality is most clearly significant in the relationship of husband and wife in marriage.

In the second creation story, Adam is created first. Then, God creates the animals to find a suitable partner. What is noticeable again is the significance given to the male/female relationship. That alone, the male is incomplete and seeks a unity, a completeness with one unlike himself. None of the other animals makes a suitable partner, so eventually God creates woman from man, and she alone then fulfills the needs of man.

The complementarity and necessary importance of the sexes is again witnessed to in the New Covenant. It is in the incarnation of the Son, the New Covenant, that the real meaning and purpose of marriage is revealed. Since he is the historical prius of the revelation of God, a revelation that is based on the perfect unity of God and man, this revelation is the basis for understanding the created order, including human sexuality. The New Covenant, as the Old one, has a nuptial order. Marriage is an analogy for the New Covenant, but it means more and this marital structure finds its complete revelation in the Christ, in his life, death, and resurrection. In this revelation, Christ is the Second Adam who stands in relationship to the New Eve, Mary, as Bridegroom to Bride. Likewise, the New Covenant reflects Christ's relationship to His Church, the Bridegroom to the Bride. It is in the New Covenant, that the believer is led to a deeper understanding of human sexuality, since it is only in the activity of God that the mystery of human sexuality is revealed. This knowledge of sexuality is not merely a conceptual knowledge, but the knowledge and wisdom that come from the heart of reality, the love of God.

b. The Meaning of the Human Body

Before one can discuss the distinctive meaning of male and female in the tradition of the Church, it is necessary to say something about the human body and the physical nature of human sexuality. Within the great intellectual traditions of the world, one of the primary questions concerning human life has to do with the meaning and purpose of physical existence. In particular, what is the meaning and purpose of the body? This may seem like a strange question, yet, it is one of the primary questions that we face as humans, since the answer, in whatever form, will include some answer to the question of death and possibility of human immortality.

The most common answer given in human history to this question is that the human body is an impediment, a limit, the source of seduction, leading man away from truth into the darkness of sin. The reason one might hold this is that in human experience, physical existence, including bodily existence, is experienced as limiting, as the sources of pain and sorrow. The body ages, becomes ill, suffers and dies. The body has also been traditionally considered the seat of the passions, and despite the great pleasure that the passions produce, they were thought to lure man away from the "higher goods" that would fulfill his being. In the light of this experience of physical existence as limiting, man realizes that his real destiny is eternal life, eternal bliss or happiness, things not ultimately found in this world, since earthly things in this world are constantly fleeting and changing. Many of the great religions of the world proposed as a solution to this dilemma of man's existence in the world that one escape or transcend the limits of material existence, so that one can encounter the divine. The dualism evident in such philosophies is cosmic dualism, isolating spirit and matter, but this dualism is extended to the body. Body and soul are understood to be antagonists. Any harmony within human life in the world is an illusion.

The prevalence of dualist thinking throughout history is almost constant. It has even influenced Christianity to the point where, during certain periods of history, some Christians have believed that the body and human sexuality were evil. Linked to the suspicion of the body was the belief that sin had its sources in the bodily passions. Among Christians with such manichean tendencies are those who rejected marriage as a way of life. These gnostic interpretations of Christianity were, of course, heretical, usually exaggerating the evils of the temptations of human sexuality and the power of sin.

At the heart of this gnostic interpretation of Christianity is the tension between those who belong to Christ and those who belong to the world. The gnostic Christians interpreted this to mean that one must totally forsake the world if one is to belong to Christ. Belonging to the world and belonging to Christ are at odds, as antithetical principles. In this gnostic interpretation of the faith, human sexuality, as the whole of the created order is understood to be totally corrupted by the fall. Because of the radical nature of the fall, nothing of the goodness of creation remains within the now fallen created order. Consequently, rather than seeing the Christian faith as a matter of conversion or a redemption of the fallen creation, salvation becomes a separation from all that belongs to the physical, fallen world. Of course, the effects of this dualism on the manner in which one understands sexuality and marriage cannot be denied. From this perspective, sex will of course be seen as negative, since it includes the body and the passions, leaving celibacy as the only option for the "true" believer.

A modern dualism is quite the opposite. It likewise separates the body and the soul, not in order to deny the passion, but in order to give free reign the bodily passions. One form of the argument presupposes that, no matter what I do with my body, it does not affect me. The modern dualists argue that the actions one engages in with the body do not affect the whole person. For example, in the past it was thought that if one slept with someone out of wedlock, that was a moral evil and that person was a sinner. Today however, no matter what one does, you hear people say things like " I am still a good person." But what does that mean? On one level it is true: God still loves you and you have a dignity as a creature of God. On the other hand, certain acts are considered sinful, and doing them makes you less than fully human; they make you a sinner in need of redemption. Dr. William May refers to this manner of interpreting human sexuality as *separatist sex.* "By this I mean that the separatist understanding has severed the existential and psychological bond between the life-giving or procreative meaning of human sexuality and its person-uniting, love-giving, unitive meaning."[92] By extension of its logic, separatist sex presupposes that one can divide the psychosomatic unity of the human person. They would argue that what one does with one's body has no effect on the person. But the Church has held that such a separation of the person from the act is not possible.

Often today, traditional Christianity is characterized as having a negative attitude towards human sexuality. Those who make such critiques cite the emphasis of past generations on the dangers of human sexuality and the consequent sense of guilt that such attitudes engendered. Or, in some instances, they allude to the Church's teachings on artificial contraception or chastity as further evidence of its hostility toward human sexuality. It is true that in the history of the Church in certain places, a negative attitude towards sexuality- almost a scrupulosity- has raised its head from time to time. And there is no doubt that such an attitude could be destructive of any normal healthy sexual life. Yet in her doctrines, the Church, understanding the difficulties of concupiscence, has defended the goodness of sexuality. The insistence upon marriage as a sacrament and the goodness of children affirms this. In fact one should argue that the Church's teachings really promote a very positive attitude toward sexuality, but an attitude that does not belie the fact that there are certain dangers surrounding human sexuality.

Perhaps what is most important here is neither the criticism of the western tradition as being too conservative in the sexual matter, nor the criticism by many that the contemporary view of sexuality is too liberal. What is important is to understand that human sexuality is a very powerful force that touches upon the very basis of human existence, and that this force needs to be guarded and

---

[92] William May, *Sex, Marriage and Chastity* (Chicago: Franciscan Herald Press, 1981), p. 3.

guided to its proper ends, and in some cases, controlled. The dangers of lust and the unbridled use of human sexuality have always been understood to be destructive of human life, and the Church has always fought against it. The destructive nature of the abuse of human sexuality is all too evident today. The modern attitude toward an almost unlimited freedom in this area is not only dangerous, but it makes the proper exercise of human sexuality difficult, if not impossible. Today, the problem is not so much the fact that sexuality is oppressed, but that it is no longer ordered to its proper ends.

Again, despite the great dangers and possible abuses of human sexuality, the Church has always taught that in and of itself sexuality is good. It is constitutive of our existence as free creatures to be fully sexual. But to live in such a way that our sexuality reaches its completion, it is necessary that it be exercised in obedience and service to God. This may sound rather foreign today, but the essence of the matter is that the exercise of one's sexuality is a religious matter, for in it, one either accepts or rejects the offer of God's grace.

The reasoning that supports the view that sexuality is good comes from a certain understanding of physical existence and the existence of the body. Within the Judeo-Christian tradition, the physical existence was thought to be good. This is affirmed in creation, the incarnation, and especially, the resurrection.

1. The Body and Creation

The doctrine of creation asserts that the whole of existence is created by God. As a creation *ex nihilo*, the creation includes the whole of the physical order as well as all of the other dimensions of reality. In the act of creation, initiated by the Father, the Son brings all things to be. This creation is understood to be good, issuing from the divine love of the trinitarian life. Thus, when one speaks of human life, one needs to understand it in terms of its foundation in the trinitarian life of God. But this is not always the case today. For instance, it has become common in the West to see religious things as having to do with the spirit, with the soul, as if these were the only concerns of the faith.[93] Influenced by some of the philosophical positions that now dominate the West, most Christians fail to see the religious dimensions of all of reality. Today, in the West, religion is understood to be a private matter, since it is not rational, and there-

---

[93]The separation of the human person into body and soul cannot really occur. The distinction between body and soul is a logical distinction, not a real one. They simply are useful categorizations to help one point out different dimensions of the human person.

fore, some argue, no longer viable in the public square.[94] But the Christian revelation contends that the faith is concerned with the whole of the created order.[95]
At the same time, these Christians claim that not only did God create all things,
but that the whole of human existence will be included in the process of salvation. As human beings, this includes our bodies, since we cannot separate ourselves from our bodies. What we do with our bodies, how we treat them, has an
intelligibility that cannot be separated from the rest of our lives. In fact, as noted
earlier, "we are our bodies." The integrity of the human person, then, rests
upon, or at least includes, the integrity of the corporeal dimensions of reality.

The underlying meaning of the human body, as established in creation, reflects the covenantal order of reality founded upon the Trinitarian love of God:
the Father sending the Son to give the Spirit. The covenantal order of creation is
based on the Christian belief in creation *ex nihilo*, where God, in his infinite
power, creates something that is not God. Within this understanding of creation,
the created order is not simply the extension of the divine, as one finds in pantheism, but it is other than God and has a freedom to stand before God, as indicated by the story of Adam and Eve. And because it is both other and free, the
created order stands in relationship to God, a covenantal relationship. What is
significant here is that the covenantal ordering does not lend itself to some "objective interpretation" in terms to forces of nature or other physical powers;
rather, it is best understood in terms of the free creation of a loving God. It is
primarily within this context that one needs to understand the mystery of human
existence. Likewise, since bodily existence is our mode of being in the world,
any understanding of man's relationship with God must include a description of
bodily existence.

Again, it should be noted that not only are humans created as bodily creatures, but they are also created as sexual beings. They image God in and through
their sexuality. What one finds from the very beginning is that the meaning of
our bodily existence is linked to the marital structure of the New Covenant, and
therefore, to the "one flesh" marital union of Christ and his Church. In and
through our sexuality, we stand in relationship to each other in the midst of the
created order as male and female, and by means of this relationship, we image
God. What is significant is that the meaning of our bodies then, from the beginning, is associated with this marital union and ordering.

---

[94]To trace such influences would be beyond the scope of this work. Suffice it to say
that with the advent of modernity, a "reinterpretation" of Christianity has occurred. Basically, it has attempted to undermine the historical nature of the Christian faith, relegating
religion to the realm of myth or private opinion. Some of the intellectual figures responsible for this work are Hobbes, Spinoza, Locke and Rousseau.

[95]See the description of the economy of redemption cited in Ephesians 1. Here, the
whole order of the created order is included in the redemptive act of Christ.

Notice that within the created order humans are free, but they are not free to violate the order established at creation. Life is not simply about choosing a "life-style" that is meaningful to them. Rather, the order of creation is an order that ought to be obeyed by the free creature. The assurance is that if they follow this created order, they will do the will of God, while at the same time fulfilling the meaning and purpose of their lives. To attempt to signify something other than the order of the good creation is bound to lead to destructive consequences.

2. The Body and the Incarnation

If the truth about man is given in Christ, the Christian needs to look to the Christ-event to understand the meaning and purpose of human existence and the meaning of the body. In the Christ-event, the meaning of the created order lost to sin is reestablished and now brought to perfection. This "re-creation" of the "new man" in Christ is based on Christ's restoring the unity between God and man, thereby revealing the true meaning about man. What the incarnation affirms is that the Son of God, the second person of the Trinity, was born, suffered and died. He became man. Being born of the Virgin Mary, he suffered and died. The significance of His bodily existence reveals the true nature of human bodies. Two points of focus in helping to understand the significance of His life for understanding human sexuality are His relationship to Mary and His relationship to the Church.

It was noted in the previous section that to understand a human being one cannot "objectify" him, but one must see him in relationship to God and others. Within the covenantal order of the New Covenant, Christ reveals who He is in His relationship with Mary. The Christ-event, as the center and source of the whole economy of redemption, is the final word about human life and the final word about existence. Yet, despite the absolute power of God, his authority is not despotic. In the light of the New Covenant, the creation of the world is a free act, the overflowing of the fullness of the Trinitarian life of God. He did not impose His redemption on the world, but offered it to the very order He created. In the course of that offer, He chose Mary to participate on behalf of humanity in the process of redemption.

Just as the incarnation is not an afterthought, but part of the plan of redemption from all eternity, Mary's role in the process, likewise, is not accidental or incidental to the plan of salvation. Mary, as freed from original sin, freely accepts the offer of salvation given in Christ for the whole of humanity. In Mary, one sees the complete human response to the plan of salvation, a response made possible by the redemptive grace of Christ. Thus, just as Adam and Eve brought sin into the world, it is through the New Adam and the New Eve, Christ and Mary, that redemption enters the world.

What is significant for our discussion here is that Mary, as fully feminine, reveals the proper human response of the feminine to the offer of God's grace. In her response, Mary remains both virgin and mother, signifying both the complete love for God and the purity of her life in perfect obedience, an obedience that is also fruitful. Her sexuality, as all feminine sexuality, finds its completion in obedience to Christ and service to God. Her actions are a response to the marital structure of the good creation, responding to the free offer of grace, bringing her humanity to perfect fruitfulness.

Mary's life, as every human life, is ordered by the mission of the Son. She gives herself over to the mission of the Son, dying to herself so that the Son may enter into the world. In this, she is perfect Mother, free from sin, obedient in her love of God. In her obedience to the Lord, she freely accepts on behalf of humanity this offer of redemption. Her love for the Son is born of reverence for Him and His mission, His being sent by the Father. In this, she is the New Eve whose free obedience gave birth to the one who can save history. In her free resignation to the will of God, she extends the salvation of the created order into the world in a new and concrete manner. Under the Old Law, Israel had a historical covenant with the Lord of history. In Mary, the New Eve, the Lord of history becomes incarnate in history. Through her bodily life, her maternity, the grace of God is extended into the created order, thereby completely incorporating what is human into the life of faith, now redeemed in Christ.

In the economy of salvation, Mary's response to God reveals the significance of the body in the process of redemption. In and by the sacrifice of Christ, the final redemption of the world is given. He dies, giving Himself over to the Father in perfect obedience. In that act, He overcomes sin, reclaiming for the Father that which had been lost to sin. Note that although He had absolute power, He did not simply command that sin be overthrown, but He freely gave His life. Like us, He suffered the full effects of sin, yet did not sin, remaining ever faithful to the Father, thereby establishing a human and, therefore bodily integrity that all others lack. And because of that integrity he was the perfect sacrifice, whose sinless sacrifice alone is pleasing to the Father in such a way as to overcome the effects of sin. But the act itself, His death on the Cross, reveals both the difficulties and significance of the body. Only by His body being broken does the real redemptive meaning of the body become evident. By His death on the Cross, all assurances of the physical world pass away. In His death, He hands Himself over to the Father in this act of perfect love. This dying to oneself is the essence of the Christian message.

Again, the heart of the Christian message is to sacrifice oneself in love for God and neighbor. This is a free act through which real human integrity is possible. Consistent with the nuptial imagery found in the scripture, His act is focused solely on His aiding of others. It is the perfect act of self-sacrificial love. Only in this act does the body find its significance. The body, then, finds it's meaning in Christ, who by becoming man and dying for us, reveals to us the one flesh unity of the New Covenant.

Just as Mary mediates that physical presence of Christ in a definitive manner into history, the Church as the Body of Christ continues to mediate His presence in fallen creation since the time of the Ascension. In the Scriptures, the Church is referred to as the bride and the body of Christ. As the Bride of Christ, the Church is called to unity with Christ, not by some external authority, but a unity that is free, and marital and therefore, covenantal. Like Mary, the Church is free to respond as the Bride of Christ, to Christ's offer of grace. Within this covenantal relationship, Christ is the source of the Church's holiness, giving her integrity. By His grace, she is continually called into existence, and by her free response, she continues to mediate the grace of Christ in fallen creation. It is precisely in the Church's visible existence in the world, in her receptivity as feminine, in her virginity and motherhood, that the nature of her being as the Body of Christ is revealed.

Some might argue today that the Church in the world is a changing and evolving Church, subject to the ambiguities and sinfulness of being in a fallen creation. Consequently, the real Church, unstained by sin, must be outside of history, transcending history, or at the end of history. Because of sin, history is fallen and cannot mediate the fullness of the divine. But if this is the case, that history is fallen and because of the radical nature of its sinfulness is unable to mediate the fullness of the divine, then how can one make sense of the Church? Moreover, how could one make sense of incarnation? Was the incarnation an anomaly, incongruous with the rest of history? One would also have to ask, if creation and the physical are now under the effects of sin, does the body of Christ have any significance in such an understanding of Christianity? That is, if the grace and love of God are essentially separated from the physical world, what difference did Christ's death really make? One might have to ask of every human being, does the body really matter? Or, is the conjugal love between a husband and wife in any way redemptive? Against the tendencies to undermine the ability of the fallen creation and the physical world to mediate the redemptive activity of Christ, the Church has insisted upon the unity of Christ, both God and man, the unity of the Church as Body and Bride of Christ, (Head and Body), the unity of human beings as body and soul.

If the meaning of the "fallenness" of creation is understood to be a distancing of God and man, then the goodness of the created order is reflected in the fact that the created order can mediate the divine. Within the tradition, this mediation took place in the events of salvation history, culminating in the incarnation of Christ and continuing in His Body, the Church. The image of the Church as the Body of Christ is an image that links the Church intrinsically to Christ. Different from the image of the Church as the Bride of Christ, which emphasizes the free covenantal acceptance of Christ's offer of grace, the image of the Church as the Body of Christ indicates that the Church is organically linked

Christ. He is the source of her life and holiness. Their unity is the "one flesh" unity of the New Covenant. Yet, even though the Church is the Body of Christ, Christ is not the Church, nor is the Church Christ. As Body, she is the visible sign of the presence of Christ in fallen history. She is the extension of the redemptive activity of Christ into history. As visible, she points beyond herself to the Head, the Christ, while at the same time she remains His Body, His continued presence in fallen creation.

The fullest expression of the meaning of the Church as the Body of Christ is given in the Eucharist. The Eucharist is the source of the historical life and continuity of the Church. In the Eucharist, the one sacrifice by which all are saved is represented. Therefore, in the historical worship of the Eucharist, the Church continues to be formed and made holy by the one grace of the Cross of Christ. In turn, Christ continues to remain present in the Eucharistic sacrifice offered in history by the Church, the Body of Christ.

Within the tradition, there was a threefold unity between the incarnate Body of Christ, the Body of Christ present in the Eucharist, and the Body of Christ that is the Church. In each instance, the presence of Christ has a historical concreteness through its unity with the created order. Notice how the matter can mediate divine grace. One way to view this relationship is to say that what is revealed in the Eucharist is the sacramental nature of the good creation, and in particular, the sacramental nature of the body.

If one extends this analogy, that the meaning of the human body might be found in understanding the incarnation of the Christ, this would indicate that the human body is a sacrament. And as a sacrament, the human body is not only a sign of some deeper reality, but participates in that reality. This is especially the case when one considers the sacramental nature of the mediation of the one flesh unity in marriage, where the unity of the husband and wife reflects the unity of the order of redemption, the one on flesh unity of Christ and his Church. In marriage, like the Eucharist, the sacramental event is not simply transtemporal, an internal or "spiritual" experience, but a historical event. In the case of marriage, it is the conjugal union of the husband and wife that expresses the free unity of the New Covenant.

The body, then, finds it's meaning and full integrity in Christ. In the perfect obedience of the Son to the will of the Father, through His love of Mary and of the Church, the true nature of the body is revealed. In each case, the body is given over to the mission of the triune God. In each instance, the body is sacrificed out of love. In reverence and love, He hands himself over to this plan of salvation, in the process bringing history to completion. That is the meaning and purpose of the body. The body becomes the visible sign of the continued redemption in Christ.

3. The Body and the Resurrection

Perhaps the one event in the life of Christ that reveals more about the meaning of the body than any other is the resurrection. In the economy of salvation, the resurrection brings to completion the mission of Christ, which is revealed in the Cross. Only in the light of the resurrection do the events of Christ's life and death come to be understood. As a matter of fact, the resurrection, although never separated from the Cross of Christ, is the central event of salvation history. The resurrection reveals the power of Christ and is the sign of the fullness of redemption that awaits the whole creation at the end of time. Without this event, as St. Paul notes, the gospel message would be radically different (1 Cor. 15). In the resurrection the significance of the body is revealed as it relates to the past and points to the future.

The bodily resurrection is one of those tenets of the faith that most Christians today do not think really seem to think about. Most Christians tend to assume that when one dies, one is immediately judged and sent to heaven or hell. Yet, the language of the faith has always been more nuanced than that, pointing to a future resurrection in which all Christians will share. This doctrine of the bodily resurrection seems to indicate two important points about the body. The first point is that the body is significant. Notice that in the gospels, the witnesses to the empty tomb and the post resurrection accounts, are adamant that the Christ who was born of the Virgin Mary, lived in Nazareth, and died on the Cross is no longer dead, but raised from the dead. The tomb was empty. Christ is alive. And, if Christians are to share in that resurrection, they too need to undergo the bodily resurrection. After all, Christ comes to save human beings in history, as beings whose lives are physical and whose physical existence is ultimately part of the "good creation," even though it is presently under the bounds of sin. Because of this, the human body is not simply discarded, but redeemed. The whole of the life of each person is saved, including his history, which is taken up into the history of God. Thus, the bodily resurrection indicates the continuity of the historical existence and the recreation of that existence in Christ. As bodily creatures, human beings are brought into the kingdom.

There are many today that do not believe in the bodily resurrection. They believe that somewhere in Israel there are the remains of the body of Jesus. They would argue that the resurrection was a "spiritual" event in the lives of the believers, not a physical event. Accordingly, they say that, although they had not seen Him with their physical eyes, the early Christians experienced the risen Christ to be alive in their hearts. This way of thinking assumes that since in our experience the dead do not rise, they cannot imagine that Christ rose from the dead either. They would argue that it is a mistake to place such a physicalist interpretation on Christianity. Instead, such a view of Christianity understands religion and faith as internal, immaterial realities. But does such a point of view adequately explain the importance of the physical world, the body, and the resurrection?

Second, while the resurrection points to a continuity with the past, at the same time it points to the future, when the body will be glorified. Just what this glorified body is can only be surmised from what Christians know about the resurrection of Christ. It remains a mystery; yet, knowledge of this mystery is given in the revelation of Christ. What one learns from the resurrection is that the body will be saved and brought to wholeness and holiness in Christ. In the order of redemption, the body is important and will endure. Although as St. Paul points out, in heaven there will not be marriage (Matt. 22:29ff). In the end, the perfect covenantal relationship to Christ will be enjoyed by those who are saved. Man will do this as male and female according to the order of creation, but there will be no marriage, since the nuptial order of salvation will be fully realized.

If our bodies are significant and have a "sacramental" role in the economy of salvation, a role that is sustained in the Church's teaching on the resurrection, then human sexuality has an important role to play in the economy of salvation. Not only do they play an important role, but the very meaning of being male and female must be considered in the light of the bodily resurrection of Christ.

c. Man as Male and Female

If one were to study most of the ideological movements of this century, one would soon discover that most of them at some point touch upon the questions of human sexuality, and often directly upon what it means to be male and female. According to many of these ideologies, the traditional roles and identities associated with men and women are thought for the most part to be confused, in many instances simply wrong, and need to be abandoned in order to bring about a new and more complete view of human sexuality. In most of these ideologies such redefinitions of human sexuality are thought to be a matter of justice. Over the past twenty years, many of the feminist movements, the politically correct ideologies, and the proponents of diversity all attempt to redefine the nature of human sexuality. If what has been said about the importance of human sexuality in human life is true, it is no wonder that contemporary ideologies have focused much of their effort on controlling human life by means of their theories of human sexuality. It enables them to gain power over individuals.

As noted earlier, most of the ideologies today that attempt to redefine what it means to be male and female begin with the idea that the roles that men and women play in society are socially determined. They are cultural products, made up by human beings, and thus, can be changed by human beings. For instance, since the recent past, the general feminist criticism of our culture is that the sex-

ual roles have been determined by men to the detriment of women.[96] According
to them, what is needed today is to redefine the sexual roles to be more inclusive, that is, to define them from a feminist perspective. Once these redefinitions
are achieved, it is believed, a more equitable social order will result with men
and women assuming an equality of sorts.

The exact success and influence of such efforts are difficult to evaluate at
any particular historical time. This is especially true today. For instance, one
must ask what forms the redefining of male and female should take? Whose
definitions are correct and ought to be embraced? Or one can ask questions
about the results of recent effort. Have women really been empowered by such
liberation movements? How is such an empowerment measured? Are men more
sensitive and willing to treat women differently than in the past? Are women
better off being treated in this more "enlightened" manner? Are both sexes really
freer? Or, has such discussion simply initiated a new hostility and suspicion between men and women? It is difficult to tell.

From a Christian perspective, the great danger of such ideologies comes
from their incomplete understanding of the human person, in particular their
understanding of the human person in terms of the idea of power. By beginning
with power, one moves from a Christian perspective, where the intrinsic worth
of a human being has a metaphysical and historical basis rooted in the creative
love of God and the redemptive love of the Son, to a political model of the human person, where humans are understood in terms of power. From this ideological perspective, human relationships are understood in terms of power and
all differences are defined as the result of inequalities in power. According to
such a Hobbesean model, life is fundamentally a struggle for power. To live
well is to have power. So men oppress women because they have more power,
whites oppress other races, etc. The solution to these inequalities, of course, is to
balance power so that no one is able to oppress another and one is free to do
what one wants. That is the only basis for real justice. But the balance of power
is a precarious, if not impossible, task. Furthermore, one might ask whether any
group is satisfied with the balance of power and does not implicitly seek to have
power over others. Are humans, then, not simply doomed to continual struggles
for power?

The difficulty with this position from a Christian perspective is twofold.
First, Christians do not understand human life, including sexuality, to be meas-

---

[96]It is difficult to give a full account of such ideological movements. They are so
varied. Yet, like Karl Marx, the father of many of these ideologies, they share the idea
that there is a fundamental injustice at work in the world. The world is separated between those who have power and those who do not. It is assumed that human relations
are governed by power and what one tries to do is to balance the power as best as possible through political and social ordering. Individuals are reduced to pawns of the so-
cial/political environment.

ured primarily in terms of power. This analysis in terms of power is foreign to the Christian message itself. For to be male and female is not about freedom to do what one wants, nor is it about power over another, but it finds its basis in the self-sacrificial love of men and women to each other. In essence it is about love, not control. When power enters in, the paradigm shifts from a Christian a perspective to a pagan one. [97]

Second, if men and women are different creatures, not reducible one to the other, then what is essential to living a good Christian life is not about the balance of power, but the complementarity between the sexes. For instance, in the androgynous model of human sexuality, men and women are ultimately the same. The unique goodness of each sex is denied; all such differentiation must be overcome. Since there is no substantial meaning to the distinctions between men and women, the only real source for human distinctions must be social convention. And to overcome differences attributed to each sex according to such social conventions, one simply needs to change the paradigm operative in society so that the differences between the sexes is negated. For instance, today, in our economically based culture, balancing power often means enabling men and women to do the same work. At issue here, of course, is a kind of egalitarianism that trivializes all distinctions between the sexes, as well as the sexual differences themselves. But the Christian view of sexuality preserves the sexual differences, understanding them to be good and constitutive of our existence in the created order. The question, for the Christian then, is not the question of equality, but what does it mean to say that man and woman image God?

Contrary to those ideologies, which undermine the created difference between men and women, Christians believe that the meaning of male and female is given in the revelation, in the full offer of redemption given in Christ, the New Covenant. In this order, what it means to be male and female is derived from the symbolism of each sex in the order of creation and redemption. What is assumed is that in salvation history, maleness and femaleness have a meaning and significance that is unique and irreplaceable. They cannot be redefined by a particular culture, but they transcend any culture, since in them is contained a great mystery that each and every culture should attempt to embody.

1. The Significance of the Feminine

The meaning of the feminine is one of the great mysteries of the created order that that certainly continues to be a matter of debate in western culture to-

---

[97]This account here is too short to be satisfactory. Power may be redefined in Christ, but in most instances, the modern use of power has a Hobbesean meaning which cannot be reconciled with Christianity. See Joyce Little, *The Church and the Culture War*, pp. 23ff.

day. The concern over articulating the precise meaning of the feminine has, in
part, happened as a response to some of the ideologies that have been extremely
influential in the academy and in political life. At the same time that this general
cultural discussion concerning the nature of human sexuality is going on, the
Church has joined in the reflection of the nature of the feminine, its purpose and
meaning. And although some of the investigation of the meaning of the feminine is prompted by a need to respond to contemporary cultural changes, the
Church's effort has a starting point beyond that. For the most part, the theological reflection on the part of the Church began long before Vatican II, and has
found itself incarnated in the theology of that council. Not surprisingly, the
Catholic theological reflection on the feminine dimension of the faith finds as its
focal points Mary and the Church.

Within the Church's tradition, Mary is the one that reveals the nature of the
feminine in the order of redemption. Mary is the mediatrix through whom the
Son of God became incarnate. She is the sinless one, who in the midst of human
history is free to accept the complete offer of the redemption of all creation. She
is the New Eve, the one who stands before God, through whose *fiat* the New
Covenant enters into history. In the covenantal structure of a free creation, there
needs to be the one who stand before God, accepting or rejecting His offer of
salvation. In the Christian tradition, Mary is that person.

The dogmatic importance of Mary is a matter of fact. According to these
teachings, Mary has an essential role in the unfolding of salvation history. She
has a unique relationship to God, and in this relationship, the truth about God
and man in the economy of redemption is revealed. As noted earlier, it is the
whole person that stands before God, thus, her sexuality must play a constitutive
role in the relationship with God in the economy of salvation. Since in and
through this relationship of Christ and Mary the definitive relationship between
God and man is established - the New Covenant - consequently, in her actions
she reveals the truth about the nature of the feminine.

According to the tradition, Mary places her whole life at the service of God,
including her sexuality. As called by God at the very center of her existence, her
faith is the very foundation of her life. It forms the basis for her understanding of
who she is and what it means to be feminine. On account of this her faith, Mary
is able to recognize the hand of God in her life and trust in what God has done.
This trust was so complete that God entrusted to her His Son. To her was given
the gift, not only of life, but the responsibility to bear the Savior of the world.
This faith defined her life.

Note that in her relationship with God her sexuality is not by-passed or denied, but exalted. In and through her sexuality, she serves God. The eternal
God, the Lord of Israel, entrusts Himself to the virgin girl from Nazareth.[98] God

_____

[98]See Joyce Little, *The Church and the Culture War*, pp. 147ff.

gives His Son to her and she freely accepts that offer of grace. Mary, in the fullness of her femininity, places herself at the service of God by becoming pregnant, by carrying in her womb the Son of God, the savior of the world. Her faith includes the whole of her being. Her obedience literally takes a bodily form, defining who and what she is.

Consistent with the feminine character of Mary, her faith, trust, and openness to the plan of God, is Mary's fidelity. Noticeably, in the scripture stories concerning Mary, she is never coerced by some external authority into obeying God, but gives herself freely to the love of God. According to the scriptures, there are times when she does not seem to understand fully, yet she remains faithful. For instance, in the account of her "fiat", she freely responds to God's definitive offer of grace. She trusts in God in this most difficult request. At other times, such as the wedding feast of Cana, she seems to understand her relationship with her Son in a more complete sense. Yet, even at those times, Mary understands her own place in terms of the more complete and definitive ministry of her Son. In faith, Mary receives from the Father the fullness of the redemption of Christ. Her life is not given over to her own desires, but to the will of God. In her fidelity to his will, she lives a perfect fidelity to God that reveals the meaning of her life.

To understand more clearly the significance of Mary in the economy of salvation, it might be helpful to mention three points. First, despite the importance of the role that Mary plays in salvation history, the scriptures have very little to say about Mary. If she is so important to the economy of salvation, why is not more said about Mary? To this, Joyce Little responds that it is in accord with the nature of her faith to be unobtrusive. She notes that, "Perhaps discipleship requires us to embrace the silent, the hidden, the inconspicuousness, precisely because only there will we discover what is really important to us."[99] Mary seems to embrace this inconspicuous life, not drawing attention to herself, while at the same time representing all of humanity in the most important event in history. She faithfully submits to the will of God, out of which comes the full revelation of God. It is such virtue and wisdom that are the defining possessions of Mary, revealing her feminine nature. Ever-patient, waiting, ever-present, continuously loving, that is the nature of the biblical understanding of the feminine. No one can doubt that such virtues are worthy of praise and essential to the life of faith.

Today, exalting such virtues as quietude, silence and unobtrusiveness stands in direct contradiction to many of the ideologies that claim that human happiness lies in the way of power, wealth and the assertion of one's self. There are plenty of shrines to this form of idolatry in every age, but against those beliefs Mary stands quietly and humbly, asserting not herself, but mediating the Son of God

---

[99]Ibid., p. 134.

into history. In a real sense, Mary is the one who is wise, the one who is able to see things for what they are, recognizing the true hand of God in the midst of history. And as a result, she can see clearly her own place in the order of salvation. Her achievements stand at the center of history while all other shrines to human achievements pass away.

Second, the quietude, the silence that enables one to see what is important, becomes the source of stability in the present time of the Church. Only one who, like Mary, is deeply rooted in God can provide such stability. Only a person with such a faith is able to empty oneself of those paganisms that lead one from one place to another, promising the fruits of the fullness of life, yet never delivering. Most people refuse to give themselves over to the truth, or even the search for the truth. Instead, most people prefer to "float" amid the many opinion, ideas and passions that a particular culture offers. Only the wise and faithful servant of the Lord can stand against such distractions and idolatries, and focus on what is fundamental to human life. As such a wise servant, Mary remained faithful to her Son, even to the foot of the Cross.

During the present time, it is the Church, as the bride of Christ, who provides the wisdom and guidance for the faithful on their journey in which world. As guided by the Holy Spirit, the Church is the womb in which the faith of the Church is protected and in which the faithful are nourished. In the midst of every age, she remains stable, bearing witness to the truth of the gospel amid all the distractions of fallen history.

Third, what is further revealed about the faith by Mary is not only that one discovers the truth of the faith in quietude, or that this becomes the basis for stability in the Church, but that at its center, the act of faith is a personal act. Mary is not forced to follow orders or believe in an ideology, but freely gives herself over to God. This act is the ultimate personal act, the immediate gift of herself, by means of which her life is now freely given over to God, and she is to do his will. In this act of faith, she is neither oppressed nor exploited; rather, her freedom not only remains intact, but also is brought to completion. She could have said no to God. But more than the mere preservation of freedom took place in her act of faith. In her faith, she is made freer by the intimate union in the love of the Son. She is made holy. And in her *fiat*, she continues to stand in the freedom of the grace of Christ, a grace that will continue to inform her life, as evidenced by the assumption.

Perhaps the way in which the feminine in the order of salvation might best be described is by the terms virgin and mother. Mary is the only woman in human history to perfectly embody both virginity and motherhood. For people living in the fallen creation, these two ideas appear to be antithetical. Yet, it is in these terms that the meaning of the feminine nature of the faith in Mary is best expressed.

The Church has taught from the earliest times that Mary was a virgin. The Church understands this to mean that Jesus was conceived by the power of the

Holy Spirit. This is no doubt a great miracle made possible by her sinlessness and her free response to God's offer of grace. But soon, the idea of the virginity of Mary was understood to be more than that. "The deepening of faith in the virginal motherhood leads the Church to confess Mary's real and perpetual virginity even in the act of giving birth to the Son of God made man. In fact, Christ's birth 'did not diminish his mother's virginal integrity but sanctified it.'"[100] As the Church came to understand more clearly the role of Mary in the economy of salvation, eventually Mary's whole life and mission came to be characterized by her virginity. The virginity of Mary stems from her obedience to God. Her virginity is *"the sign of her faith,* 'unadulterated by any doubt,' and of her undivided gift of herself to God's will."[101] In her faithful response to the will of God, she conceives Christ in the flesh. Her maternity bears witness to the personal and complete nature of her response to the offer of God's grace. In her virginity, she is the spouse, the New Eve whose purity and holiness remain intact. In her acceptance of this holy virginity, the New Covenant enters history, issuing forth in a definitive manner in the good creation and the redemption given in Christ. As the New Eve, ever faithful to the Second Adam, Mary's virginity comes to signify the whole plan of salvation.

Within such an understanding of the faith, Mary must be understood to occupy a central place in the economy of salvation. Her quietude, patience, fidelity, stability, and personal engagement, are neither secondary additions to the faith, nor, as feminine, are they thought to be secondary in quality. Quite the contrary; they represent the feminine response to the fullness of the offer of grace. In Mary, the meaning of the feminine is revealed as the spouse of Christ, issuing in and promulgating the New Covenant.

Within the tradition, the Church too has been understood as feminine. As a matter of fact, Mary is the paradigm for the Church. Like Mary, the Church is understood to be holy and virginal. She can stand before God and receive Christ, not through her own efforts, but by the power of the Holy Spirit. Her purity, the result of being made holy by the one sacrifice of Christ, frees her to participate in the redemption offered by Christ, and as a sacrament, to mediate that grace in fallen creation. Her virginity, then, her integrity, like Mary's, is founded solely upon the freedom given in Christ. In the economy of salvation, the mediation of the Church is central; there is no way to Christ apart from that representation in the sacraments.[102]

---

[100]*Catechism,* 499.

[101]Ibid., 506.

[102]This does not mean that those who never receive the sacraments cannot be saved. It does mean that all grace is given in Christ who is the one true sacrament and means to salvation. This is salvation offered *ex opere operato* in history in the sacramental life of the Church.

Despite the importance of virginity for describing the femininity of Mary, and therefore of all women, it is the motherhood of Mary that best describes the unique character of the feminine. In Mary, virgin and mother come together, unified by her reverence for God. It is a reverence so complete that in it, her will and the will of the Father are one.

The motherhood of Mary, like her virginity, is born of faith. And although the fruitfulness of the faith is offered to her and made possible by the grace of Christ, yet she is not merely passive in her act of faith. It is not as if something merely done to her; rather, her faithfulness is completely fruitful free act, resulting in the incarnation of the Son. At the same time that the redemptive grace of her motherhood is given in Christ, the free entrance of this grace into history is contingent upon the free activity of Mary, her response as the New Eve to the offer of the restoration and redemption of the world now fallen. Without this acceptance, her free response to the free offer of grace, God could not enter into history. Note that such fruitfulness uniquely constitutes the feminine nature of Mary.

If what is said about Mary is true for all women, the essence of being feminine is tied to maternity. In a very real sense, it is analogous to God's creative act. As God acts to generate the world, so too the woman is the source of life. "The woman in her humility stands in the same relationship to the man as God in his humility stands in relationship to all of humanity. For God in creating, just like the woman in conceiving, engages in an activity which remains largely hidden and anonymous: God is a hidden, a silent, an invisible God. In His creation, He remains in a sense anonymous. This helps us to comprehend our previous assertion, that the power which collaborates also co-creates. Woman, therefore, as the hidden collaborator, represents the anonymity of God; she represents it as one side of all that is creative."[103] Such creative love is not oppressive or limiting, but becomes the center of reality and life in a special way.

In a unique way, a woman stands in relationship to God as an extension of His creative love in the created order. If life is ultimately a gift that comes from God, the author of all life, then woman mediates that life and grace in and through her sexuality. Just as Mary's giving birth to the Son of God was an act of grace, the birth of each human is also a great gift, issuing forth from the womb of the mother. In this very fundamental way, new life is created, continuing the plan of salvation, whose author is God.

This creative act on the part of the woman, like the activity of God, is often hardly perceptible. As noted, this "unobtrusive" character of the feminine act of faith is often like the anonymous acts of God. At the same time, it is both the most private of all acts and the most profound of all acts. And, despite their hid-

---

[103] Joyce Little, *The Church and the Culture War*, p. 136. Here, Little is quoting Gertrude von le Fort, *The Eternal Woman*, trans. Marie Cecilia Buehrle, with a preface by Max Jordan (Milwaukee: Bruce Publishing Co., 1954), 14.

denness, the significance of the acts and the authority of the actor are not diminished. This understanding of the feminine stands in contrast to many of the values that have dominated much of history, and is especially contrary to many of the dominant values in the world today. In many of those philosophies those who deserve praise are only those who accomplish things only in the public. Accomplishments in business, politics, and other social and cultural achievements alone are given human acclaim. As a matter of fact, today, more than ever before, there is a grave prejudice against motherhood. Or better, in the West there seems to be a mother hood, a schizophrenia about fertility and the bearing of children. Many see the bearing of children to be a great inconvenience; thus, it is put off until one is "comfortably" able to have children. Fertility, rather than treated as a normal state of human health, is often treated as a disease, with innumerable men and women rendering themselves infertile through the use of artificial contraception or sterilization in the belief that that will decrease or end the risk of pregnancy and increase the quality of their lives. This attitude towards pregnancy and the issuing of new life is definitely reflected in our attitudes towards children, where today there are so many wonderful opportunities for children, on the one hand, and on the other, children are seemingly neglected and abused perhaps more than ever before. Yet, for the most part the birth of a child is a matter of great joy, continuing to signal hope for the future. And despite all of the difficulties surrounding the bringing of children into the world and raising them, people continue to do so. In fact, most parents would claim this to be the most important thing that they have done in their lives and bravely continue to take on that responsibility.

The fact that despite all the negative attitudes about motherhood, it continues to survive, and indicate the real depth and significance of that act. It is the act that alone is feminine. Recently, it has been popular for a couple to say, "we are pregnant," indicating, the responsibility of both the mother and the father for the pregnancy and the subsequent responsibility for the child. Yet, it is quite obvious that it is only the woman who is pregnant. The man can walk away, or die, and the woman will still be pregnant. The pregnancy is intimately hers. In the most personal manner, in motherhood, the woman's whole being, including her body, becomes the means by which the creative grace and redemptive activity of Christ are extended into the world. In this sense, maternity is more than the unique bodily "extension" of the woman's existence, for the child is more than the mother, and from its very conception, exceeds the very being of the mother. It is new life. And as new life, the child is a participation in the grace of Christ that encompasses, yet transcends the life of the mother. In the most profound sense, the child becomes a symbol of the continued presence of the creative grace of Christ, and procreation is related to the One Flesh unity of the New Covenant which lies at the heart of the created order. In that order, it is the fruitfulness of the marital union of Christ and his Church that is the source of all that is created. The marital union of husband and wife participate in that redemptive love of Christ and it is from that New Covenant that their life and love flow. Yet, in the love of husband and wife, it is essentially the woman, whose essential being embodies the fruitful "yes" to the offer of salvation, the answer which alone is representative of the whole order of creation. This "yes" to the creative love of Christ is manifest most clearly in her willingness to give birth to children.

The meaning of motherhood, likewise, transcends the significance of simply the biological act of giving birth. It is a relationship that extends to the raising of children. In this task, the life-giving process begun in the womb continues. Traditionally, the focal point of the family was the married love of the husband and wife that issued forth in the procreation of children. As the children were born, another dimension was added to the family where the mother and her children were given precedence. The mother was thought to be closer to the children that she bore than the father, establishing a relationship that is prior to the relationship between the father and the children. The mother and the children were at the center of the family and needed to be protected from the dangers of public life. The family was a safe haven where children learned the meaning of love and the lessons of their faith. And thus, the family was the context in which the education and growth of children took place. The mother was the one who sacrificed herself for the protection and growth of their children in the home.

If this articulation of the meaning of the feminine is at all accurate, the meaning of sexuality reveals its depth and importance for human existence. If the faith is covenantal and marital, the feminine has a central role not only in the individual faith life of each woman, but also in the whole economy of redemption itself. Consequently, a woman's vocation to motherhood and the work of a mother is more significant than any other professional vocation. Maternity is the activity in which the sexual life of the woman finds its completion and the criteria by which the Christian vocation of all women is defined. One wonders whether in a culture such as ours, where motherhood and virginity are rarely, or arguably, no longer respected, can there ever be a real respect for women.

2. The Significance of Being Male

In the economy of salvation, it is not Joseph who is the male counterpart of Mary; it is her Son, whose integral masculinity stands in relationship to the integral femininity of the sinless Mother of God. Unlike Mary, He is divine; like Mary, He is fully human and without sin, living in the full integrity and freedom of the New Covenant. It is in the relationship between Christ and Mary that the New Covenant comes into existence, an act which is at once both creative and redemptive.

Christ is the one who became incarnate, the perfect unity of God and man. In the incarnation, Christ takes on the whole of human life, including human sexuality. He is a man, and His sexuality is neither diminished by His divinity nor relegated to a place of secondary importance. Just as Christ embraces the fullness of human life, so, too, He must embrace human sexuality. And in this perfect union, the whole truth about man is revealed. Therefore, the real meaning of being male can only be found in the revelation of Christ.

In the New Covenant, Christ, although born of Mary, has an authority that transcends Mary's since His redemptive death becomes the means whereby the grace of the New Covenant becomes possible. So despite the fact that Mary is dependent upon Christ, the freedom and integrity of Mary are not destroyed or subjected to an alien power, but are made possible and brought to their fullness by her relationship to her Son. This means, first, that the covenant is instituted in and by the offer of God's love given in Christ. Neither Mary's fruitfulness, nor her human holiness is generated by her own effort. All sanctity is made possible by the grace of Christ. But this reliance upon Christ does not undermine the freedom of the one who responds. On the contrary, such complete love does not dominate, but seeks the perfection, wholeness and integrity of that which is the object of His love. The love of Christ, His grace, seeks the good of that which He loves. Only such a love is the basis of all truth, beauty and integrity, both in the order of creation and in the order of redemption. There is no other reality. The New Covenant offering of grace is made possible by the death of Jesus. In that redemptive death, the meaning of being male is revealed, while at the same time, it is in response to that act that the feminine is brought to fulfillment.

Second, it is important to note that the basis of this covenantal understanding of human sexuality is the love of God, not power. It is on account of the love of the Father that He sends His Son. Christ does not come to place the world under His despotic power. Christ does not come to dominate Mary, to use her, or to dominate the Church, but He acts to redeem them in and through His love, and in the process makes their freedom possible. This point touches clearly upon the nature of masculinity, which like the revelation of Son, moves beyond itself bringing unity and freedom to others.

The unity of all Christians is a unity where God is father and the Church is mother. As noted, the motherhood of the Church is essential to the nature of the faith. There can really be no faith apart from it. In the maternity of the Church, the believer comes to participate in the paternity of God, whose gracious personal love for us becomes the basis for the order of redemption and creation. In both of these acts, God moves beyond Himself, extending Himself towards that which is not God. This movement of God is the creative act. The masculine creative act on the part of God reflects the trinitarian life in which the love between the Father and the Son and Holy Spirit issues forth beyond the trinitarian life into the created order. In this sending, this other-directedness, the nature of the Father and Son is revealed. As masculine, the Father and the Son move beyond themselves and brings order to what is disordered. In the relationship of the Father to the Son in the act of creation, it is through the Son that all things come to be. In the stages of trinitarian economics, it is the Father who sends the Son who sends the Spirit. The Spirit flows out of the love between the Father and the Son, a free relationship, not one governed by power, but by love.

This view of God, understands Him to be the source of all things, the origin of the whole created order, an order that is not closed in upon itself, but an order that has its origin that is trinitarian life of God whose very nature is love. It is not a static order, but a covenantal order in which God continually moves beyond himself, creating and sustaining that which is outside of his own existence.

The Fatherhood of God, then, is not simply what some contend today: an image created by a certain patriarchical culture, whose time is now past. Rather, it reveals to us something distinctive and true about the nature of God, and consequently, about the nature of reality. Through the revelation of the Son, we come to know that God is the Father. In the activity of the Son, we come to understand the meaning of the Fatherhood of God. Through both the Father and the Son, the meaning of human sexuality is revealed; the real meaning of human sexuality is given in the revelations of the Triune God.

In the order of creation, the masculine is characterized by its distance from the "other."[104] Different from the feminine whose character is more private than not, more closely held, more directly related to the body, the masculine is "outer" directed. It moves beyond itself to that which stands outside of it. As the Father and the Son, whose love overflows in creating and redeeming, the nature of the masculine is to act in a like manner, to bring the new into existence, claiming for Christ that which has fallen away. The particular nature of masculinity is, therefore, to stand in relationship to the others, bringing unity and freedom to that to which it stands in relationship to.

One of the biblical images that is useful for understanding the nature of masculine sexuality is the image of Christ as the Head of His Body - the Church. In this image, Christ stands in relation to the body. Christ is not the body, the body is not Christ; yet, both are in perfect harmony. As head of the body, Christ causes the body, the Church. He is the source of her life. At the same time that Christ brings the Church into existence, he gives her an identity and guides the Church as she completes her mission in the world. As Head, He is the source of the free unity of the body. This is a free unity offered by Christ and consistent with the "nature" of the Church: never imposing something foreign on her life. This unifying activity of the Head is essential to the process of redemption in a world that is fallen and fragmented. Since the created order is presently under the power of sin, the body, the Church, is affected by sin, a process only reversed under the authority of the head, whose headship alone has the power to conquer sin. Here, to be head is not simply to be part of some larger whole, but

---

[104] See Little, *The Church and the Culture War*, 174 ff. She makes reference to Ong's argument.

to be the source of unity and integrity, drawing things into being. In precisely such activities, the nature of the masculine becomes evident.

It is true that in the incarnation, Christ becomes man, entering into creation; therefore, he is part of the larger whole. At the same time, he transcends the created order as the very author of that created order, "through whom all things came to be, apart from him nothing came to be" (Jn. 1:3). He is the source of all meaning and the unity of being. Not only do all things come to be through him, but through him, the redemption of all things will be brought to completion.(Eph 1:10) At the end, all things will be brought to fullness in Church.

At the same time, it is not only in the beginning and end of time that the salvation is given in Christ, but it is in the Cross of Christ that the mission of the Son culminates. According to Christian teaching, it is the Cross that is the center of all history. Here, Christ pours Himself out, sacrifices Himself, for the redemption of mankind and the whole of the created order. Christ is both the sign and the sacrament through whose historical existence all things come to be and all things are redeemed. In the Cross, sin, with all of its destructive consequences, is overcome. It is precisely in this sacrifice that the headship of Christ is restored, sin is overcome and the order of the good creation is restored. Unity, therefore, is restored in the Body of Christ, where His headship has made that unity possible. This recapitulation, reclaiming all things under the headship of Christ, means that in the end, He will return all things to the Father. This is the mission of the Son (Eph. 1:17). In this process, He restores that which is lost in Adam, offering to the created order the freedom and truth of existence in God.

It is precisely the nature and meaning of the masculine that one finds revealed in this redemptive action. In the Cross, Christ, imitating the Father, assumes the headship of the Church. In and through His headship, the whole created order is restored and ordered once again to the Father, from whom all things originally came. The image of headship, as informed by the sacrifice of the Cross, reveals that the head is the servant of all. He is the one who extends beyond Himself, not in order to attain power or some other selfish end, but in humility, dying so that others might live. This is consistent with His mission as the cornerstone upon which the building rests. That is, to be male means to build up the life of faith through extending beyond oneself into the world. Such acts not only build and support the life of faith, but also have a unifying character, just as Christ is the head of His flock. As the shepherd, He is willing to lay down his life for His flock.

Another way to that the scriptures look at this is to see Christ terms of his mission. Every individual vocation has its authority and meaning in the light of the mission of Christ. In reality, there is no mission besides or apart from the mission of Christ. It alone is complete. Thus, even apostolic authority is understood as an extension of the mission of the Son. The apostles do not have a mission of their own, only the mission of Christ.

Mary, on the other hand, whose vocation must be understood in terms of the grace of the Son, is never described as having a mission. Her free response to the call of God is necessary and her *fiat* makes possible the mission of Christ; yet, her service to God does not extend into the world in the same way. Her role in the economy of salvation Mary is not to go out into the world, but to bring Christ into the world. Her vocation is subsumed under the mission of Christ. Her passivity neither negates her freedom nor diminishes the significance of her free decision to do the will of the Father. It is this quietude, this passivity that characterizes her feminine response to the offer of grace, the establishment of the New Covenant. On the other hand, Christ is the New Covenant. In His actions lies the cause of the New Covenant, revealing the true nature of the covenantal and spousal ordering of creation. The act on His part that corresponds to Mary's free acceptance is the Cross. Again, as masculine, Christ in His mission extends beyond himself into the world, as He does on the Cross. In this process, He makes known the truth, establishes order, and initiates the kingdom of God. On the Cross He pours Himself out for the salvation of all, establishing the freedom and the unity now lost to sin, freeing humans from sin, including Mary, so that the grace of Christ can enter into human life.

It is appropriate in an age such as ours, which stresses power and leadership as a means of controlling others, to assert that the Gospel understanding of "headship" and "leadership" are found in the ideas of service and love. This love is not weak, acting without convictions or living without integrity. On the contrary, this love is rooted in the truth, just as all real strength comes from living in the truth and carrying out that truth in one's actions. It comes from putting on Christ. In this case, it means, like Joseph, quietly submitting to that truth and acting upon it. It is precisely this attitude which is woefully absent today, especially among men. Today, the idea of self-sacrifice is replaced by self-fulfillment, where responsibility is replaced by the continuous search for pleasure, where fidelity is replaced by the desire for immediate gratification; and strength, courage and the willingness to do the good is replaced by any number of trivial pursuits. One needs only to look at the popular male figures today to see evidence of this, or the failure of so many fathers to pay child support. What is needed today is a real revolution, a new evangelization, in the process of which the Christian understanding of being male and female will be established, supplanting all those perennial ideologies that continually attempt to undermine the truth about human sexuality. Only in solidarity with Christ can that which is lost be restored.

Within the Roman Catholic tradition, this understanding of masculinity has not only been extended to fathers and husbands, but also to the priesthood. To be a priest is to stand in the *persona Christi*. They are members of the Church who stand in a unique relationship to the Church. In their ministerial priesthood, they do not represent the congregations that they lead, as an elected delegate might, because they are not elected by the membership, but are chosen by God to administer the sacraments, and in particular to offer the sacrifice of the Mass. It is precisely in the event of the Eucharist, the one sacrifice of the Cross by means of which all things are saved, that the Church finds the source of its life. It is this one sacrifice, offered here and now by the sacramental priesthood, that is the center of the life of faith. By their sacramental ordination priests stand in the person of Christ, and by their ordination they participate in the obedience of Christ to the Father, taking on the identity of Christ.

Their ordination does not make them asexual, but according to the covenantal structure of reality and the covenantal meaning of sexuality, they stand as males representing in and through their sexuality the meaning of paternity of God. By their ordination, they receive a sacramental character, undergoing a metaphysical change representative of the place they stand in the economy of salvation. Included in their vocation is their masculinity. As masculine, their mission takes on the character of offering to the Church the holiness of grace mediated by the sacramental life. The priest, in the person of Christ, stands outside the Church, mediating to the Church the very grace of Christ. They are able to offer the one sacrifice of the Cross to the Church which finds its life in that sacrifice.

Again, the heart of the Christian faith and the source of all grace is the New Covenant. That covenant is nuptial in character and the meaning of human sexuality is derived from that order. Whether one is celibate, or a virgin, or chaste, or married, each vocation is defined by and a means of participating in the grace of the New Covenant.

Today, it is interesting to note that in an age where there is a great deal of confusion about human sexuality, there are also very few men being ordained priests and some theologians are still discussing the possibility of women priests, or married priests. Those who argue for the ordination of women usually argue that either a man or a woman can signify Christ. They focus not on the sexuality of Christ, but on His humanity. Thus, any human being, simply as human, represents Christ. Those who oppose the ordination of women argue that humans exist only as male and female, and that it is dualistic to abstract humanity from its concrete bodily existence. They would argue that one can only understand man as male and female. Therefore, anyone who holds to the integrity of the whole human person, body and soul, would argue that within the sacramental order of creation, male and female are not reducible to an identity. They represent different, unique, irreducible dimensions of the covenantal economy of salvation. The defenders of a male priesthood would argue that this insight is a matter of great significance and should be cherished and nurtured by the Church, instead of, as it is so often today, made a point of derision by feminists and other proponents of the ordination of women. The importance of this revelation for the tradition is immense, since it is the basis not only for priestly celibacy, but also for the sacrament of marriage.

It should be further noted that the Church's defense of the distinctive role of male and female in the order of creation and in the order of redemption is more than simply an appeal to tradition; rather, it reflects a consistent view of the world. Again, in their teaching, the Church affirms that the masculine can signify Christ and therefore stand in the *persona Christi*. The foundation of this teaching is that each sex has its own unique meaning that is given in creation and revealed more completely in the New Covenant. As standing in the person of Christ, the ordained minister stands in relationship to the Church (the feminine), mediating the grace of Christ to the Church who is called to respond. For example, in the sacramental mediation of the grace of Christ, the forgiveness of sins is offered. The Church does not forgive sins; Christ does, and it is the priest who mediates that forgiveness. Again, the masculine is described as reaching out beyond themselves, sacrificing themselves, bringing the other to unity in the love of Christ.

By their celibacy, priests represent the same obedience to the Father that the Son gave to the Father. There are, no doubt, practical reasons for celibacy, but the theology of the spousal meaning of body also indicates the importance of celibacy. Celibacy is not an imposed restriction, but a genuine calling, sustained by the grace of Christ. And although today celibacy is often characterized as juridical restriction imposed during a certain historical period to solve certain sociological difficulties, it must also be noted that from the very beginning of the priesthood continence was understood to be part of the priestly discipline.[105] In the early Church, preparation for the celebration of the Eucharist required the abstinence from sexual relations. Continence was a constitutive part of priestly sacramental ministry from the very beginning, reflecting the unique priestly relationship to the one sacrifice of Christ. The Church came to understand the priesthood in terms of its role in the sacramental economy; celibacy came to be understood as an essential component. Thus, if the primary action of the priest is to offer the Eucharistic sacrifice and that becomes the defining characteristics of the priesthood, and therefore at the heart of orders, it is easy to understand how periodic continence was extended to include the whole of the priestly life.

This theology of orders is consistent with and reaffirms the view of human masculinity as ordered to the spousal meaning of the New Covenant. As Christ gives himself completely to his bride the Church, so too the priest gives himself totally over to the will of the Father, dedicating his life to the love and service of the Church. The meaning of celibacy, then, is in part derived from the fidelity of this spousal relationship. The priesthood is not simply a "vocation" or a mere function that he performs, but the priesthood becomes a means of participating in the redemptive love of God wherein the total self-donation of the priest

---

[105]See Roman Cholij, Clerical Celibacy in East and West, foreward by Alfons Cardinal Stickler, S.D.B.; preface by Michael Napier (Leoministe, Herfordshire: Fowler Wright Books, 1989). I am indebted for this information to Fr. Donald Keefe.

shapes his identity according to his unique relationship to the Church. As Christ loves his Church and remains faithful to her, so too must the priest stand in relationship to the Church.

In its final account, human sexuality takes its meaning from the structure and order of the New Covenant: in and through his sexuality man images God. This is true of the masculine, whether it be represented by the husband or by the priest. In each case, they reflect the masculine aspect of the marital covenantal, which in turn is rooted in the very order of the good creation. As male, they are directed beyond themselves, understanding themselves in terms of the love which demands that one die for another as Christ died on the Cross. One might say that the Cross is the normative symbol of masculine giving. The man does not carry life, but offers life, and he continues to guard and guide that life in a world filled with sin. His relationship to the feminine is one of love, not domination, moving outside of himself, risking his being for the sake of the gospel. He needs to be steadfast in the face of external challenges, brave in defending what is good, and relentless in the preaching of the gospel. In one sense, it is perhaps this apostolic character that most visibly demonstrates the nature of the male. Following Christ into the world, each man is called to die to himself to bring to Christ that which has been lost. As an extension of the work of the Cross, the mission of man is to offer to others the possibility of truth, holiness and happiness. This offer is mediated in and through male sexuality, a sexuality whose final meaning and purpose is derived from its participation in the New Covenant.

3. Chastity – Virginity

It has been argued in this chapter that the truth about human sexuality and its meaning is given in the Gospel, and that the fullest form of sexual expression is marriage, where the unique and total gift of the man and woman to each other reflects that truth and order of existence as created by God. By teaching this, the Church affirms that sexuality is sacramental, representing and mediating the deeper reality of God's redemptive love. Our sexuality, then, is not merely a means by which we express love for one another, but through our bodily existence as human beings, we come to share in the triune love of God. In the spousal relationship signified and now redeemed in the love of Christ for His Church, human beings as male and female are made holy. As noted, not only is the married couple redeemed in this manner, but also the celibate priest. Likewise, chastity has a role to play in the development and the manner in which humans serve God through their sexuality.

Chastity has often been looked upon in a negative manner. Some have considered it as denial of sexuality, creating a dualism between soul and body. Others presuppose that human sexuality is an evil that needs to be overcome, even suppressed, so that the traditional understanding of chastity was not adequate for dealing with human sexuality. Many today, believing the human sexual drive and activity to be "natural," consider chastity to be an unhealthy imposition on a very natural drive. Against these negative views of chastity, Christians have understood chastity see chastity as a virtue essential to living a good moral life. Christians see it as positive. For instance, members of religious orders take the vow of chastity, thereby freely agreeing to live a certain way: i.e., not engaging in sexual activity. As a result of this choice, religious are freed from the corresponding responsibilities of marriage and are now free to serve God according to their vocation. Also, in the name of chastity, young people are counseled not to be sexually active until marriage. The time prior to marriage is not merely one of sexual repression, but considered to be a time of preparation, a quiet space where, freed from the demands of sexual activity, the young are allowed to grow in understanding and integration of their sexuality. Yet, chastity is more than simply the product of some special dedication or a guard for a special time in life. Rather, it entails in a most essential way the truth about human sexuality and its meaning for human existence.

The good that chastity aims at is the successful integration of sexuality within the person, and thus, the inner unity of human beings in their bodily and spiritual being. Sexuality, one way in which man's belonging to the bodily and biological world is expressed, becomes personal and truly human when it is integrated into the relationship of one person to another in the complete and life-long mutual gift of a man and a woman. The virtue of chastity therefore involves the integrity of the person and the integrity of the gift of human sexuality in relationship to others.[106] It therefore is an essential virtue for anyone at any stage of life.

As noted, the virtue of chastity is less about denial and more about the integration and development of human sexuality. For instance, most adolescents, although physically capable of being sexually active, are far from being mature enough to understand the real significance of their actions. As matter of fact, even some adults never achieve that kind of integrity or they lose the integrity that they once had. One needs only to think about the middle-aged man, faithful husband and father, who suddenly turns to a life of sexual license. The Christian understands such a loss of integrity to be the result of his submission of his sexuality to the power of sin. Against such actions, chastity enables one to identify the proper use of sexuality and to begin to live according to that order.

There is, no doubt, a dimension of the virtue of chastity that requires what the *Catechism* calls an *apprenticeship in self-mastery*.[107] But such a time is not

---

[106]*Catechism*, 2337.

[107]Ibid., 2339.

a mere denial, but it is described as a "training in human freedom." This presupposes that, in part, the integration of human sexuality includes the struggle with the passions. Within this process, one needs to either learn to master one's passions or one will be mastered by them. If the latter occurs, there is a resulting loss of human freedom. If, on the other hand, one is able to master the passions by the grace of Christ, one is then freed to live out one's sexuality according to the order designed by God in creation. The effort for self-mastery is a life-long and arduous task, requiring continual effort.

There are all sorts of admonitions within the tradition to help people to attain a chaste life. For instance, in the past, modesty was thought to be an important virtue. It was a way of moderating sexuality through the way in which one acted. Certain forms of behavior or dress were simply not acceptable since they tended to incite certain kinds of reactions that were thought to be harmful to an individual. Today, of course, such social prohibitions are ridiculed, believing that the individual should be able to absorb anything and keep his or her passions in check. Yet, the evidence seems to indicate that that attitude has not worked all that well. Perhaps the moderation in behavior will return some day.

According to the Christian traditions, the real key to living a chaste life is that one should dedicate the whole of one's life to God, including one's sexuality. All of God's people are called to live a chaste life, dedicating their sexuality to the love and service of God. This includes married people, who in and through their sexuality image God, coming closer to him by means of the unique love between a man and a woman. In this instance, chastity does not mean that they refrain from sexuality (although there may be times within a marriage that continence may be the most loving act), here it means that one approach the other in love, seeking not one's own fulfillment but the good of the other. Within marital sexuality, this means that one should never treat the other as a means or an object, but engage the other in the manner and ways appropriate to Christian marital love. Consequently, one should never use one's spouse, but approach the other in friendship and love, seeking always to move towards a more complete loving union. To do otherwise is unchaste and destructive of the very marital commitment that one has made.

Perhaps the best way to put this is that one's sexuality must always be governed by charity. In this context, chastity becomes an extension of the life of charity, extending into the realm of human sexuality. This means that chastity needs to be based upon the truth of human sexuality given in the New Covenant. (For there is not real love apart form the truth.) As all charitable acts, they find their foundation not only in knowledge of the true order of God's good creation and redemption, but also in the reception of the grace necessary to act upon that charity. Consequently, the Christian in living the life of chastity needs prayer. This may seem like an odd thing to say today, in an age where it is argued that the proliferation of knowledge about human sexuality is bound to solve all of the problems concerning sexuality. But against such utopian perspectives, the

Church has maintained that chastity, as charity, is a gift. It requires the grace of God. In prayer, we ask God to give us that gift. Thus, a necessary part of one's sexual maturity as a Christian requires that one pray, at once asking for the gift of God's grace, at the same time forming one's mind and soul according to the laws of love.

It should likewise be noted that while marriages need to be chaste, chastity could also take the form of one dedicating one's life to the state of virginity. Here, in a very real sense, just as in marriage, one places one's whole self, including one's sexuality, at the service of God. In virginity, the truth of one's very being as a creature before God is confirmed. Like all things Christian, this way of life is a gift of God, a way of life to which one is called, a calling alone able to be sustained by the grace of Christ.

Summary:

In his writings, Pope John Paul II notes that living the married life according to the truth of the gospel creates what he calls the "ethos of marriage."[108] This means that marriage, as the fullest form of sexual expression, is the norm for understanding human sexuality, and that the morality of human acts as they pertain to sexual matters is judged according to that norm. Within marriage, the truth about human sexuality is communicated clearly. Sexuality is ordered according to the nuptial structure of the New Covenant, thereby being firmly rooted in the creative and redemptive acts of Christ. Today, the meaning of human sexuality is clouded by certain social movements and various other modes of sexual expression, each with its own view of human sexuality. Yet, Christians have insisted that the truth of human sexuality is given in the revelation of the New Covenant, where the New Adam and the New Eve establish with authority the creative and redemptive activity of Christ once and for all. During the present age, the New Covenant is mediated by the Church, which as the Bride of Christ is made holy by the blood of Christ, and is therefore free to mediate the grace of Christ under the conditions of fallen creation. Since the New Covenant is the source of all grace and truth, it reveals the meaning of human sexuality.

In the Christian tradition, the manner in which humans image God must include the body and, therefore, human sexuality. In and through our bodies, as male and female, human beings signify different aspects of the order of creation and redemption. The incarnate Christ, who became flesh, lived in this world, and died and rose from the dead, reveals the true meaning of the body. On the one hand, the incarnation points to the fact that God can enter into the finite world. This entry into history is, of course, made possible by the acceptance of

---

[108] John Paul II, *Marriage and Celibacy* (Boston: St. Paul Edition, 1986), pp. 276ff.

the divine offer of grace by Mary. In the incarnation, the significance of the physical order is once again affirmed.

This event demonstrates that material existence is able to mediate the divine life and be taken up into the divine life of God. This latter truth is particularly evident in the resurrection, where the body is not discarded as something useless, but remains as the body of the risen Christ. In Christ's resurrection, the "new creation" is initiated and our own salvation is revealed. In the end, as Christ's body was raised, so will all of those who die in Christ.

What this means is that bodies are significant. They are essential to human life since humans come to be who they are by means of their bodily existence. We exist in no other fashion. In fact, one could say that we are our bodies. We stand before the Lord as bodily creatures. This is essential to our relationship with Him. As St. Paul says, we are "to glorify him with our bodies" (1 Cor. 6:20). We image God through our bodies, as male and female.

One consequence of this emphasis on the body is that the differences between the sexes are significant. Each sex signifies something different in the order of creation and redemption, neither interchangeable nor reducible to the other. Marriage presupposes these historical differences, thereby basing the marital union on the complementarity of the sexes. Marriage is the concrete sign of the sacramental nature of human sexuality, revealing the significance of the body and the truth that it reveals. Through the marital imagery of the New Covenant, the very spousal nature of the order of creation and redemption is revealed. It is from this marital and sacramental order that the meaning of the feminine and the masculine are discerned.

In the New Covenant, to be female is to image the New Eve, Mary, the one who stands before God, as sinless, representing the whole of the created order. She freely accepts on behalf of humanity the redemption of Christ. In her *fiat*, the complete truth about the feminine is revealed. As both virgin and mother, she embodies the fullness of the meaning of the feminine. Like Mary, the female is called to be holy, as the virgin, giving herself completely to the love of Christ. As mother, she must entrust herself to God, bringing life into the world and providing a safe haven in which to nurture that life.

Masculinity finds its model in the revelation of Christ. Unlike Mary, whose body becomes the means through which the Son of God enters into history, Christ freely enters into history in perfect obedience to the Father, willing to die for the sins of the world. There is no disharmony between Christ and His mission, a mission that includes the personal disclosure of who He is through His preaching, miracles and death on the cross. This movement of the extension of the Father to the Son and the return of all things through the Son to the Father is what best characterizes the meaning of masculine sexuality. It moves beyond itself, trying to bring others into its life, extending the gospel into the world.

Perhaps the best way to talk about the Christian understanding of sexuality is to understand it in terms of the meaning of chastity. The virtue of chastity requires that one integrate sexuality into the whole of one's being. Accepting the difficulties of managing the passions, chastity directs human sexuality to the service of God. Under the rule of charity, both married people and those dedicated to the life of virgin, honor and serve God.

Suggested Readings:

Henri de Lubac, *The Motherhood of the Church.*
Joyce Little, *The Church and the Culture War.*
Pope John Paul II, *The Theology of the Body.*

Study Questions:

1.   What does it mean to say that meaning of human sexuality is given in the New Covenant? How is this different from contemporary interpretations of human sexuality?

2.   What does it mean to say that the meaning of the feminine is revealed by Mary, who is both virgin and mother? Can a culture that is opposed to motherhood have a positive attitude about the meaning of the feminine?

3.   What is the understanding of human sexuality that dominates our culture today? Where does it come from? What kinds of presuppositions underlie it?

4.   What is chastity? Why be chaste? What kinds of difficulties surround the Church's teaching on chastity today?

Chapter VI:
Pope John Paul II on the
Meaning of Man as
Male and Female

It is hardly possible today to speak of human sexuality without referring to the writings of Pope John Paul II. His teachings on human sexuality are one of the hallmarks of his pontificate, reflecting his continued efforts to articulate for the faithful the meaning, purpose, and depth of human life in the light of the Christian revelation. Many around the world, especially in the West, particularly in Europe and the United States, have criticized the papal teachings for their untimeliness, for his failure to get in touch with the modern world. Or, to put it otherwise, he has failed to say what they want him to say, failing to justify the kinds of sexual behaviors that many in modern western culture want justified. Instead, the Pope, consistent with the Christian tradition, has continued to teach that human sexuality has a depth and significance that cannot be reduced to the latest trends and social revolutions. Quite the contrary, he insists that the meaning of human sexuality is given in the Christian revelation. As creatures created and redeemed by God, it is through our bodies that we serve God, as male and female.[109]

One way to characterize the teachings of Pope John Paul II would be to say that his arguments weave closely together the different dimensions of human life, attempting to show the reader that human life has an integrity and unity that should not be violated. For instance, in his description of the human person, he uses what can be described as a "phenomenology" of the human person. In such an approach, the human person is seen as an agent whose actions shape the person, so that in each concrete human act, the whole human person is at stake. This does not mean that the human person is infinitely malleable, taking on any variety of shapes. Instead, he believes that there is a proper order to human life that is revealed in Christ. By our acts, we either live into the truth of Christ and thereby achieve real human integrity, or we choose something else. When applying this approach to theology to his understanding of marriage, John Paul II notes that the meaning of marriage is derived from the act of marriage, the total

---

[109]The primary sources for this section are the teachings of Pope John Paul II given at his weekly audiences between November 11, 1981 and October 13, 1982. They have been published as *The Theology of Marriage and Celibacy* (Boston: Daughters of St. Paul, 1986).

and complete giving of one person to another. Because of the significance of the human body and human actions, the meaning of the human person and their bodies can only be found with the Church's understanding of marriage. In order to unravel this view of marriage, one needs first to look at what Pope John Paul II says about marriage and then look to see what he says about the body and its significance for understanding married life.

a. Marriage and the Economy of Salvation

Unlike many secular interpretations of marriage that define it simply in terms of the relationship between individuals, John Paul II understands marriage to be a sacrament. That is, by means of the love between the man and the woman, they are opened up to the salvific activity of the triune God whose love is now present amid fallen creation in the relationship of Christ and His Church. In the dynamic love between the husband and wife, each individual is called beyond him and herself more deeply into the mystery of God's love. "Marriage, the Sacrament of Matrimony, is a covenant of persons in love. And love can be deepened and preserved only by Love, that Love which is 'pored out into our hearts through the Holy Spirit which has been given to us.'(Rom 5:5)."[110] It is within this larger process of salvation history that human life and creation find their meaning

For the pope the meaning of salvation history and the meaning of human life is given in Christ. John Paul II affirms the Christocentric nature of reality. As the central event in the whole economy of salvation, it is from the Christ-event that all things take their meaning. This means that in the life of Christ, not only are the particular teachings of Christianity established, but the meaning and purpose of all things are revealed in the order established by Christ in the New Covenant.

> Christ is "the way, and the truth and the life"
> (Jn. 1:14). Consequently, the decisive answer to
> every one of man's questions, his religious and
> moral questions in particular, is given by Jesus
> Christ, or rather is Jesus Christ himself, as the
> Second Vatican Council recalls: "In fact, it is
> only in the mystery of the Word incarnate that
> light is shed on the mystery of man."[111]

---

[110]Pope John Paul II, *Letter to Families*, February 23, 1994, 7.

[111]John Paul II, *The Splendor of the Truth*, 2.

As noted previously, man as the image and likeness of God is a mystery to himself that needs to be revealed to him. Christ, as man, reveals the meaning of human life in all its dimensions.

Also, because of sin the truth about man and reality given in Christ is no longer evident. Sin entered the world and affected the whole of the created order, obscuring the truth about man and human sexuality. Man chose to define his life for himself rather than choosing the truth given in Christ. Yet, Christ did not abandon man who freely sinned; instead, He came Himself to redeem man, restoring order to the fallen creation. The present period of history is characterized by the tension between the bondage to sin and hope given in Christ. Despite the effects of sin, the order of the good creation is not destroyed. And by the coming of Christ, man and creation are freed from the bondage of sin, an act essential to the redemption of the world.

In his teachings, Pope John Paul II uses the term *sacrament of redemption* to refer to the economy of salvation in the New Covenant. Using Ephesians 5 to describe the order of redemption, John Paul II defines the sacrament of redemption in the light of the relationship of Christ and His Church.[112] What has taken place in the redemptive act of Christ is that the infinite has entered into the historical. Not only is the truth about man revealed here, but the redemption of the whole world has taken place. Christ is the visible sign of the total gift of God to man, in him the whole order of created grace is mediated. [113]

Pope John Paul II describes the gift made to man on the part of God in Christ as a "'total,' that is 'radical' gift, as it indicated precisely by the analogy of spousal love . . .In this way, the analogy of spousal love indicates the 'radical' character of grace: of the whole order of created grace."114 The mediation of this grace takes place, first of all, in the incarnate Christ, whose life, death and resurrection are the acts in and through which the redemption of the world has taken place. But this salvation accomplished by Christ is not a one-time event relegated to the past; rather, the redemptive acts continue to be mediated by Christ in His Church.

In citing St. Paul's letter to the Ephesians, Pope John Paul II, referring to the activity of Christ, says it "... reveals contemporaneously His salvific love which consists in giving Himself up for the Church, as spousal love whereby He

---

[112]The emphasis upon Ephesians is central to the Pope's understanding of the sacramental and covenantal order of creation. References to this text are made throughout these homilies. Especially *The Theology of Marriage and Celibacy*, 215ff.

[113]*The Theology of Marriage and Celibacy*, p. 243.

[114]Ibid.,, p 243.

espouses the Church and makes it His own Body."[115] The redemptive activity of Christ expresses itself in His Body, the Church. In this theology, the Church, as His Body, cannot be reduced to a mere gathering of people or some collection of people who believe; rather, the Church is the one who, like Mary, mediates the redemptive activity of Christ, her Head. Christ dies for the Church, making her holy by His blood (Eph. 5:25ff). The love of Christ for His Church has a spousal character. By his death he makes the Church, his Bride, holy, purifying her by the Blood of the Cross, preparing her to accept His offer of love. On account of her intimacy with Christ, as the object upon which His salvific activity is focused, she freely gives herself to the mission of the Son. In this process, the Church acts like a sacrament, mediating the grace of Christ.

Moreover, in the analogy between Christ and the Church, and the Bridegroom and the Bride, Pope John Paul II indicates the central importance of this "spousal love." In the economy of salvation, Christ's grace is not a force or a power imposed on fallen creation, but a free offer of grace made by Christ to a free creature. In the donation of Himself to His spouse the Church, Christ's love is analogous to that of a husband for his wife. Here, the Church, as spouse, receives the love of the husband, Christ, and freely returns that love. The mystery that is revealed in the Church finds its meaning in her indissoluble union with Christ. "In this way the Church lives on the sacrament of redemption, and in her turn completes this sacrament as the wife, in virtue of spousal love, completes her husband, which in a certain way had already been pointed out 'in the beginning' when the first man found in the first woman 'a helper fit for him'" (Gen. 2:20).[116] It is precisely this love that stands at the heart of the redemptive order and is therefore at the heart of the reality itself. This is the New Covenant. This love not only brings the Church into existence, but remains "a permanent dimension of the life of the Church" and consequently the life of the faith.[117]

Noticeably, the heart of the Church's faith is not a set of principles, rules or ideas, but a personal relationship. In the same way, the created order, which has its origin in Christ, has this personal relationship- the New Covenant- at the center of reality. That is, the spousal order of the New Covenant is not limited to the period after Christ, but can be found in the order of creation from the beginning. The created order, then, is not simply based on a set of laws of nature, as science would have us believe, but ultimately it is based in the activity of the triune God. The whole Christian revelation finds its unique character in this truth, requiring a new way of thinking about the created order. In the activity of the Son, as sent

---

[115]Ibid, p. 237.

[116]Ibid, p. 259.

[117]Ibid, p. 259.

by the Father, the transcendent one enters into history, revealing the intimate unity of the created order and the divine. It is a personal act, an act of love. At the same time, this spousal love of Christ for His Church is a historical act, continually taking place in the life of the Church. Since it is precisely in the Church that this spousal love continues to be present in history, one must again affirm that the Church, as the continued presence of Christ, acts like a sacrament.[118]

John Paul II notes that in the tradition, sacraments referred to the "mystery" of the divine that is present and mediated through the visible sign. Within this theology, the visible order, including the whole of creation, has a sacramental significance, since the whole of the created order partakes of the order of redemption given in the one grace of the New Covenant. Within this context, the sacrament is more than mere proclamation; it is an action, an event requiring, even demanding, a response from those who participate in the sacramental action. "The sacrament consists in the 'manifesting' of that mystery in a sign which serves not only to proclaim the mystery, but to accomplish it in man. The sacrament is a visible and efficacious sign of grace."[119] The Church acting as a sacrament mediates the mystery of man's call to holiness in history. This mediation finds its most concrete expression in the sacramental life of the Church. It is within this context that the Pope understands the particular sacraments, especially marriage.

Before beginning to speak about marriage as a sacrament and its relationship to the Church, it is important to note that within the order of redemption there is a unity and continuity between the act of creation and the act of redemption. In what Pope John Paul II has labeled the "Great Mystery" of redemption, what was hidden becomes revealed. In this process of redemption, the original goodness of creation is restored and brought to completion by the salvific acts of Christ. The original order of creation, now affected by sin, is not abandoned for some new distinct order, but is restored by the grace of Christ. The relationship of Christ and his Church (Eph. 5:23), the New Covenant is fullness of the whole order of grace. All grace, all goodness, all truth is the given in the Christ-event, which finds its historical locus in the death and resurrection of Christ. This is the central act of history in which sin is overcome and the fullness of salvation is given. It is the one grace of Christ that both creates and redeems. The fullness of life is found in him.

One way in which the Church speaks of this central nature of Christ is her insistence that Christ is fully divine and in full unity with humanity, there can be no further revelation, since this revelation is complete.[120] In that case, the reve-

---

[118]Ibid., p. 259.

[119]Ibid., p. 219.

[120]Ibid., p. 258.

lation not only fulfills the present when it comes to pass or prepares one for the future consummation, but it also stands in continuity with the past, bringing it to completion, revealing its meaning now lost to sin. Thus, there is a unity and continuity between the order established at the beginning and that completed in the Christ-event. The First Adam precedes the coming of the Second Adam in the order of history. But in the order of reality, the metaphysical level, the Second Adam not only brings to completion what was lost in the first Adam, but he is the creator, the Son, sent by the Father, through whom all things are made. The whole created order and the economy of salvation finds its unity and continuity in the Christ. The New Covenant, relationship of Christ to his Church, stands in continuity with the past, completing it, revealing the truth about it, while at the same time mediating in the present the redemptive event of Christ and promising the future consummation of all things in Christ.[121]

According to Pope John Paul II, since the whole created order stands in relationship to Christ, this means that it is a visible sign of the order of the good creation, brought to completion in the sacrament of redemption. While speaking of the sacrament of redemption as "analogous to the indissoluble covenant of spouses," Pope John Paul II explains that,

> Therefore, in speaking about the eternal mystery being actuated, we are speaking also about the fact that it becomes visible with the visibility of the sign. And therefore we are speaking also about the sacramentality of the whole heritage of the sacrament of redemption, in reference to the entire work of creation and redemption, and more so in reference to marriage instituted within the context of the sacrament of creation, as also in reference to the Church as the spouse of Christ, endowed by a quasi-conjugal covenant with Him.[122]

Here, he affirms that the same mystery is at work in both the created order and the order of redemption. In his description of this process, he affirms different phases of the redemptive process, yet always emphasizing the unity and the continuity of the process.[123] In the order of redemption, the unity of Christ and the Church, being the very image of spousal love, reveals the truth about the whole of creation, including man.

---

[121]Ibid., pp. 257ff.

[122]Ibid., p. 261.

[123]Ibid., p. 219.

As noted in the above quote, this unity between creation and redemption has a special significance for marriage. Marriage must first of all be understood in terms of both the sacrament of creation and the sacrament of redemption. Priority must, of course, be given to the latter, since in Christ the fullness of grace is given. Yet, marriage is not simply a new order established with the coming of Christ, but is from the very beginning part of the good creation.[124] At the same time it would be improper to understand marriage as simply a "natural estate" or part of the natural order; rather, it needs to be seen as sacramental from the very beginning. Its sacramental character is obscured by sin, but even in the Old Covenant, the true nature of marriage was foreshadowed it the covenantal relationship between God and his people, although it awaited the future fullness to be given in Christ.

In speaking of this dynamic, John Paul II says,

> If Christ, in the presence of those with whom He was conversing in the Gospels of Matthew and Mark (cf. Mt. 19: Mk. 10), confirms marriage as a sacrament instituted by the Creator "at the beginning' - if in conformity with this he insists on its indissolubility - he thereby opens marriage to the salvific action of God, to the forces that flow "from the redemption of the body" which help to overcome the consequences of sin and to constitute the unity of man and woman according to the eternal plan of the Creator. The salvific action which derives from the mystery of redemption assumes in itself the original sanctifying action of God in the very mystery of creation.[125]

By the redemptive activity of Christ, marriage is not redefined but restored to the original intention for which it was created. Divorce is no longer possible since the grace necessary for living out the original order of the marriage is now available in the redemptive death of Christ. This "confirmation" of marriage as a sacrament is not simply the restoration of an order lost to sin, but at the same time marriage is revealed as part of the "new creation" - "it signifies the assuming of all that is created."[126] As a participation in the New Covenant, marriage unites the order of creation and redemption.

---

[124]Ibid., p. 267.

[125]Ibid., p. 277.

[126]Ibid., p. 274.

Notice that implicit within this understanding of marriage is a denial of the adequacy of all political, economic and sociological definitions of marriage. Any adequate understanding of marriage must begin with the radically graced nature of the whole of the created order with its radical dependence upon God, the Creator, from whom all things come. Much like what was described in the earlier chapters of this book, Christ is portrayed as having a hand in all things, unifying the order of creation and the order of redemption. As a matter of fact, Pope John Paul II makes reference to the fact that the "original sacrament of creation draws its efficacy from the 'beloved Son' (cf. Eph. 1:6 where he speaks of the "grace which he gave us in his beloved Son.")[127] From this perspective, all other approaches to marriage will not be adequate, since the primary dynamic in human life and the whole of the created order is the relationship of Christ and His Church. This is the New Covenant, apart from which the meaning of human life cannot be found.

This way of thinking may sound strange to us in the West at the close of the twentieth century. For the most part, our culture teaches us that religion is at best a part of life, at most a private consideration to be separated from public life, having nothing to do with the "secular" aspects of reality. Yet, this bifurcation of reality is false and can only be sustained to the detriment of Christianity, since in truth, religion is foundational to human life. There is no higher or more important end to human life than the salvation given in and through Christ. Again, there is no dimension of life outside of the grace of Christ; therefore, the human response to the call to grace is at the foundation of human life, especially marriage.

Perhaps what is most notable at this point, beyond the comprehensive nature of the economy of salvation, is the spousal nature of this order. In an important sense, marriage really "fits" into the order of redemption since the very order of creation is covenantal, and therefore, nuptial in nature. At the same time, this nuptial order in creation mirrors the spousal love of Christ for the Church. Both the order of redemption and the order of creation have this marital structure, the order of a free covenant requiring a free response in faith to the offer of salvation. As noted by Pope John Paul II in his commentary on the text of Ephesians, in this great mystery of redemption, two important ideas come to overlap: the mystery of Christ and the Church, and the Christian vocation and the plan of salvation. This relationship between Christ and the Church is a nuptial relationship, which order the Christian life in the plan of salvation. The spousal love, then, is not a claim to power over another, as is so often common today with the Hobbesean emphasis upon the self: self-assertive, self-fulfilled, etc. Rather, the key components to this relationship are reciprocity and communion; *communio*

---

[127]Ibid., p. 253.

personarum.[128] As such, this spousal love is not based on a community of external things such as social, cultural or economic factors, but on the most fundamental dimension of community, the true communion of persons in the redemptive love of Christ.

Human beings are persons who are said to image God who likewise is a
personal God. The Father loves the Son and the Son loves the Father, the Spirit
is the product of that love and returns that love. To image the triune God, human
beings must enter into human communion; the primary mode of this human
communion is marriage and the family. Only persons are capable living in
communion, the free complete gift of one self to another.

In his *Letter to Families,* Pope John Paul II cites Vatican II, which calls attention to the fact that there is "a certain similarity between the union of the divine persons and the union of God's children in truth and love."[129] Every man
and every woman not only have the capacity to live in truth and love, but have
the "need" of love and truth as an "essential dimension of the life of the person.
Man's need for truth and love opens him both to God and to creatures: it opens
him to other people, to life 'in communion,' and in particular to marriage and
family."[130] This communion to whom persons give themselves is drawn from
the mystery of the Trinitarian life.

Within the Catholic tradition, the most human and freest act is the personal
gift of oneself to another in love. The greatest atrocities and dehumanizing acts
are, therefore, those that deny this total giving, such as artificial contraception,
genetic manipulation, abortion, et al. Such manipulations place boundaries on
and destroy the free act of love that constitutes the nuptial order of the communion of persons. The real nature of marriage, as all spousal love, is the gift of
one's total self. Spousal love should not be given to idolatry, but to the donation
of the husband and wife to the other for the good of each other.[131] The final
unity is the "one flesh" unity spoken of in Genesis and later in the gospels, a
unity made and achieved in love.

Such a love, while a free act of the person and in the most fundamental
sense the most personal act of any individual, at the same time transcends the
individual, moving toward a community of persons, which is more than their
individual loves. The essential communitarian nature of the faith manifests itself in the life of faith in two important ways. First, one comes to faith only
within the Church. As a participation in the redemptive love of Christ, this
movement towards community is a participation in the grace of Christ and in

---

[128]*Letter to Families,* 7.

[129]*Gaudium et Spes,* 24.
[130]*Letter to Families,* 8.

[131]Ibid., p. 209ff.

Christ's love for His Church. For it is the Church, as a sacrament, that mediates the grace of Christ. This is the grace of the New Covenant, the very grace that constitutes the sacrament of marriage. This grace is redemptive, mediating and accomplishing the mystery of this spousal love of the order in redemption in man.[132] Second, one not only comes to faith in the community of believers, but such faith moves beyond the faith of the individual establishing community. Here again, as often witnessed to in Christian life, the love of God and the love of man are inseparable. In the act of faith, man transcends himself, dying to himself so that one may live in Christ. In the act of faith, through Christ, one enters into communion with God. At the same time, one cannot love God and not love one's neighbor. Marital love is a unique expression of that love. As all love, it is spousal in nature, and as participation in the love of Christ, unites all things to Christ.

Perhaps another way to discuss this relationship of marriage to the larger economy of salvation is to understand it in terms of the meaning of the sacraments in the life of the Church. As noted, the Church is the Body of Christ, His Bride, the sacrament that not only mediates the grace of Christ, but also contains that which it mediates. Thus, the Church is holy, despite sin and death, remaining the Bride of Christ. Because it is made holy by the blood of Christ, the Catholic Church is able to proclaim that where the Church is, there is Christ. Since Christ is present in the particular life of the Church as it exists in fallen creation, the Church is the visible sacrament of this redemption, and the seven sacraments then must be understood in terms of the life of the Church. This is especially true of the Eucharist, which is the source and summit of the life of the faith.

All the sacraments have as their focal point the redemptive death and resurrection of Christ. Like the other sacraments, marriage is a visible sign in fallen creation that mediates the grace of Christ by means of its participation in the order of grace, initiated in the redemptive activity of Christ. However, it differs from the other sacraments being especially linked to the order of creation where this sacrament finds its origin. It is within this framework that one best sees the salvific significance of marriage; how it opens up the husband and wife to the larger order of grace established from the beginning, making marriage not only a means to grace, but a way of seeing the world.

b. John Paul II and the Theology of the Body

In the thoughts of John Paul II, perhaps the most notable contribution to the theology of Christian marriage has been his theology of the body. In the history

---

[132]Ibid., p. 219ff.

of the West, one cannot but notice that different anthropologies with different interpretations of the meaning of the human body have dominated from time to time. This is evidenced in the different cultural attitudes towards the human body that have been operative in different periods, most evidently reflected in dress and art. Even today there are a number of different theories of the meaning of human life that are clamoring for our allegiance. In contrast to these modern tendencies, Pope John Paul II reminds the Christian that the real significance of the body is given in the incarnation: the life, death, and resurrection of Christ.

The manner in which John Paul II indicates the profound truth about the body is in his assertion that the body has the nature of a sacrament. By saying this, Pope John Paul II places the Christian understanding of the body within the process of redemption, at the same time pointing to the depth and significance of the body. The "body" is visible; it signifies the "visibility of the world and of man." Therefore in some way, even if in the most general way, the body is a sacrament, being "a visible sign of an invisible reality." That is, it is a sign of the spiritual, transcendent, divine reality. In and through this sign, God gives Himself to man in His transcendent truth and in His love. The sacrament is a sign of grace, and it is an efficacious sign.[133] The body mediates that grace in a special way in the communion of life achieved in marriage.

The body, then, is not a mere addition to the human person, either replaceable or disposable, but essential to the meaning of human existence. This means that in the Christian effort for salvation, the body is not a mere hindrance to human fulfillment or a dimension of the human person that is left behind; rather, it is a dimension in and through which one enters more completely into the love of God. "The body, in fact, and only it, is capable of making visible what is invisible: the spiritual and the divine. It was created to transfer into the visible reality of the world, the mystery hidden from eternity in God, and thus to be its sign."[134] What the human body signifies is so much more than any biological, psychological or philosophical theory can give an account of. It is the means through which one enters more completely into the depths of reality, a reality whose fullness reflects the spousal love of Christ and His Church.

This type of understanding of the body is certainly at odds with the great disdain for the body so often encountered today. The contemporary attitude towards the human person has its roots in a "dualistic interpretation" of the body that has led to the abstracted kind of life most Westerners live today.[135] When

---

[133]Ibid., p. 175.

[134]Ibid., p. 252.

[135]For a literary examination of this dilemma, see Walker Percy's *Love in the Ruins*. In the book, Percy's main character, Dr. Thomas More, a physician, invents the Lapsometer, an instrument capable of measuring the body-soul relationship with its corresponding poles: beastialism and angelism.

the body is no longer understood to be sacramental, no longer holy, no longer the means through which one encounters the divine in the world, it becomes open to all sorts of manipulations. If the body has no real redemptive significance, only a natural utility, then the body can be used and manipulated in any number of ways. The result is, of course, that life is no longer seen as sacred by the vast majority of people and abuse closely follows. Most contemporary interpretations of human sexuality simply abstract it from physical existence, seeing it as the raw material that one needs to give meaning to. They would argue that the body and physical existence have no intrinsic intelligibility and has no meaning apart from the meaning that the individual gives to them. The result has been some of the great tragedies of our times, as is the case with abortion. Likewise, the modern Western approach toward sexuality, despite the spread of AIDS, has been rather "casual," open to all sorts of manipulations and distortions. If sexuality has minimal significance, such as only the fulfilling of a biological need, then when and whether one uses it is also of minimal significance.

Against such interpretations of human sexuality, as noted, Pope John Paul II has reiterated again and again that human sexuality is sacred. Human sexuality reflects the order of creation revealed in the redemptive act of Christ. As sacramental, human sexuality extends beyond the act or intention of the individual; thus, its meaning is not contrived solely by the individual agents, but the human body has an inherent intelligibility and significance. This order, this truth, this intelligibility of human sexuality is revealed already in the story of creation. This is the profound truth that any understanding of the human life must begin with. "So, then, the double aspect, male and female, proper to the very constitution of humanity, and the unity of the two which is based on it, remain "from the beginning," that is, to their ontological depth, the work of God."[136]   The male/female order is constitutive of the human order, not only for the purpose of reproduction. Rather, as male and female, man and woman stand in relationship to each other. In this relationship, the body expresses itself in the most profound sense, at the same time giving oneself to one another and becoming formed more concretely in one's identity as a human being.

> ... He assigns as a duty to every man the dignity of every woman; and simultaneously (even though this can be deduced from the text only in an indirect way), he also assigns to every woman the dignity of every man. Finally, He assigns to every one - both to man and woman - their own dignity: in a certain sense, the *"sacrum"* of the person, and this in consideration of their feminin-

---

[136]*The Theology of Marriage and Celibacy*, p. 95.

ity or masculinity, in consideration of the body.[137]

According to John Paul II, it is in and through our bodily existence that we come to be whom we are; this is especially true of the relationship between man and woman. Marriage, then, as the fullest form of human sexual expression, has a central purpose in the plan of God.

By pointing to the importance of male and female for our lives as human beings, John Paul II is really indicating the sacramental nature of human sexuality, and therefore, the redemptive nature of human sexuality. Yet, due to sin, the primordial meaning of human sexuality is lost to man, leading to the variety of distortions about human sexuality that have plagued man from the very beginning. Yet, despite sin, God sent His Son to redeem us. And as part of this process, the Son reveals and restores the original sacramental meaning of human sexuality.

In Christ, the *redemption of the body* takes place, affirming the original meaning of the order of the body given in creation. The redemption of the body is not a "side issue" in the larger order of redemption; rather, it is inseparable from the very salvific activity of Christ. This is first evident in the incarnation. By becoming man, the Son enters into complete union with human existence. He does not only appear to be a man, nor does He later shed His human body and become pure spirit, but He "becomes" man. Included in this, of course, is His masculinity.

The exact meaning of His sexuality is sometimes a matter of dispute today. Most theologians do not deny that Christ became incarnate, nor that He was a man, but some do argue that what is really significant is that He became a human being and that sexuality is unimportant. That is, that He became a human being is more important than the secondary or even less relevant fact that He became a man. In this argument, one often used by those who are feminists or who support the ordination of women, the maleness of Christ is unimportant. What is important is that He, the divine, was united with humanity. But what is being asserted by Pope John Paul II is that Christ's incarnation as a male is significant. Since, concretely, humans only exist as male and female, if Christ were to enter into union with man, He would need to do so in a particular man: i.e., as male or female. One cannot abstract from that fundamental reality, a reality that takes its meaning from the order of salvation, wherein male and female represent different dimensions of the economy of salvation. It must also be remembered that such differences do not imply inequality, a notion so prevalent today.

In the masculine humanity of Christ, then, the covenantal structure of the order of salvation is preserved and revealed. Christ is the "New Adam," redeem-

---

[137]Ibid. pp. 280-281.

ing the whole of the created order lost in the first Adam. As the first Adam had authority over the whole created order, so now the "second Adam" has an authority over all of the created order, bringing it to the order and completion for which it was intended.[138] This redemptive order includes individual human beings, the historical order, and the whole of the created order. What is the "stumbling block" of the faith is that this salvific order, with all of its dimensions, rests upon the existence of a particular man, who, in His death, freed us from our sins.

Perhaps it is in the resurrection of Christ more than anywhere else that the meaning of the body becomes evident. The resurrection is the great mystery that reveals the truth about man. As the central miracle of the Christian faith, it is not an aberration in nature, but represents the true meaning for man and the truth of the created order. The risen Christ is God's answer to the death that resulted from the fall of the first Adam. It is the restoration of the human life to the level of integrity for which it was created. The resurrection signifies the power of God over sin and death, leading to the fullness of life in Christ. In Christ, death is overcome, not only for Christ, but for all who believe, so that by dying and rising with Christ, all who believe will come to share in the resurrection of the dead.

Notice that the resurrection is not simply a spiritual resurrection, with the body left behind and the soul going off to heaven. Rather, it is the resurrection of the whole Christ; the full humanity of Christ is raised. Like Christ, the believer is assured of being raised from the dead on the last day. Each resurrected body, like that of the resurrected Christ, will share in a newness of life, yet a newness that stands in continuity with our bodily existence in this life. The gospels insist that there was an empty tomb that He appeared to others, that they came to recognize Him in and through His actions. It was the body of Christ, born of the Virgin Mary that was raised from the dead.

John Paul II describes this resurrected body not only in terms of a new life, but also as a completeness of the life for which humans were meant. In speaking of the resurrected body he says:

> It is therefore a perfect spiritualization, in which the possibility that "another law is at war with the law of... the mind" (cf. From. 7:23) is completely eliminated. This state which - as is evident - is differentiated essentially (and not only with regard to degree) from what we experience in earthly life, does not, however, signify; any "disincarnation" of the body nor, consequently, a "dehumanization" of man. On the contrary, in

---

[138]Ibid. , pp. 59ff.

fact, it signifies his perfect "realization." In fact,
in the composite, the psychosomatic being which
man is, perfection cannot consist in a mutual opposition of spirit and body, but a deep harmony
between them, in safeguarding the primacy of the
spirit.[139]

The integrity of the human person as a creature before God is to be found in
the harmony of the body and spirit. Notice that attempts to "disincarnate" the
human person are doomed to dehumanize man. It relegates earthly life to little or
no significance. Instead, the Christian tradition insists upon the importance of
the historical life of man and therefore the significance of the body. Such an
understanding of the place and integrity of the human body is the cornerstone
for understanding the Church's teachings on human sexuality.

According to Pope John Paul II, the body is a sign. He says that the glorifi-
cation of the body, which takes place in the resurrection, "will reveal the definitive value of what was to be from the beginning a distinctive sign of the created
person in the visible world, as well as a means of mutual communication between persons and a genuine expression of truth and love, for which the *communio personarum* is constituted."[140] Here, John Paul II notes that the body has
its "perennial meaning" within the context of this intersubjectivity. The body
becomes again a sacrament, a sign through which, as bodily creatures, the giving
of oneself to another is made possible. There is no other way in which such a
giving is possible. This is ultimately the same kind of communion which we
seek within our faith, a personal and total engagement with and in Christ.

What is again significant here is that the resurrected body reveals the true
and necessary meaning of the body. It is necessary since in human life the body
is not simply used or brought along until the end, but it is the means by which
we communicate with one another. In the most positive sense, humans are bodily creatures. We are our bodies. They represent and signify who we are. Likewise, in terms of our relationship to God, the body has a role. One way to say
this is to state that the body has a "metaphysical meaning." This means that the
body is a sign whose meaning is derived from the economy of salvation in
which it finds itself. In this economy, the body is restored to wholeness by the
redemptive grace of Christ. The body, as redeemed in Christ, is sacramental in
the economy of redemption, mediating the grace of Christ.

The extent to which the body participates in the economy of redemption and
the exact nature of that participation is perhaps best indicated by the belief that
the resurrected body remains male and female; yet in the eschaton, they are not

---

[139]Ibid, pp. 26-27.

[140]Ibid., p. 44.

given in marriage.[141] The body is not lost in the process of redemption, but saved, showing that the body has an eschatological significance. It means something, even in the end time. Even more striking is the belief that sexuality means something in the end time, even though there is no marriage. The reason for this, of course, is that that which marriage mediates during the time of the Church is immediately present in the end time; thus, sacraments are no longer necessary. The whole of the redemptive nature of the good creation restored in Christ will be directly present, no longer requiring mediation. Yet, human sexuality remains. This indicates the essentially positive nature of human sexuality as constitutive of our human life. It also further indicates the nuptial nature of the whole economy of salvation, since in the end, the complementarity of the sexes remains for all eternity.

The fact that there is no marriage in the eschaton does not denigrate the meaning of marriage; it simply indicates that the meaning of the body was given in creation and that it has a sacramental significance in the economy of salvation. Marriage and procreation, then, are "gifts" given by God to allow the believer to participate more completely in the economy of salvation, an economy that is nuptial.

c. Marriage as a Sacrament

According to John Paul II, marriage is a charismatic gift, so that even those who choose it for non-religious purposes, receive it from God.[142] It is not, then, simply one "life-style" chosen among many possible options, but it is a redemptive act to which one is called. Think for a minute what it would mean to most people who got married if they understood it as a religious vocation, a service to God. If most married couples held that marriage is not done for self-fulfillment, but that it is a way of serving God, a vocation to which one is called by God, then that would certainly change the way in which marriage would be viewed and lived. Unfortunately, this attitude towards marriage is not very prevalent today, making it ever more difficult for any enduring commitment.

Like the whole of the Christian life, marriage finds its foundation in the reverence for Christ. There is no other option since all things have their origin and authority in the grace and authority of Christ. Every way of life is measured by the way in which it responds to the call of God. There is no other criterion for measuring life that has any ultimate significance. So too, marriage, virginity

---

[141]Ibid., pp. 17, 41.

[142]Ibid., p. 154.

and chastity are measured by this same criterion. According to John Paul II, these callings find their common meaning in the mission of Christ.

Most people throughout the ages have understood marriage to be the "natural" way to live and have seen the Christian call to continence, at least, unusual and in some cases unintelligible. Such is the reaction of many today when one discusses topics like virginity, continence, and celibacy. Most people, Catholics included, can hardly imagine why someone might take the vow of celibacy or live a life dedicated to virginity. For most, they simply assume that what modern experts determine to be a "healthy sex life" is necessary for a "good life." As such, marriage or one of the other "lifestyles" (homosexuality, pre-marital cohabitation) tend to be the only options open to them. But contrary to contemporary trends, Pope John Paul II and the Catholic tradition have always been accepting of celibacy and virginity as viable ways of living. As a matter of fact, one might even wonder what sort of understanding of sexuality one has that might be so limited that it excludes celibacy or virginity.

When reading the works of Pope John Paul II, one is struck by the fact that the basis for marriage and continence is understood to be the same: perfect conjugal love.[143] Since the very nature of human love is connected with the nuptial meaning of the body, neither celibacy, virginity, nor marriage can be understood apart from it. In essence, they have the same basis in the nuptial love of Christ for His Church.

> Based on the same disposition of the personal subject, thanks to which man fully rediscovers himself through the sincere gift of himself (cf. GS 24), man (male and female) is capable of choosing the personal gift of his very self, made to another person in a conjugal pact in which they become "one flesh," and he is also capable of freely renouncing such a giving of himself to another person, so that in choosing continence "for the sake of the kingdom of heaven," he can give himself totally to Christ. On the basis of the same disposition of the personal subject and on the basis of the nuptial meaning of the body, male or female, there can be formed the love that commits man to marriage for the whole duration of his life (cf. Mt. 19:3-10), but there can be formed also the love that commits man to a life of continence "for the sake of the kingdom of heaven" (cf. Mt. 19: 11-12).[144]

---

[143]Ibid., p. 125.

[144]Ibid., p. 125-126.

According to this view, the nuptial meaning of the body is essentially inter-subjective. As intersubjective, human beings find their individual humanity only in relationship to others, i.e., by giving themselves to others. In this giving of oneself to another, the body has a redemptive significance, bearing witness to our lives before God. As bodily creatures, the body cannot simply be discarded, but signifies our personal act of faith or the rejection of faith before God. In marriage, the bodily act is of a certain kind, a response to the nuptial, interpersonal nature of our being as humans, an order created in the beginning and restored in the love of Christ. The celibate life or the life of virginity, likewise, is an interpersonal act, the giving of oneself, not sacramentally to another human in marriage, but the giving of oneself over to Christ. In the end, the only way to understand the full significance and redemptive activity of the body is within the framework of the redemptive act of Christ.

As noted in the discussion of chastity, in a Christocentric world all things are to be measured by their relationship to Christ. Continence, then, like marriage, is a charismatic choice. It is a gift from God. One is called by God to serve God. To this calling, the believer is to freely respond. Although it may seem to be an outrageous demand, the truth is that it is not a demand that one cannot sustain. God gives those He calls the means to live that way of life to which he calls them. In the call to continence, the response of the believer in the act of faith, the believer puts on Christ, identifying himself with the kingdom of God.[145]

This is, perhaps, the most important idea in living out the fullness of human sexuality: both marriage and continence, as well as all that is redemptive, require the active grace of Christ to bring them about. As such, one is never called to that which is not possible to live. That is, Christians are called to live a holy life. That is not an ideal that one strives for, never to be achieved; rather, all things are possible with the help of God. This is the optimism of the Christian vocation; it is the belief that despite all of the difficulties of sin and existence in a fallen world, the truth about God and the truth about man are now given in the New Covenant. God's grace is active in the world, and apart from such grace, the demands of continence and even the demands of married life, such as life-long fidelity, would not be possible nor could they be expected. Consequently, continence should not be seen as a negative way of life, a rejection of a part of life, but as a particular vocation within the Christian way of life.

In the same way that continence finds its meaning in Christian life, virginity likewise takes its meaning from the mission of Christ. Accordingly, virginity does not mean a lack of sexual knowledge, but the giving of oneself over to the love of Christ. As marriage and continence, it has the dimension of an eschatological sign, pointing to the meaning of the body revealed in the last things. A

---

[145]Ibid., pp. 74ff.

life dedicated to virginity takes its meaning from the nuptial meaning of the body as revealed in the glorified body of Christ.[146] Like Mary, who remained virginal in her maternity, the whole of one's being is given over to the plan of God. As such, the virginity of Mary and Joseph is reflected in the perfect communion of husband and wife. It mirrors the same order and communion that one finds between Christ and His Church.

Marriage, according to John Paul II, has much the same final meaning and significance as chastity and continence. All of them are Christian vocations to which one is called by the power of Christ. In a special way, virginity and continence point to the significance of human sexuality as revealed at the end of time. While marriage, on the other hand, indicates what was from the very beginning, pointing to the sacrament of creation and the original order and goodness of man as male and female. And even though it points to the beginning, marriage remains a historical reality, a gift, the sacrament of the bodily union of the nuptial order of the whole of creation. There will be no marriage in the end, since the fullness of the grace of Christ, as given in creation, will be immediate then. Only now is that sacrament a great gift, affirming that in the concreteness of historical existence the grace of Christ touches our very lives, opening up history in the most intimate way to the transforming love of Christ. In marriage, the believer comes to participate in the one redemptive act of Christ, the Cross, by whose act alone all are saved and from which the whole of reality has its meaning.

d. The Language of the Body

As noted in his theology of marriage, Pope John Paul II affirms the traditional biblical teaching that human sexuality takes its meaning from the plan of God. In creation and in the order of redemption, Christ reveals the true meaning of male and female. Most modern theories of human sexuality tend to fall short, since they, for the most part, interpret human sexuality apart from its redemptive significance. That is, they fail to see it as sacramental, and when this happens, all sorts of abuses of sexuality occur.

In the tradition, it was the conjugal love of the husband and wife that protected and defined the unique character of the marital union. Conjugal love, as the unique gift of oneself to another, was understood to be nuptial, and therefore, was understood in terms of the heterosexual love between the man and the woman. A constitutive part of the unique gift of self in love was the act of sexual intercourse. In this act, the marriage was said to be "consummated," indicating that it achieved some sort of completion. Here, the unique gift of self became inclusive of the body, signing in the act of sexual intercourse, the most

---

[146]Ibid., pp. 81ff.

humanly intimate interpersonal act, the complete gift of oneself to another. In this act, the word, the promises and vows made in marriage, receive a personal reality.[147] It becomes personal in that it is a subjective and bodily act, wherein the physical giving represents the total gift of self, which in the end is sacramental.

What is interesting about this kind of analysis is that in his writings, John Paul II is evidently working to get the reader to understand the personal nature of reality. Most of us have been taught since birth that there is a difference between the "objective" or real world and our own subjective world. John Paul II indicates that the very interpersonal nature of reality suggests that such an analysis of reality is inadequate. Human beings are personal beings who are engaged with the world. Through this engagement with the world, especially in the love of one another, the human person is called to transcend oneself. Real love is not an abstraction, a nice idea, but something to be practiced. It is only through such engagements, and ultimately, through the intimacy of human love that humans are called to human growth and fulfillment. Thus, in the end, there is no truth about man, about the world, about history, apart from the love of the New Covenant. This is the essence of the faith. To try to locate some other "truth" or some other realm of reality apart from the faith is doomed to fail. The real source of conversion is only from sin and false claims to wisdom to the truth of Christ; and this act is always interpersonal, an act of love. Within this dynamic relationship, human beings have an incredible dignity. They stand before God, imaging God as male and female. They are called to love God and one another.

According to John Paul II, the dynamic relationship constitutive of the act of faith is the context where the meaning of human sexuality, and especially the body, becomes clearest. As sacramental, our bodies not only have an intrinsic meaning or purpose, but as free creatures, man and woman can use their bodies in any number of ways. One either accepts the offer of salvation given in Christ, in and through certain human acts, or one rejects it. The significance of human bodily acts is referred to by John Paul II as the "language of the body."

The language of the body, according to the Pope, is not only the substratum of human life, but a constitutive part of the communion of persons. It is a language of which the body itself is not the author, but which is given meaning by the actions of the person. In marriage, this means that man and woman become the gift to each other in and through their masculinity and femininity. In the process of the mutual self-giving, the couple discovers the significance of the body, which affirms the definitive nature of their sexuality.[148] This means that the body speaks.

---

[147]Ibid. p. 304.

[148]Ibid., p. 305ff.

John Paul II says,

> In the texts of the prophet the human body
> speaks a "language" of which it is not the author.
> Its author is man as male or female, as husband
> or wife - man with his everlasting vocation to the
> communion of persons. Man, however, cannot, in
> a certain sense, express this singular language of
> his personal existence and of his vocation without
> the body. He has already been constituted in such
> a way from the "beginning," in such ways that
> the most profound words of the spirit, words of
> love, of giving, of fidelity - demand an adequate
> "language of the body."[149]

As intersubjective beings, humans seek a communion of persons. This communion of persons has a covenantal structure. Within the covenantal structure, there are two options: one is either faithful to the covenant, faithful to God, faithful to one's spouse as Israel was faithful to the Lord, or one is not. As the Pope notes, the language of the body, as any language, expresses a knowledge that contains the categories of truth and falsehood. In the latter case, the adulterous language of the body is destructive of the unity for which human life is intended. The language of adultery is false. Think, for instance, why the act of adultery is abhorrent in Christian cultures. Is adultery simply a matter of having some traditional values about sexuality that are simply one option among many? Or is adultery a really serious act, since the most intimate union between a man and a woman, a union that is permanent and exclusive, has been violated? In the latter case, the act cannot be insignificant. It is no wonder that adultery is not easily overlooked.

At the heart of this approach to the body and to reality, there is an understanding of existence that gives meaning and intelligibility, not only to the body as it exists, but also to the actions of the body. At the heart of this approach, there is the belief that it is the concrete and particular human acts that make human beings what they are. That is, our actions follow from the free decisions on the part of the believer to accept or reject the grace of God. In a particular act, then, the significance of the act is determined not solely by the actor, but by the very orders and structures within which an act is understood. For instance, in the encyclical *Vertitatis Splendor* John Paul II indicates, against the relativism of contemporary Western culture, that certain acts are intrinsically evil. That is, the moral significance of the act is not determined by circumstance or by the intention of the believer, but it is always and everywhere a moral evil. To hold such

---

[149]Ibid., p. 313.

moral stance, one needs to see the particular act within a particular order, an order that remains permanent. According to the theology of the body, that order is first that God created man in His image, male and female. Second, that man is an interpersonal being who, following Christ, seeks in the love of others and in the giving of oneself the fullness of grace. This relationship is not defined by selfish need, but by a spousal relationship whose nuptial character is determined by the love of Christ for His Church. What is revealed by Christ is that the Christian vocation calls for a total openness to the mission of Christ. At times this may include great suffering and hardship, but the faith teaches that the grace to achieve the end for which one lives is always available. So, to refuse, to hold back, to fail to give oneself completely, must be recognized as sinful.

Within the "language of the body," then, the truth of man as male and female, as redeemed in Christ, is lived out. It is precisely in this language that the nuptial order of creation and redemption becomes concrete. As Pope John Paul II indicates, the language of the body then becomes the language of the liturgy.

> We can say that through the one and the other the "language of the body," reread in the subjective dimension of the truth of human hearts and in the "objective" dimension of the truth of living in union, becomes the language of the liturgy.[150]

This means that in the spousal love of a man and a woman, what becomes concrete in history is the "great mystery," mediated in marital love. John Paul II, following the text of Ephesians 5, notes that the truth of this great mystery is "reread" in terms of the truth of the spousal love, in the end mediating that mystery into fallen creation. Against Manicheanism or other Gnostic interpretations of the human body, which render a "non-personalistic" consideration of the body, the Christian understanding of the body holds that the interpersonal love between a unique man and woman acts as a sacrament. In the sacramental action, in this case marriage, the objective truth of the order of redemption is made accessible. That is, my own marriage no longer simply represents what I feel and experience, but takes on a life larger than my own. The married couple's love is not only like the love of Christ for His Church, but it exists as all love does: in and through Christ. Marriage, then, not only participates in that love and truth, but mediates them.

> The sacraments inject sanctity into the plan of man's humanity: they penetrate the soul and the body, the femininity and the masculinity of the

---

[150]Ibid., p. 362.

> personal subject, with the power of sanctity. All
> of this is expressed in the language of the liturgy:
> it is expressed there and brought about there.
>   The liturgy, liturgical language, elevates the
> conjugal pact of man and woman, based on the
> "language of the body" reread in truth to the di-
> mensions of "mystery," and at the same time en-
> ables the pact to be fulfilled in these dimensions
> through the "language of the body."[151]

Within the unity of marriage, the "language of the liturgy" becomes the "language of the body." The basis for this truth is that from the very beginning, man and woman were not only attracted to one another, but masculinity and femininity were infused with the *sacrum* (the holy) which corresponds to the "great mystery" as described in Ephesians.

Summary:

To say that the "language of the body" is the "language of the liturgy" is a significant shift in emphasis in the discussion of the sacrament of marriage. Remember that the only real source of truth in the Christian tradition is the liturgy of the sacrament. This means that the truth, and what is even more significant, the salvation wrought by Christ, are not mediated by the hypothetical meanderings of theologians, but in the concrete liturgical life of the Church. In the Catholic tradition, the Eucharist has always been the locus of the presence of Christ. It mediates an unambiguous presence where Christ is present completely by the power of Christ, *ex opere operato*. One significant dimension of this teaching is that the truth and grace of Christ continue to be fully present in the midst of history. This sacramental faith stands in continuity with the Christ-event, mediating the fullness of grace that was present in the historical life of Christ to us here and now. There is no lapse in the mediation, no fragmentation, even today for us living years later in a much different culture. That continuity, that unity, and that complete holiness which Christ brought into the world continue to be the great gifts of Christ, enabling history to continue to be open to the redemptive act of Christ, the source and end of all things.

When speaking and trying to articulate the profound meaning of masculinity and femininity, what John Paul II simply does is remind the believer of the profound mystery of Christ. It is within this mystery that the marital love between a man and a woman find it meaning and source. To say that conjugal love is liturgical is to ultimately place human sexuality in the realm of the sacramen-

---

[151]Ibid. p. 364.

tal, not as a subsequent occurrence after the death and resurrection of Christ; rather, from the very beginning this order reflects the redemptive love of the New Covenant. This love is always nuptial, always free, always redemptive. There is really no other love, no other place to turn. In this sacrament, the body "speaks the language of love" and finds the meaning for which it was intended. In and through our bodies, the believer's stand before God, each giving oneself over either to the redemptive love mediated by the body or to despair of such love.

The depth and significance of the Church's teachings on human sexuality escape most of the modern readers. Pope John Paul II understands that there are significant cultural forces aligned against his message, but he continues to speak, in hope and courage, the profound message of the Christian understanding of the human sexuality and marriage. By taking this position, John Paul II stands against those gnostic traditions that fail to understand the sacramental significance of the body, while at the same time, bearing witness to the holiness of the body as understood within the Catholic tradition; thereby, bearing witness to the holiness and sanctity of femininity and masculinity.

Suggested Readings:

Pope John Paul II, *The Theology of the Body*.
Pope John Paul II, *Love and Responsibility*
Richard Hogan and John M. LeVoir, *Covenant of Love*

Study Questions:

1. According to Pope John Paul II, what does he mean by the term *sacrament of redemption*? How is this helpful in understanding the work of Christ?

2. What is the theology of the body? What is unique about it? What does it say about the meaning of the body and its importance for marriage?

3. What is the relationship between a particular human being and his or her body? What is the meaning of the term the "language of the body?" What does it mean to say that the body speaks?

4. John Paul II says that marriage needs to be understood in terms of the sacrament of creation and redemption. What does this mean? What lies underneath these two aspects of the same reality? What holds them together?

5.   According to John Paul II, what happens to the body when it is not longer understood to be sacramental? How does the incarnation protect the true meaning of the body and help protect it against abuse?

Chapter VII:
Conclusion

Undoubtedly, one of the more difficult tasks of the contemporary world will be to recover the mystery and depth to human life that modern man has appeared to have lost. There are many reasons for this loss of the sense of the mystery of human life. Pope John Paul II in the encyclical *Fides et Ratio* indicates that some of the responsibility for the present crisis lies with the deficient philosophies now operative in the West.[152] As a result of the current situation, western culture is experiencing what he calls the "crisis of meaning," which is caused by the proliferation of philosophies of life that lead to the "increasing fragmentation of knowledge." Not only has such an approach to reasoning led to increased fragmentation, but it has also led to a certain superficiality in the way in which contemporary philosophy approaches human life. "In consequence, the human spirit is often invaded by a kind of ambiguous thinking which leads it to an ever deepening introversion, locked within the confines of its own immanence without reference of any kind to the transcendent."[153] On account of the lack of any appeal to some transcendent order, modern philosophy now suffers from eclecticism, historicism, scientism, pragmatism and nihilism that result in an inadequate view of human life.

In response to the deficiencies of modern philosophy, John Paul II does not despair of the value of philosophy but states that philosophy needs "to recover its sapiential dimension as a search for the ultimate and overarching meaning of life."[154] A philosophy with its foundation in this "sapiential dimension" is especially necessary today in the face of increasing technical and scientific knowledge, since these latter forms of knowledge are limited and need to be ordered to some higher purpose. Contrary to those fragmentary approaches to philosophy and knowledge, sapiential knowledge presupposes as its object the truth of the whole of reality, including metaphysical truth and the truth of the faith. This understanding of philosophy assumes first that there is a truth, a universal order that can be known by human beings through the use of reason. This truth becomes the foundation for all real understanding. So to live well one must understand this order and live "into" it. Simply, if one refuses this truth, one cannot live well. Those who hold that there is a transcendent meaning to the created

---

[152]Pope John Paul II, *Fides et Ratio*, 80ff.

[153]Ibid., 81.

[154]Ibid.

order are open to exploring that order, thereby moving towards the ends of life for which man was created. Such a "sapiential" approach to knowing enables humans to find meaning and purpose for life and is not confined to the narrow parameters of empirical knowledge.

Since sapiential knowledge is open to the truth about the whole of reality on the most fundamental level, it must be open to the truth of the faith. For the revelation of God given in Christ is the full revelation of the truth about God, humanity, and the whole of the created order. The revelation does not deny or suspend the rational dimensions of the human intellect; rather, it opens up human rationality to the mystery of the infinite love and being of God. "Revelation therefore introduces into our history a universal and ultimate truth which stirs the human mind to ceaseless effort: indeed, it impels reason continually to extend the range of its knowledge until it senses that it has done all in its power, leaving no stone unturned."[155] The revelation of the mystery of God, then, is the means by which one is freed, not from the use of reason, but from the faults of reason. As the tradition says, *credo ut intellegam*, that faith proceeds understanding and only in the light of faith can one understand the true meaning of the created order.

Perhaps the best way to explain the benefits of faith for philosophy is to note that; first of all, faith frees reason from the narrowness of being closed upon itself. It frees the human reason from the parochialisms that struggle to dominate it. As in any age, the modern age is fragmented by inadequate views of life and the human person. Many have a limited view of the human person, failing to see the mystery of each human being. The effects of such reductionistic philosophies have been all too evident in this century in the destructive acts of groups, nations, and individuals motivated by such philosophies. Only a philosophy open to the depths and transcendent purpose of the created order avoids the narrow rationalisms that identify the truth with some political agenda.

Second, at the same time that the faith acts to preserve the truly transcendental dimensions of the world and human life, it enables the philosopher to recognize the truth among the many competing claims to truth. Therefore, faith acts to free human beings from those idolatries that prevent the person from seeking those "goods" that completes human life. The faith "illumines" human life. In the end, as the Christian tradition holds, faith brings all things to completion to the one universal and final truth, the truth of Christ.

The discussion of marriage in this book looks at marriage from the perspective of faith. As noted in the first chapter, there is today a "war" about the meaning and purpose of marriage. One side sees marriage and family as primarily social constructs that are subject to the forces of social change. Those who hold these philosophies would argue that because of changing social forces, the meaning of marriage and family has changed, or as some have argued, they may

---

[155]Ibid., 14.

even pass away. Is marriage a social construct open to constant redefinition? Can its social usefulness pass away? On the other side are those who view marriage and family as normative forms of human society. In their view, marriage represents an order that is more profound and enduring than those described as social construct. Some would argue that marriage has its foundation in nature, or the will of God. This "traditional' view of marriage and family recognizes that a person or a culture can vary from the normative expressions of marriage and family, but such expressions are variations or even aberrations, and in the end, marriage and family remain the same because they have a particular meaning and order not subject to social, political or historical changes. They reflect the true order of human existence. As is often the case today, those who defend the normative nature of marriage and family have a view of the world rooted in the Judeo-Christian tradition. Accordingly, they understand that marriage and family reflect an order created by God in the beginning, and which remains normative for human life in every age.

The difference between these two interpretations of marriage and family is not simply that they look at the same thing from different perspectives, but that they have very different views about the nature of reality. The first view, usually founded in sociological analyses, sees marriage and family only as social realities. This view tends towards seeing the way one views and structures the world as the product of human culture alone. It is at best descriptive of marriage and family life from their present social manifestation. The sociological analysis cannot make any judgments as to the truth or adequacy of marriage. The second perspective understands marriage and family to be established by God in the order of creation. From this point of view, marriage is not simply what any individual or culture believes it to be, but it has an intelligibility of its own. But if this is the case, one must look at the nature of that larger order to understand the meaning and purpose of marriage.

In the end, the difference between the two perspectives comes down to this, either the reality in which we live is created and defined by human beings or there is some larger order into which each human is called to live. In the former case, the danger is that life has no essential order and meaning, and is therefore subject to the endless manipulations of those in power. In the latter case, the difficulty is that one must discover that larger order and find the appropriate meaning and purpose of the different aspects of human life within this whole of the created order.

The latter is the Christian position. It holds that human beings do not name and order things, but God does. Therefore, in order to live well, each human being is called to live in the truth of Christ in whom the whole truth about humanity and creation is given. Just as the Church contends that one needs faith in order to understand reality as a whole, so too one needs faith in order to understand the meaning of particular human actions; i.e., marriage. Without faith, one does not achieve a complete understanding of the meaning and purpose of marriage. Within the Roman Catholic tradition, the way in which the faithful have come to express the understanding of marriage in the light of faith is to say that marriage is a sacrament.

To say that marriage is a sacrament is to say that it is salvific and that it takes its meaning from the acts of God in the orders of creation and redemption. Marriage, as all sacraments, is a sign that mediates God's grace to us. In and through this sacred sign, the gift of Christ's love, the recipient is able to participate in the grace of Christ by which we are redeemed. Since that revelation is historical, given in the concrete acts of God in history, the sacraments become the means by which the believer is united with God in these revelatory and salvific actions. In the case of marriage, the Judeo-Christian tradition understands it to have its origin in creation. There is a sense in which this is true of everything within the created order. That is, if everything comes from God and is redeemed in God, then all things take their meaning from the order established in creation.

When one studies the doctrine of creation what is revealed is the radical dependence of everything on God. The doctrine of creation *ex nihilo* teaches the absolute sovereignty of God and the radical dependence of all things on God. This means not only that all creatures have their origin in the creative act of God, but that each creature is ordered to some purpose within the plan of creation. This includes man, who is not only brought into existence by God, but who is ordered by God to union with God. And as a constitutive component of his very being, man is created in the image and likeness of God, male and female. For marriage this means that through the love of man and woman for each other, they image the triune God. But this relationship between man and God must not be seen as a "component" or aspect of human life isolated from the rest of life, but it reflects the very order of creation itself. Therefore, as all that it created, it reflects the order of the creation, the covenantal order of reality. There can be no dimension of reality that does not have its foundation in the creative act of God.

Yet despite the insistence on the absolute sovereignty of God, the Christian tradition teaches that God's creation is a free creation. Out of his love, God creates that which is other than Him. He creates man as the crown of creation and calls him to live in communion with God. At the heart of this act of creation, then, is an act of love. But as an act of love, creation must in essence be a personal act, not an act of sheer power. It is the life-giving love out of which God creates, and it is to that very love that every human being is called. The way in which the outpouring of the divine in the creative act of God and the response of the created order might be best described would be to say that creation, then, has the structure of a covenant. The relationship between man and God, a relationship born of love, is at the heart of reality.

Marriage, the actualization of man in the image and likeness of God, has the structure of the covenant given in creation. From the beginning, man and woman are commanded to unite with one another in a "one flesh union." This unity is not the abolition of one party by the other, but the union of the two, each freely giving oneself to the other in love. In the love between a husband and wife, they mirror the love of God for Israel. As in the act of creation, in the covenant it is the love of God for His people that brings them into existence and calls them to respond freely in love to His offer of love. Thus, from this point of view, marriage is "natural" in the most profound sense of having its order in the original good creation, and through marriage, one is able to continue to live in that order. At the same time, as a means of imaging God, marriage is graced and therefore redemptive.

Within the economy of God's actions, marriage not only takes its meaning from the creation but also from the redemptive acts of Christ. As a matter of fact, it has already been noted that to say that marriage is a sacrament is to say that it is redemptive. Because of sin, the original harmony of the good creation is lost. Man freely rejected God's offer of grace and chose to place something else before God. As a result, man lost his way and is in need of being redeemed. Because of the radical nature of sin, the Father sent His Son to redeem mankind from sin. There is no redemption apart from the redemption of Christ; thus to understand marriage as a sacrament, one needs to understand it in terms of Christ, the New Covenant.

As noted, Christians often make the link between marriage and creation. But to say that it is redemptive means that it ultimately needs to be linked to the one sacrifice of Christ, since it is in and through Christ, whose sacrifice constitutes the New Covenant, that all men are saved. The New Testament describes how this salvation works in a number of different ways, but primarily through the use of nuptial imagery. According to this, the good creation has the order of a covenant. In the scriptures the covenantal love of Christ for His people, from creation until the end of time is described in terms of marital imagery. In Ephesians, for example, the relationship between Christ and the Church is described as the relationship between a bridegroom, Christ, and the bride, the Church. This analogy not only says something about the nature of the Church, but also about the nature of marriage.

Christ, as the bridegroom, gives His life for His bride, "that he might sanctify her, having cleansed her by the washing of the water with the word." (Eph. 5:26) In the New Covenant, Christ alone has the power to initiate the order of redemption. Thus, to say that our free gift of oneself to another in marriage is a sacrament means that it must be a participation in the one cross of Christ. Such a participation must be more than the mere following of the example of Christ; rather, it means that in marriage one participates in the New Covenant and is transformed by that participation.

The graced character of marriage indicates that, as a participation in the redemptive act of Christ, marriage is holy and cannot be overcome by sin. Therefore marriage cannot end in divorce. One way to define the complete and redemptive nature of marriage is to say that it is a permanent, exclusive, heterosexual relationship. This means that it is a total gift of oneself to the other in a unique, irreversible and definitive manner. In the fallen world of our experience, many people are doubtful as to the possibility of such a complete human relationship. The "realists" argue that the world is fragmented and partial and the idea of a total gift of one to another is only an ideal, perhaps to be approximated, but never realized. Against that pessimistic way of thinking, the Catholic tradition has held that despite sin, man and woman can be united in marriage in such a way that they can give themselves completely to one another. But this presupposes that the complete gift of the spouses to one another is not simply a matter human effort, but that their love is taken up into the love of Christ on the Cross and purified so that their love for their spouse, as all true love, is redemptive. Only by being transformed in the divine love of Christ does marital love become redemptive.

The effects of this marital love are concretely present in the lives of the couple who receives the sacrament. The first primary effect is the bond of marriage. In and through the free gift of oneself, the man and woman are united as husband and wife. This union places them in a more intimate relationship with the other and at the same time with themselves. It allows them to grow more deeply in their love. Another good of marriage is fidelity by which the husband and wife are given a "space" in which to grow as individuals through their love for one another. Noticeably, in a world where there is no fidelity, there is no room for growth in love since the other may be gone or one might be replaced by another at any moment. Within such transient relationships, the most one can look for is the immediate physical and psychological gratification of only extrinsic needs. Marital fidelity, on the other hand, provides a context in which the husband and wife can give themselves completely over to the love of the other and therefore to the love of Christ.

The third good of marriage and perhaps the most obvious is the good of children. In many ways, although this is an obvious good, today it is the most controversial. Pope John Paul II has noted that with the advancements of modern culture has come what he calls the "culture of death." That is, as our atheistic, secular and technological culture has advanced, the significance of the sacredness of human life has diminished. As this pertains to children, this first of all refers to the slaughter of millions of children each year by abortion. From the Roman Catholic perspective, life begins at conception and must be protected. But life is not only a good that needs to be protected; it is a "good" that married couples ought to pursue. That is, married couples have an obligation to bring new life into the world. Consequently, the Church has not only understood abortion as a refusal of the good to which mature married couples ought to aspire, but also artificial contraception. In the end, against the proponents of many contemporary ideologies, the Church bears witness to the blessing that children are. Often today, people are unwilling to sacrifice themselves for the good of others, especially children. Instead, they often place more value on jobs, social freedom and any variety of other pleasures. Yet, the Church has always borne witness to the fact that children are a greater good than any of these lesser goods and ought to be pursued as an end in itself.

At the same time that the Church teaches that children are a good in and of themselves, the Church argues that children are also good for the couple. In the giving of themselves to each other, the couple grows. That is, as social beings, humans become "more human" by responding to the love of the other. Initially, it is one spouse that calls the other spouse through his or her love to greater maturity and wholeness. Then through the loving procreation of children, the spouses move beyond themselves in another manner. Now they need to provide for and educate their children. In this process, the mother and father learn the true nature of Christian love, which as sacrificial and creative, always moves beyond itself, opening the individual to the deeper   dimensions of reality.

An essential component of this marital unity, of course, is the sexual component. That is, marriage is not an abstract love, but a form of love firmly rooted in our bodily existence. As total gift of self to another, it includes the whole of one's being, including bodily giving. One could then define marriage as the fullest form of sexual expression, the goal towards which all sexuality moves. Because of the comprehensive nature of marriage, it provides the context in which the most profound elements of human life are brought to completion. And, therefore, because of this, all of human sexuality is "judged" by marriage. That is, in the light of completeness offered by marriage, other forms of sexual expression are thought to fall short; e.g., pre-marital sex, homosexuality, artificial contraception, etc. The problem with them is not only what they do, but what they do not do. In the end, they fall short and frustrate the drive for the total gift of self to which each is called in marriage.

In addition to saying that marriage is the norm for understanding what are sometimes called today "sexual expressions," marriage at the same time reveals the meaning of the masculine and the feminine. According to the biblical accounts, in the beginning God created man unto the image and likeness of God, "male and female he created them" (Gen. 1:27). In time, the man and woman were joined, reaching a higher level of completion. Yet, throughout history, other interpretations of the meaning of human sexuality have given rise to competing views of sexuality. For much of human history, what it means to be male and female has been a matter of dispute, and the variety of theories as to the nature of this relationship are legion, both in the past and still today. Contrary to such theories, Christians have held that the truth about human sexuality is given in the New Covenant. The mystery that lies at the heart of each human person is revealed in Christ: the whole truth about man is given in Christ. What is revealed in the New Covenant is, first of all, that human sexuality is complementary and therefore each sex cannot be understood in isolation from the other. Like the New Covenant, which finds its expression in Christ and Mary – the New Adam and the New Eve, human sexuality reveals itself as a nuptial relationship. Just as the incarnation of Christ is not possible apart from the *fiat* of

Mary, so too human sexuality requires the free offer of grace and the free response in love to reveal its essential nature.

Second, since the nature of human sexuality is revealed in the New Covenant, the meaning of both male and female are found in that truth. According to the covenant, the feminine takes its meaning from Mary, whose role in the economy of salvation is essential to the New Covenant. In her free acceptance of the offer of God's grace, she acts definitively for the whole of humanity. Entrusted to her safekeeping is the savior of the world. The masculine, on the other hand, is revealed in the life of Christ, who not only became man, but became a man, thereby revealing the true meaning of being a man. By His death, He overcomes sin and initiates the kingdom of God, thereby transforming the fallen creation by incorporating it into His eschatological kingdom. To be male, is to act like Christ. Men are likewise called to go out into the world transforming it by the power of God's grace.

Third, to say that human sexuality finds its meaning in the New Covenant is to say that human sexuality is sacramental. That is, in and through human sexuality, men and women enter more deeply into the love of Christ and they are transformed by that love.

One of the important decisions that one will have to make in life is about the exact importance of human sexuality in human life. One can opt for what might be called the "shallow" view of human sexuality, which reduces it to an animal appetite that needs to be fulfilled. People who hold such views might be heard to say something like, "its just sex. What's the big deal?" Or others might say, "What is wrong with having sex as long as it's by two consenting adults?" But most people, even if many say things like this, do not in the end believe it. If it is "just sex," then why be angry if their spouses or partners are unfaithful? Why is rape such a radical violation of the human person if sex is simply the expression of an impulse? To this, the Catholic Church teaches that in human sexuality more is at stake than simply mere sexual release. It touches upon the whole of one's being, and is therefore, sacramental.

The one person in recent history who has probably said some of the most profound things about human sexuality is Pope John Paul II. In his work on the "theology of the body," John Paul II holds that the body has a fundamental significance for the life of the faith. The basis for this particular understanding of the significance of the body rests in his philosophy of the human person. That is, he understands human beings as agents who through their actions determine the type of persons that they are. Accordingly, he speaks of the "language of the body." In and through our actions, we speak who we are and at the same time come to realize whom we are. For instance, in the faithful conjugal love between husband and wife, the man and woman move towards the truth about male and female as redeemed in Christ. Adultery, on the other hand, is a false language, destroying the truth of human sexuality. One of the primary purposes of this analysis by John Paul II is to indicate the integrity of human life. One cannot act one way and claim to be really different. In each human act, the whole human being is engaged and thus what one does is what one becomes.

In the end, perhaps the simplest way to define marriage is as a Christian vocation. Through the unique spousal love of husband and wife, the begetting and raising of children, people serve God. In the most concrete manner, it is the means of preaching the gospel and bringing others to salvation, giving life spiritually and physically. By the love of one's spouse, you bring him/her to a greater love of God. By having children and educating them in the truth of Christ, parents are serving God and His Church. Again, it is good to remember that what is ultimately at stake in human sexuality and marriage, in particular, is the salvation of the human person. If sexuality and marriage are viewed in the light of the Christian revelation, one cannot separate them from what God has ordered in creation and what he has accomplished in the order of redemption. Marriage, then, is sacramental because in and through the love of husband and wife, they enter more deeply into the love of the Triune God by whom they are saved. In this process, the spouse is never a means to an end, but the means *and* the end. For in marriage, the love of God and love of neighbor find their unique and complete expression.

Bibliography

Catechism of the Catholic Church. Libreria Editrice Vaticana, 1994.

Chesterton, G.K. *Brave New Family: G.K. Chesterton on Men & Women, Children, Sex, Divorce, Marriage & the Family,* ed., Alvaro de Silva. San Francisco: Ignatius Press, 1990.

Cholij, Roman. Clerical Celibacy in East and West, foreward by Alfons Cardinal Stickler, S.D.B.; preface by Michael Napier. Leoministe, Herfordshire: Fowler Wright Books, 1989.

Christensen, Bryce. *Utopia Against the Family.* San Francisco: Ignatius Press, 1990.

Crichton, J.D. "The Sacraments and Human Life," in *The Sacraments: Readings in Contemporary Sacramental Theology* ed. by Taylor. Alba House: New York, 1981, pp 31ff.

D'Souza's, Dinesh. *Illiberal education : the politics of race and sex on campus*, New York: Free Press , c1991.

Ebeling, Gerhard. *Word and Faith*. Philadelphia: Fortress Press, 1963.

Gaudium et Spes. In *Vatican Council II.* Edited. Austin Flannery. New York: Costello Publishing Co., 1988.

Hugo, John. *St. Augustine on Nature, Sex and Marriage.* Chicago: Scepter, 1969.

Pope John Paul II. *Fides et Ratio.*

Pope John Paul II. *Marriage and Celibacy.* Boston: St. Paul Edition, 1986.

Pope John Paul II. *Veritatis Splendor.*

Kasper, Walter. *Theology of Christian Marriage.* Trans.by David Smith. New York: Seabury Press, 1980, pp. 37ff.

Keefe, Donald. *Covenantal Theology: The Eucharistic Order of History.* New York: University Press of America, 1991.

Leeming, Bernard. *The Principles of Sacramental Theology.* Westminster, MD: Newman Press, 1956.

Little, Joyce. *The Church and the Culture Wars.* San Francisco: Ignatius, 1995.

Lubac, Henri de. *The Motherhood of the Church.* San Francisco: Ignatius Press, 1982, p. 156.

Lumen Gentium. In *Vatican Council II.* Ed. by Austin Flannery. New York: Costello Publishing Co., 1988.

May, William. *Sex, Marriage and Chastity.* Chicago: Franciscan Herald Press, 1981.

Miller, Monica. *Sexuality and Authority in the Catholic Church.* Scranton: The University of Scranton Press, 1995.

Miyakawa, Toshiyuki. "Ecclesial Meaning of the *Res et Sacramentum*." *Theological Studies* Vol. 31, October 1967, p.389.

Mowinkel, Sigmund. *Religion and Cult.* Trans. J.F.X. Sheehan. Milwaukee: Marquette University Press, 1981.

Pope Paul VI. *Humanae Vitae.*

Rad, Gerhard Von. *Old Testament Theology.* Trans. D.M.G. Stalker. Vol. II. New York: Harper & Row, Publishers, 1965.

Rawls, John. "Distributive Justice" *Philosophy, Politics and Society*, 3rd series, ed. By Peter Laslett and W.G. Runciman. Basil Blackwell, Oxford: Barnes & Noble Books, Div. Harper & Row, Publishers, New York, 1967.

Edward Schillebeeckx, O.P, *Marriage: Secular Reality and Saving Mystery*. Trans. by N.D. Smith. London: Sheed and Ward, 1965.

Solzhenitsyn, Alexander. "A World Split Apart: commencement address delivered at Harvard University, June 1978." Translated from the Russian by Irina Ilovayskaya Alberti. New York: Harper & Row, c1978.

Strauss, *Leo. Natural Right and History*. Chicago: University of Chicago Press, 1953.

Strauss, Leo. "The Three Waves of Modernity," in *Essays in Political Philosophy: Six Essays by Leo Strauss*. Ed. Hilail Gilden. Indianapolis, 1975.

Wicks, Jared. "The Sacraments: A Catechism for Today." In *The Sacraments: Readings in Contemporary Sacramental Theology*. Ed. by Taylor. Alba House: New York, 1981.

Index

Author's Biographical Sketch

Dr. Daniel Hauser is a professor of theology at the University of St. Francis in Joliet Illinois. He received doctorate from Marquette University in systematic theology and has a Master's in Theological Studies from Harvard Divinity School. His primary areas of interest are sacraments, ecclesiology and the theology of history. His first book, *Church worship and History: a Catholic Systematic Theology*, was published in 1996. He is also the author of a number of articles: *Origen and the Historicity of the Church, Roman Catholic Ecclesiology and the Problem of Historicity: Insights from Origin Scholarship*, and *Catholic Education and Cultural Diversity*. For the past twenty years, he has been teaching mainly undergraduates at the University of St. Francis